LETTING GO AS CHILDREN GROW

BY THE SAME AUTHOR

BABY WISDOM: THE WORLD'S BEST-KEPT SECRETS FOR THE FIRST YEAR OF PARENTING

EVE'S WISDOM: TRADITIONAL SECRETS OF PREGNANCY, BIRTH AND MOTHERHOOD

THREE IN BED: THE BENEFITS OF SLEEPING WITH YOUR BABY

DO NOT DISTURB: THE BENEFITS OF RELAXED PARENTING FOR YOU AND YOUR CHILD

LETTING GO AS CHILDREN GROW

From Early Intimacy to Full Independence
A Parent's Guide

A *twenty-first century update* of
DO NOT DISTURB

DEBORAH JACKSON

BLOOMSBURY
LONDON · BERLIN · NEW YORK

First published in Great Britain 1993
This paperback edition published 2003

Copyright © 1993, 2003 by Deborah Jackson

The moral right of the author has been asserted

Bloomsbury Publishing Ltd, 50 Bedford Square, London WC1B 3DP

A CIP catalogue record for this book
is available from the British Library

ISBN 0 7475 6576 7
9780747565765

Typeset by Hewer Text Ltd, Edinburgh
Printed in England by Clays Ltd, St Ives plc

10 9 8 7 6 5 4

In memory of my father, Tom Newton.
And to Paul, Frances, Alice and Joe.
With all my love.

NOTE ON GENDER

Most of the parents in this book are stereotyped as 'she', in deference to the large number of female readers who write me wonderful letters and meet me at workshops around the world. And to aid clarity, most babies have been classified as 'he'. I intend no disrespect to the many fathers who are intimately involved with the raising of their children, or to any baby girls – my own included.

CONTENTS

PREFACE TO THE 2003 EDITION

My own words occasionally echo around my oh-so-busy brain: 'children . . . just don't know the meaning of the word "hurry" . . . When a child is hurried along, or chooses to hurry in order to feel effective, he may grow up to be too speedy for his own good.' It was 1993 and my son, Joseph, was yet to be born. Frances had just started school and Alice was still toddling between playgroup and the park.

'[The children] fail to appreciate that you are usually hurrying *on their behalf* to ballet, Brownies or football training, or whatever activity you have organised for them.' I was being ironic. The idea that we might all calm down, do a little less, empty our schedules and put away our kitchen wall planners seemed achievable back then.

It was all a matter of balance – and of giving choices to the child. In those early days, 'Would you like to learn the violin, darling?' was a question marinated in hope, not in horror. It seemed like a good thing to offer a range of varied hobbies which the children could adopt or drop as it suited them. Of course, given the extreme independence of my own brood, I might have guessed what was in store: a lot of adopting, hardly any dropping, and a family itinerary that's busier than the flight chart at Heathrow. ('Are you flying past today, dear?' 'Yes, I'll be landing briefly between orchestra and school play dress rehearsals – if you could just throw a cooked dinner my way . . .')

Searching for a metaphor, I think back to *Three in a Bed*.

The children have taken over the comfortable centre-fold of the mattress and we parents cling dutifully to the sides. How did it come to this?

The problem with Western child-rearing is that it takes place in the context of Western life – and that is getting faster by the year. As we hurtle through the twenty-first century, we scarcely have time to mow the back lawn, let alone sit in a deckchair and watch the weeds grow. We have more gadgets than ever before and less inclination to use them. We can buy in almost every human activity, from gardening to cleaning, painting the walls to making food out of raw ingredients. And yet . . . and yet, we're always in a hurry. In a hurry and tired. In a hurry, tired and desperate to escape from our self-imposed misery. Sometimes it feels as though we're clinging to the sides of our own lives.

Children are not to blame for the stresses which assail the average modern parent. They've just become addicted to the pace of life we helped them create. It is up to me whether or not I play the role of twice-hourly chauffeur, funding an extra-curricular timetable which could have paid for an education at Eton. As middle-class parents, we choose to do these things because of the benefits they bring; because all their friends are busy too; because to grow up in today's world without ever having had a tennis lesson or a Scout uniform, a music certificate or a gym badge is, in some bizarre way, to be left behind.

I did not manage to protect my three from the lure of the After School Activity and part of me did not want to. Some of the most important people in my children's lives include their piano, ballet and violin teachers. These women give a wonderful example and open doors to new possibilities, new ways of using their creative skills. They have become our friends. But then, we do see them rather a lot. The weekly ballet lesson didn't stay weekly for long: it soon turned into ballet-and-tap with jazz and modern and all the exams and dance shows that are a part of the scene. Piano practice, likewise, proliferated into an area of intensive involvement and – as Alice's aptitude increased – high stakes. It's rather like signing up for a mobile phone without reading the small print. All the rest of your life, you're paying the service charge. But you also get to make a heap of interesting phone calls.

Re-reading and re-writing this book has given me the chance to follow once again the journey I took when my children were small. I have rediscovered ideas and questions which I thought I had off by heart but realise I forget to apply. And it strikes me that we need these ideas more than ever. As the world speeds up, we can see parents trying desperately to regain a semblance of control by doing more. They put their babies through increasingly rigid routines; farm their children out to an ever-widening band of experts; juggle more and paradoxically manage less. But our lives are as full as an old computer hard drive and it's time to stop and reload. It's time to do a little less.

I hope this completely refreshed, re-titled book will help you to let go as your children grow – and that you will find the escape route to whatever form of family bliss you seek.

Deborah Jackson
Bath, 2003

'Hannah saw Mona needed only to realize she was now riding the bike on her own, so she lowered her fingertips and fell back. As their fingertips touched for the last time, and brushed apart, Hannah felt a pang of joy and pride, mixed with anguish – at the loss of the little girl who couldn't ride a bicycle. As Hannah and the other children cheered, as Mona rode back, her eyes bright with triumph, Hannah first understood that parenting was a series of such small daily deaths, and that learning to let go of your charges was as crucial as learning to take them on.'

Lisa Alther, *Other Women*

INTRODUCTION

People will tell you where they've gone
They'll tell you where to go
But 'till you get there yourself you never really know

Joni Mitchell, 'Amelia'

When my first daughter, Frances, was four months old, I used to take her swimming. We had just moved house and had yet to make many friends, so our afternoons were calm and uncluttered. The local baby pool was often empty as we splashed about. Frances soon grew to love the water.

I had read a book about teaching children to swim. A treasured find from a jumble sale, it contained photographs of babies floating, blowing bubbles and swimming by themselves. On the basis that mother-love is the child's best teacher, it described exercises through which mothers could guide children towards safety and skill in the water. On no account were the children to wear armbands, as this falsified the feeling of the body's natural buoyancy.

Frances and I embarked on this programme with enthusiasm. At least, I embarked on it; Frances was too young to understand. I blew on her face and ducked her under. I taught her to blow bubbles rather than swallow the chlorinated water. By the age of five months, she could float on her back for up to a minute, not minding if her head bobbed briefly under the waves.

1

But 'success', represented by a swimming baby, eluded us. The pool was closed for repairs, we made new friends, and once we started swimming again, our trips to the baths were infrequent. They were also a little fraught. As Frances grew older she began to resist my instructions, refusing to try out her water-baby exercises and clinging fearfully to me.

Instead of responding humanely to Frances' rebellion and acknowledging her fears, I became irritated. 'But you've always loved the water,' I pleaded. Her rejection of my enthusiasm felt threatening, and I in turn would threaten her: 'If you're not going to do anything, we might as well go home.' I knew that what I was saying was counter-productive, because it made her cling all the more, and venture less. Yet I found it extremely hard not to react.

I did not see events with much clarity or objectivity at the time. My feelings in the heat of the moment were of fear. I was afraid that I could not control our relationship, and that Frances and I would become alienated. In times of reflection, my main emotion was of dissatisfaction with my mothering. I would realise I had been harsh on her and would make resolutions to change. But as soon as we set out for the swimming pool, we somehow rubbed each other up the wrong way.

A few years later, my attitude had changed considerably and my self-understanding had grown. Enough, anyway, for me to realise how easy it was to impede Frances' natural progress. In many situations (not just the swimming pool) I learnt to let myself and Frances off the hook, and to relax. I tried wherever possible to keep my mouth shut, my arms open, and to allow communication to flow.

By the time Frances was four, our swimming afternoons were shared by her baby sister, Alice. Because I could not offer Frances my full attention, she swam in armbands (contrary to the advice of my little book). Although she liked the water, she was still cautious, or so I thought. On one of our weekly swims, I was playing with Alice in the middle of the pool and looked down to see Frances doggy-paddling past me. She had cast off her armbands and was dodging fearlessly between swimmers. To my delight, and despite my earlier interference, she had taught herself to swim.

This episode was one of many in which my first daughter taught me a necessary lesson: she is able to signal when I am becoming over-involved in any aspect of her life, protect herself from my undue desire to control, and emerge with the skills she herself wants to pursue. She teaches me constantly that we are really on the same side. She wants to strike forward in life and fulfil herself, just as I would wish her to do, but she will move in her own time and from her own initiative.

These days I try not to define success (or failure) in terms of the behavioural patterns of my children. As Adele Faber, co-author of *Liberated Parents Liberated Children* says, 'The point is that the process is the product.'[1] If parents and children are not enjoying life, and each other, we are probably neglecting the process of parenting. Success, if it means anything, has more to do with happy memories than goals achieved.

Becoming entangled with Frances in this way also brought me face to face with my own emotions, many of which I had not felt since childhood. I was amazed by the range of emotions in me, triggered by her growing independence. It was apparent I had to give these feelings some attention.

Yet I learned not to blame myself too heavily. I don't believe the words 'right' and 'wrong' are helpful when applied to relationships, not even the parent-child relationship that carries such a huge responsibility and is open to judgement from all sides. When Frances swam off by herself, she was rediscovering the confidence she had known when only a few months old; although I had complicated the process at times, I had at least allowed her that.

The out-of-print, Australian swimming handbook was not to blame either. Teaching children water safety is an admirable aim, and the author was merely sharing her own experience. As a parent and swimming teacher, she had realised, quite rightly, that children like to learn from their mothers. Unfortunately, it is not simply what a mother does, but *who she is* that matters.

My problem was that I had put more faith in the method

than in my daughter's natural ability to swim. Frances had tried to communicate her needs to me, but I had found it hard to respect what she was saying: 'I don't need to be taught.' With my adult vision of the joy she would get out of swimming, I was reluctant to hear her point of view. Frances was not motivated to reach any goal, only to enjoy the moment.

I have always been quite hard on myself, and there were times when I left Frances correspondingly little room for manoeuvre. I could have learned a lesson from pioneer doctors at London's Peckham Health Centre in the 1930s. They

> . . . discovered that quite tiny children could be safely left in the sloping shallow end of a swimming bath. Provided no adult interfered with them, they would teach themselves to swim, exploring the water gradually and never venturing beyond the point at which they began to feel unsafe.[2]

It simply did not occur to me that children could teach themselves to swim, as they teach themselves to crawl and to walk. Frances, absorbed in the process, understood this better than me. Now, watching my second daughter, Alice, gain confidence in the shallow end with me merely *nearby*, I began to realise the beauty of this easy way of growing up. My role is simply to be around for the times I am needed.

THEORY IS NEVER ENOUGH

This book is about the dialogue between parent and child, a dialogue that needs no words. It is about the child's struggle for independence, and the parent's difficulty in letting go. It is about the ways in which we disturb our children. Inevitably, this means facing up to our mistakes.

Mistakes, as we shall see, are to be welcomed, not feared. In the words of the nineteenth century American diplomalist Edward J. Phelps, 'The man who makes no mistakes does not usually make anything.'[3] Our mistakes offer us an opportunity to learn.

We all have ideas about how children should be raised. Every society has its ideology, and no person is exempt from its pressures, for good or bad. But an idea is like an empty house, perfectly constructed, undisturbed but lifeless. As soon as people cross the threshold, the house ceases to be immaculate and things get broken. This is how people inhabit theories.

I was inspired by certain ideas when I became a mother, but always felt that I was somehow ruining their perfect form. What I had to learn was that my child did not judge my mistakes, but she did appreciate my attempts to mend them. Failure is human, and our children are not surprised by it. Frances needed me to be genuine, and was happy to accept me the way I was.

Unfortunately, many parents find it hard to accept themselves, and do not realise that it is OK to *be* themselves with their children. In the absence of trust in our feelings, we rely heavily on tactics supplied by others who are supposedly more expert than us. We buy books on 'how to' bring up babies, and allow their wisdoms to service, or even displace, our own intuition and our personal knowledge. We allow ourselves to believe there is a correct, or an ideal, way of parenting and thus, inevitably, lay ourselves open to feelings of inadequacy and guilt.

The dichotomy between method and reality turns many a household into a place of misery. When we feel unhappy after a fractious family day, we do not say 'hey, ho' and start again, as children do. Instead, we tend to blame our children for their deviant behaviour, or ourselves for not being good enough at the job. Communication breaks down, and we become ever more reliant on methods of control that may not be our own. Paradoxically, to restore a true balance, what we need is less control.

ADVICE AND HOW TO TAKE IT

When you first learn to cook, it's just as well to follow the recipe. But you can't become a chef until you experiment for yourself, and create a few gastronomic flops along the way. Only through practical experience can we learn the limits of what is and what is not possible. The only people able to avoid making mistakes are theorists without children. There has, at some time, to be chaos in the kitchen.

I don't believe parents really want to be told how to bring up their children. A first-time mother may appreciate information on practical matters, but she is in danger of learning that experts know best. When a health visitor gives advice before acknowledging a mother's feelings, she is showing little faith in the mother's ability to feel her way through. Some doctors and health workers even tell parents how to relate to their children, an area in which they can have no specialist knowledge whatsoever.

There are, of course, midwives and health visitors who genuinely believe in the instinctive sense of the average new mother or father. They are not panicked by the frightened parent into looking for quick solutions. Such professionals might say: 'You carried your baby, you gave birth to your baby. What do *you* feel you would like to do?' In so doing, they relegate themselves to the secondary, or support position which is rightly theirs. It takes a great deal of inner strength to hand over power in this way.

No method or ideal should get in the way of our personal dialogue with our children. As Frances grew older, I struggled to behave towards her as certain books had suggested, and not as I felt inside. Until I realised what was happening, I would not have thought this possible. Confident and strong as I was, some of my convictions were brittle because they were based on knowledge (rationalisation), not on understanding (the inspirational 'knowing' that enhances our lives).

Alexander Lowen, the American psychoanalyst and originator of Bio-energetic Therapy, believes over-adherence to theories and concepts disturbs the mother-child relationship:

The mother who attempts to raise a child on the basis of what she has learned about child psychology will invariably go wrong. She will misinterpret the child's needs according to her preconceived ideas. She will fail to respond to the child's bodily expressions because these can only be understood with feeling. She will be confused when her feelings conflict with her precepts.

It has been said that a little knowledge is a dangerous thing, but all knowledge is 'little' when it deals with life or personal relationships. The knowledge of the ego must be tempered with the wisdom of the body if behaviour is to retain a human quality. I would rather see an ignorant woman raise a child with feeling than an educated woman raise it without feeling.[4]

FULL OF DOUBT?

'But,' some parents say, 'I don't know what my feelings are – it's all so new to me. I do need advice.' This is a very common reaction to parenting, but it is essential not to confuse lack of practical experience with lack of emotion. The modern parent may lack useful, everyday experience of handling babies, but she is not devoid of feeling.

Even the parent who has arrived at a state of 'not knowing' is acknowledging an emotion. Having children can strip us of many of our prejudices, and reduce us to a state of doubt and uncertainty. If we embraced parenting with our ideas all sewn up, there would not be much room for growth, for learning and for genuine communication with our children. Breastfeeding counsellor Norma Jane Bumgarner endorses the 'don't knows':

Some part of the equipment built into good parents keeps us questioning and evaluating what we are doing, especially during that first 'experimental' time we try a new (to us anyway) approach in parenting. You will do best to realize that your doubts are completely normal. In fact they are solid evidence that you are a good parent on the way to becoming even better. You are watching and evaluating, striving to allow life for your child to be the best it can be. How fortunate your children are to have parents with doubts![5]

Unfortunately, few parents get the chance to dwell quietly on their doubts, before someone with a 'sewn-up' opinion comes along and tells them what they should be feeling or doing. 'You should have this all sorted out by now,' people insist. Well, people are wrong. If and when they feel in need of technical information to help them make a decision, parents are perfectly equipped to ask. They have only become so dependent on a constant stream of advice because there are so many people out there eager to offer it.

A PLEA FOR UNDERSTANDING

We should beware of thinking that the person with the most information has the answers that will solve all our problems. Take, for instance, one of the most problematic areas of modern mothering: breastfeeding. While some mothers find this as natural and joyous as they hoped they would, many others struggle through pain and pressure to make it work. Very often, what transforms the experience is understanding and support from another breastfeeding mother, not detailed advice from a doctor who has never breastfed. Alexander Lowen:

> Pediatricians have studied the dietary needs of infants for a long time and have acquired some knowledge of this subject. Primitive people lacked this knowledge, but they had an understanding of how to nurse their children, and it worked. However, as our knowledge increased, breast feeding diminished. People seemed to put more faith in knowledge than in understanding.[6]

Knowledge is power, says Lowen, 'the power to control the results by manipulating the causes.'[6] A mother struggling to do the 'natural' thing with her child may be bombarded with advice from those in the know. But all their intervention cannot make her feel good about her baby and the things she does with him. And it is that inner positive feeling which is the key to constructive and flexible parenting.

It is no coincidence that many thousands of mothers are helped to breastfeed each year by a support group that puts the emphasis on sympathetic understanding, rather than on encyclopaedic knowledge. La Leche League, the international breastfeeding support group with representatives in sixty-three countries, has built its counselling philosophy on a basic respect for mothers' feelings. Its counsellors (all themselves experienced breastfeeding mothers) are trained to sense the emotions behind a woman's request for help, in order to respond usefully to her appeal.

Child psychiatrist and psychoanalyst D.W. Winnicott had more faith in mothers than many mothers have in themselves. I do not believe his trust was misplaced. In a paper published in 1968, entitled 'Breast-feeding as Communication', he wrote:

> It is a question of getting doctors and nurses in general to understand that while they are needed . . . they are not specialists in the matters of intimacy that are vital to both the mother and the baby. If they start to give advice about intimacy, they are on dangerous ground because neither the mother nor the baby needs advice. Instead of advice what they need is an environmental provision which fosters the mother's belief in herself.[7]

I remember once driving up to a set of traffic lights at a busy junction in Manchester. Two young boys were running along the pavement, and the first one darted into the road. The second child followed. But while the leader was in comparative safety – he judged the traffic well and dodged the cars with confidence – the second child was very nearly run over. He was following his mate, not judging the road at all.

The danger is that, instead of following our own noses, we play follow-my-leader with another person's ideas. This is *not* good enough for our children, who try desperately to get us to focus on their needs and to listen to them.

Whatever ideas you find in this book, please do not feel obliged to follow them blindly. Allow yourself to be the chef in your own kitchen. And if, sometimes, you find the place in chaos – well, most children prefer things on the messy side.

1

THE INTIMATE CONVERSATION –

BABIES ARE NOT BLANK SHEETS

I have no hesitation in saying that one cannot spoil a child with love, but it must be genuine, that is, it must be tender feeling which responds to the needs of the child and not what the mother thinks the child needs.

Alexander Lowen, *The Language of the Body*

This book is about separation: the growing apart of children from their parents. It is a subject that has long concerned parents and their advisors. In many cultures the process of separation is begun swiftly, before bonding has even taken place. In a worldwide study, primal health researcher Dr Michel Odent found that most societies, including traditional ones, found ways of disturbing the early, crucial bonding between mother and baby. This was done, for example, by claiming that a mother's colostrum, or 'pre-milk', was somehow bewitched or bad for the baby.

One effect of such premature separation, says Odent, is the toughening up of the child. With some notable exceptions, most societies have historically used aggression as their strategy for survival. This includes exploitation of the environment as well as warring with other tribes. But the Efé Pygmies – and other cultures whose strategy for survival is harmony with the environment – allow mother and baby their privacy in the early weeks. Breastfeeding begins with the colostrum and may continue for years, until another baby comes along.

Our child-rearing techniques have more in common with the 'train-them-young' attitudes of the Victorians than with the Efé Pygmies. We know our children must grow up, so we prod and persuade them to grow up as soon as possible. Great store is placed on a parent's ability to dominate and tame her child, however young he may be.

Since the aim of growing up is to move from dependency towards autonomy, Western society looks for early evidence of a child's separation from his mother. The toddler who does not cry when his mother leaves him and the teenager who does not rebel are both models of 'good' behaviour, with the implication that they are a product of 'good' parenting. The same assumptions are not necessarily made by parents with other traditions. Infant crying and adolescent attempts at independence are often simply interpreted as expressions of age-appropriate need. They are labelled neither 'good' nor 'bad'.

DYNAMIC BABY

Babies really are a nuisance. They are so needy, or demanding, to use the vogue word. Our lives are often simply too busy to be doing with them. There's the shopping, the housework, the job to go back to, the social life, the yoga class, the abandoned hobby, the long-suffering partner to appease . . . It would help enormously if our babies could hurry up and grow up, so we could get back to normal. As American pop star Madonna put it, when she began nursing her first baby, Lourdes: 'She only gets a couple more months, and that's about it. Then I want to be able to fit back into my shirt.'[1]

But the beginning of life demands intimacy. Closeness comes before separation. Before our children can properly claim *in*dependence, they must have their fill of dependency. In the 'intimate conversation' between a baby and his mother, this is what the baby is trying to communicate.

A newborn baby has plenty to say from the start. His tiny, quivering body expresses his helplessness urgently to any person who greets him. Only if we come to a new baby with our minds already made up does his message become distorted. A baby's demands are not specific. His attitude of helplessness is an open question, to which there is an infinite number of responses.

He gestures towards the world, and his mother gestures back with a tentative reply: 'Shall I rock you? Would you like to feed?' Her response is like a question in return, not an answer, because she is fluid and open to change.

Twentieth century psychiatrist D. W. Winnicott studied the silent early communications between mother and baby. In his view, the mother appears to complete the baby's half-finished sentences:

> The baby says (wordlessly of course): 'I just feel like . . .' and just then the mother comes along and turns the baby over, or she comes with the feeding apparatus and the baby becomes able to finish the sentence: '. . . a turnover, a breast, nipple, milk, etc., etc.' We have to say that the baby created the breast, but could not have done so had not the mother come along with the breast just at that moment.[2]

The baby's expectations, however vague, become specific as his mother meets his needs. It follows that whatever a child's personality, his early experiences play a great part in his understanding of the world. At birth, he is neither a blank page nor a complete person. He asks the questions, but his mother's responses become incorporated in his growing self. Jerome Kagan, a psychologist from Harvard University, explains the relationship between nature and nurture:

> There is a wonderful and permanent interaction between the biology of the child and that child's environment . . . We must remember . . . that the behaviour of every human being can be likened to a pale grey fabric: black with biological threads, white with experience, but these threads are so thin and so intricately woven together, that

13

you can never see any black threads, nor any white threads.[3]

The child's environment is in dynamic equilibrium with his personality, each shaping the other at all times. A baby has a history even though he may be only a few days old. He is already learning from experience, and his environment, in the form of his parents and other members of his family, is adapting to his personality. This shaping continues until we die, or for as long as we are open to experience and change.

So it is almost impossible to take one aspect of a child's behaviour and attribute it entirely to nature or nurture. This does not, however, stop many people from trying. They might see a child once a year, and claim he has his father's temper, or spot a beleaguered woman with her screaming child in the shopping trolley, and decide she's an awful mother. Either way, on-the-spot analysis is often judgemental and destructive. As one commentator says, it all depends on our viewpoint:

> Nurture theories are associated with optimism in everything from civil rights to child rearing. Nature theories are more skeptical about the possibilities of change, whether for individuals or for society as a whole.[4]

Parents who believe that personality is set in concrete may be apt to blame the child: 'He's always been a bad boy'; while parents who believe nurture is responsible for every behavioural quirk tend to blame themselves: 'I should have given him more . . .' Guilt often comes from an over-emphasis of the part parents play in making or breaking their children.

WHAT ARE BABIES TRYING TO SAY?

The first clear view of the development of personality and intelligence was proposed by Swiss philosopher and developmental psychologist, Jean Piaget, in the 1930s. Professor Piaget identified the built-in reflexes that allow babies to reach out to their world. He realised that logic develops as a result of many layers of experience throughout infancy and childhood.

Magical Child, a work inspired by Piaget and other scientific research, outlines nature's plan for the baby and growing child. It is an astounding vision of human potential. The American philosopher Joseph Chilton Pearce describes how the human infant is propelled by intent that will one day be transformed into controlled, conscious activity:

> We adults move through our own volition. We decide to move, walk, or whatever, and our body-knowing just does it for us . . . But this is not the case with the infant or child. He has no volition. The infant-child has only *intent*, and this intent comes from the older-brain processes. The surprising and disturbing fact about the early child is that for the first three years or so, he has no volitional control, no will, in the adult sense. That child is moved by his intent much as a puppet is moved by its strings . . . The early child cannot knowingly disobey a parent or wilfully misbehave. The early child can only obey the inborn intent that moves him.[5]

This revelation chimes with the instincts of many traditional cultures, where adults assume there is no point in disciplining very young children, as they simply would not understand. In Africa, for instance, the Ganda people of Uganda are happy to train their babies gently, but will never rebuke or punish them for their mistakes. Before a child can talk, it is believed he 'has no sense', a theory which protects him from destructive discipline.[6]

Ganda parents' respect for the pre-verbal stage is significant here. Before they talk, babies' communications are quite unlike our own. Speech pins us down, forces us into corners, reveals our prejudices and limitations. Pre-verbal babies are much more open and unhindered. Their meaning is rarely specific, but hopeful, eager and unfettered. A variety of different responses could meet their needs.

Austrian/American psychoanalyst Wilhelm Reich was

another observer to emphasise the importance of babies' reactions. Allowing a child his part in the conversation was called 'self-regulation', a process described here by Reichian therapist Peter Jones:

> The self-regulating baby or child is able to satisfy her core needs, the deep, instinctual needs that we are all born with. When she is a dependent, helpless baby, the parents or other carers have to provide the conditions in which she can do this . . . This is often misunderstood as 'letting the child do exactly what it likes', or 'total freedom'. This is very misleading, because 'freedom to' is of little use to a baby in arms. Self-regulation for a very young child demands an awareness in her adult carers of her needs and an ability to respond to them in the right way. This regular satisfaction on a deep level of her core needs does give a child a real feeling of freedom, a freedom from the inner stress brought about by frustration and depriva- tion. This 'freedom from' is far more important for a child's emotional health than any 'freedom to' . . .[7]

Peter Jones helped me to see the dangers of a dogmatic attitude. Most dogma comes when we choose to ignore babies' distress signals – the whimpering, the crying, the outright screaming which other cultures respond to as swiftly as a telephone call (by picking the baby up . . .) But dogma can be applied to any theory, as we found after the birth of our second baby, Alice. My husband, Paul, and I embarked on an experiment of total carrying, where Alice was almost never put down or left alone. This was not as arduous as it sounds – much-carried babies are a delight to hold, as they are inevi- tably soft, yielding and cling obligingly to their parents' form. I knew Alice was happy, because she did not learn to cry out loud before she was around six months. However, we were still following a theory.

One day Alice, then about four months old, was lying on her back on the floor after enjoying a massage from Peter. Her face was beaming, and she kicked her legs with evident joy.

She had never lain like this before. Naïvely, I asked Peter if he thought lying her down could possibly be doing her any harm. He said, 'Follow your baby – ask yourself, is she enjoying it, or not?' Suddenly it struck me, I had been reading books instead of my baby's face. Of course Alice enjoyed being carried in my arms, but the carrying had become something of a dogma. I was not open to alternative measures, or fully aware that I could trust such a small baby to tell me what she needed.

Genuine respect for children is so rare that it may seem ridiculous to suggest we respect a newborn baby. Yet respect is central to the philosophy of many of the world's most important paediatric pioneers. Consider, for instance, the work of French obstetrician and philosopher Frédérick Leboyer. Leboyer's sensitive approach to babies in the 1970s provided a remarkable contrast to the then highly clinical, unresponsive world of the modern hospital. In order to get a better view of the baby, he stood back. In other words, he was able to respect the baby, to see him as a 'separate reality'. He found that adult egos usually overshadow a baby's introduction to the world; that respect for the newborn is sadly lacking . . .

When the child makes its first appearance, emotion is at its height. And everyone's breathing – already tense – stops altogether.

'Will the baby breathe?'

Everyone is holding their breath. Identifying with the baby, however unconsciously.

We have all *returned* to our own births – fighting for breath just like this newborn baby; on the verge of suffocation. We have no umbilicus to supply us with oxygen. So things soon become unbearable, and we feel we must take some action. The easiest, the most sensible, the most obvious thing for the onlooker to do would be simply to breathe.

Instead of which, he cuts the baby's cord.

His own emotional involvement has made him quite irrational.

Naturally, the baby shrieks.

17

Everyone present exclaims in relief: 'It's breathing.'

But in fact, it is just they themselves who have found relief.[8]

CRYING, CONFUSION AND GUILT

The baby's helplessness, his cry, are potent signals that we should listen to his side of the story. If we cannot face his distress, we may leave him to cry alone. Or, if we want to try and relieve his suffering, we may clasp him to our bodies over-anxiously.

I recall feeling submerged by Frances' cries when she was tiny, unable to separate from them while holding her calmly. My friend, experienced with babies, and not intimately attached to mine, could calm her in seconds. Our styles of holding were the same, but Frances responded instantly to my friend's relaxed body. A baby's crying is intended to set our alarm bells jangling, but it warrants neither panic nor retreat.

Babies *will* have their difficult moments, whatever we do with them. Infants in traditional cultures may not cry much, but that is because the mother and her support network are poised to supply their needs before they reach that stage. My second baby, Alice, did not cry during her in-arms phase, but nevertheless she would get edgy and whiny at times, attempting to tell me something new or to get me to change my tack. Had I not been able to interpret her voice, she would, I presume, have learnt to cry sooner.

Most Western babies cry at birth and liberally from then on. One study of 400 British babies in 1989 discovered that on average babies cried for two hours a day, with two-month-olds crying the most.[9] The researchers then pronounced crying as 'normal', which indeed it is in our society.

But some scientists have concluded that crying in babies not normal at all:

Klaus [Dr Marshall Klaus, American paediatrician and – with Dr John Kennell – pre-eminent researcher into infant bonding] – makes the astonishing claim that if properly bonded with the mother, the child should *never* cry. Crying, he states, is, an unnatural, abnormal, uncommunicative expression, an emergency distress mechanism only. And in those societies where bonding is practiced, crying is, indeed, quite rare.[10]

Bonding' is used here to denote the traditional practice of allowing a baby to be with or near his mother (or father, aunt, grandmother or older sibling) at all times, usually carried on her body. If anthropologists have observed cultures where babies do not cry, then crying cannot be considered physiologically 'normal' for human babies. But to say that babies should never cry is akin to saying that there should be no ill in the world: it's an ideal.

If we approach parenthood expecting our efforts to produce perfectly happy babies, then we are likely to feel guilty, confused and anxious when crying occurs. We are also less likely to embrace the crying child with patience, kindness and the necessary element of detachment. Guilt and anxiety may produce unnecessary reactions, such as anger or (at the other extreme) an overwhelming empathy which makes us unable to cope. Certainly I believe that crying should be taken seriously, but if we treat every cry as an emergency then we may become as distressed as the baby himself.

Developmental psychologist Dr Aletha Jauch Solter believes it to be essential for babies and children to vent their feelings through crying – but says it is equally important that parents do not get sucked in by their children's emotions. Nor should they feel guilty. She says:

'It is important to remember that when a baby cries, it does not in any way imply that the parents are doing a bad job. The baby may not need anything at all, but may simply be discharging past hurts . . . Once this is fully understood, then parents will no longer need to have quiet babies in order to feel confident.'[11]

A crying or jumpy baby is not merely the product of mismanagement by his carers, though they may have a lot to do with it. The equation is more complex. If we begin to list the factors that are not immediately in a parent's control, for example his inter-uterine experiences, the society into which he is born, the kind of birth he had, his mother's emotions or his own digestive system, we can be sure that no method will, in itself, override all circumstances.

Take, for instance, the experience of American mothers living in a West African tribal community. The diet, lifestyle and methods of child-rearing were the same for both the American and African families, but the 'product' (the baby) was not identical. Sherri Saines, a mother from Clarion, Pennsylvania, takes issue with those who would turn anthropology into method:

> I want to reply to . . . one of several articles implying that carrying our infants will make us all better people and the world a better place. I, too, believe that wearing our babies is a great benefit to mothers and children. I lived for three years with the Lobi people of West Africa. West African babies are carried basically until they are weaned; they are generally calmer, cry less, and squirm less than American babies. But . . . cross-cultural comparisons are much too complex to assume cause and effect so easily.
>
> My first child was born in Africa. He, too, was carried much of his first year, passed around and held constantly, and not allowed to cry if possible. Our pace of life was slow and calm. He was healthy and grew well. But he was just as jumpy as other American babies, and other Americans there had the same experience.[12]

Ms Saines believes that culture forms our basic being in ways we do not understand, and this may certainly be part of the puzzle. One of the obvious differences between a traditional village culture and post-industrialised society is that belonging to the former offers a clear-cut way of doing things, while the latter offers choice. While the villager struggles against a harsh environment for survival, the urbanite struggles to know himself and to live harmoniously alongside others. The ancient lifestyle may be simple, offering great freedom from stress, but it cannot tolerate alternative behaviours: dissent interferes with survival, the single and urgent purpose of the tribe.

THE UNCONSCIOUS PARENT

Looking at Sherri's jumpy baby, it seems likely that the infant responds to the chronic tensions and unconscious attitudes in his carer's body. It is as if culture is in our bones, directing every muscle, seeping into every pore of our being. American Analyst Alexander Lowen believes unconscious assumptions and behaviours, not child-rearing methods, are by far the greatest influence on a child's well-being:

> Parents . . . overlook the fact that it is not what they do but how they do it that spells the difference between acceptance and rejection. Most parents are unwilling or unable to see the importance of unconscious attitudes to which the child is sensitive.[13]

Elsewhere, Lowen explains why babies react to our hidden feelings. 'Many people,' he says, 'especially those who are characterized as intellectuals, have mainly a head consciousness . . . They communicate their thoughts easily, but they have great difficulty in knowing or expressing what they feel.'[14] Reaching ego consciousness is a natural part of growing up. A baby, equipped only with body consciousness, has insights into his mother that even his mother may not know about:

> Body consciousness . . . is characteristic of children who live in the world of the body and its feelings and of adults who retain a close connection to the child they were and still are inside. A person with body consciousness knows what he feels and where he feels it in his body. But he can

21

also tell you what you feel and how he sees it in your body. He senses you as a body and responds to you as a body; he is not misled by the 'emperor's new clothes'.[14]

A baby may not understand people's moods, but he responds to them in a heightened way. For some parents, the thought that a baby can read their unconscious attitudes is off-putting, even frightening. It means there is no escape. Whatever child-care methods they employ, however many brave faces they put on, the baby sees right through them to the real person underneath. But once appreciated, this realisation can be hugely liberating. A parent can stop trying to create a charade, or live up to unreal expectations. She can begin to accept herself, and her moods, both good and bad. She can start to feel the power of her unique relationship with her baby.

There is absolutely no danger in a mother's fluctuating messages to her child. He does not judge her moods, and expects to get to know the emotional landscape that is his mother. Far more dangerous than our 'real' selves to our children, is wearing an unreal mask displaying only the emotions we think they need to see. As John Holt, one-time teacher, author and spokesman for the home-school movement put it:

> Children, unless they are very unlucky, and live at home with adults pretending to be model parents (which may be a growing trend), are used to living with real, capricious, up-one-day-and-down-the-next-adults – and their sharpness of observation and keenness of mind, they *learn how to predict these strange huge creatures*, and to read all their confusing signs. They know the complicated emotional terrain of the adults they live with as well as they know their room, their home, their backyard or street.[15]

THE EYES HAVE IT

It is not what we do with our babies that matters, so much as the way we do it. Take, for instance, the 'detail' of eye contact between a mother and her baby. This is a part of the intimate conversation that health professionals rarely bother with, fortunately, which means that it is relatively undisturbed.

British zoologist and baby watcher Desmond Morris reports that, once babies have recovered from the trauma of birth, they will spend up to an hour staring intently at the mother's face. While the use of his eyes is not yet mature, a newborn baby can focus on objects up to twelve inches away, and responds most strongly to curvy, moving objects – in other words, his mother:

> Some hospitals routinely ignore the importance of this primary eye-to-eye contact. They favour the idea that both mother and baby 'need a rest' after their exertions. This may appear reasonable on the surface, but if both parent and child are fit and healthy it is far better for them to be in close eye-contact during the first hour. In this way the deep bond of attachment between them can start to take root at this key moment.[16]

Note the pseudo-medical concern of the late twentieth century hospital, which ensures the separation of mother and baby 'for their own good'. Many forward-thinking maternity units now ensure that the privacy of the new mother and infant is not disturbed unless absolutely necessary. They realise that early intimacy can play a vital part in the initiation of breastfeeding and feelings of maternal satisfaction. As Joseph Chilton Pearce reports, the newborn baby's skill of focusing on the human face is soon lost if it is not practised:

> For a short period, the newborn cannot only focus on and recognise his mother's face but also follow her visually when she moves about the room. The qualifications are – and this is so obvious, yet devastating in implication – that the infant must be undrugged and undamaged, and this innate brain pattern must be *given* that face to focus on if the patterns are to be fully activated. If furnished with the stimuli to bring that

pattern into play, the infant will spend some 80 per cent of his waking time locked in on that face. The brain's pattern for organising visual data will thus be strengthened. If not brought into play and continually stimulated, that brain function will quickly disappear, not to be regained for days or weeks.[17]

The eyes are an active expression of the inner person. Far more important than setting aside time for eye contact, which happens naturally while holding and feeding, is being aware of the messages we send out casually with our eyes. Lowen believes hostility, ambivalence and depression to be as easily conveyed through the eyes as mother-love:

Eye contact is probably the most important factor in the relation of parents and children, especially in the relationship of a mother to a baby. One can observe how a nursing infant regularly looks up to make contact with its mother's eyes. If the mother responds lovingly, there is a sharing of the pleasure in the physical closeness that reinforces the infant's sense of security. However, this is not the only situation where children seek eye contact with their mothers. Every time a mother enters a child's room its eyes will rise to meet hers in either pleasurable or fearful anticipation of what the contact will bring. A lack of contact owing to a mother's failure to meet the child's eyes is experienced as rejection and leads to a sense of isolation.[18]

Interestingly, each culture places a different emphasis on the importance of eye contact. In Africa and Asia, where babies are carried almost constantly, the infant is expected to be the passive observer of an ever-moving world. He receives loving eye contact from those around him and especially from his mother during nursing, but there is little sense of this being an educative experience. The calm, quiet Gusii mother of Kenya, in particular, is one who makes very little eye contact with her much-carried baby.[19] Her aim is to produce a calm, quiet child.

By contrast, the American mother is more likely to place her baby at a distance (in a high chair, stroller or rocking seat) and to engage in playful, engaging eye contact, with the specific aim of eliciting an active response. Neither approach is right or wrong, but side-by-side they demonstrate the infinite variety of our communications with even the youngest child.

A child who is nurtured with genuinely loving looks and in loving arms will not be damaged by the occasional glance of anger or despair. But when a mother is consistently disapproving of her baby, or ambivalent, then the effects can be long-lasting. A deep and overwhelming depression on the part of a mother is the condition most likely to create a vacancy in her eyes. Winnicott described the mother's face as a mirror, reflecting the child back to himself:

> It is possible to think of the mother's face as the prototype of the glass mirror. In the mother's face the baby sees him- or herself. If the mother is depressed or preoccupied with some other ploy, then, of course, all the baby sees is a face.[2]

To take a quite different example, a baby might be having the time of his life with a mother who holds him sensitively, exchanges loving, playful and meaningful looks and allows him to feed at her breast whenever he wants. This same child may have no cot, an erratic weight chart and not a shred of routine. Health professionals frequently interrupt such a relationship with well-meant but inappropriate advice, designed to bring the mother 'into line'. It takes a special kind of expert to know when and when not to interfere.

Of course eye messages are not merely a one-way track from mother to baby. Babies convey their love and fear quite clearly in their eyes. They do not convey judgements, as adults do, because they have not learnt to judge, but some parents interpret their babies' behaviour in this way. As developmental psychologist Dr Daniel Stern describes, it is possible for a mother to feel rejected by the eyes of a six-week-old baby:

At this age, babies often stare at things as if their gaze has indeed been captured and they are obliged to stare at one spot. A baby in this state appears ... to be active mentally – not lost in vague reverie, as an adult would be.

Parents can feel challenged, even upset by such moments in a baby's life. Imagine holding your six-week-old baby girl in your arms. You're face to face. You want to play, but she is transfixed by a spot where your forehead and your hairline meet. You, wanting her to look into your eyes, smile at her to divert her gaze. But your smile is not successful. You may – as most parents do – go on trying to divert her. You may make silly faces or even shake your baby from side to side, hoping the physical movement will unhook her gaze. But she may well continue to gaze at your hairline. Many parents interpret this gaze aversion as real rejection and may even give up trying for the moment to make eye contact. This is not any kind of rejection, however, but a normal phenomenon. It has been called *obligatory attention*.[20]

If a baby's behaviour really is no more than a set of reflexes, the bare bones of personality, then he is open to all possibilities. He *cannot* reject his mother, his context for life. Only the neurotic adult, with her child-like needs and sophisticated arguments, could possibly interpret his behaviour as rejection.

SPONTANEOUS REACTIONS

Our babies do not reject us, judge us or mistrust us. In an ideal world, we in turn would free them from our prejudices: accept them as they are, and trust that whatever they are up to is a part of growing-up. The attitude with which we approach our children affects all aspects of our behaviour towards them, and whatever child-rearing methods we choose, babies sense whether or not they are welcome in our world.

For some parents, it may be liberating to feel that their emotional landscape is a haven where their children can find refuge and courage. On good days, it is wonderful to sense one's inner strength, and the corresponding strength of the child. But many parents are understandably daunted by the idea that they cannot rely entirely on models for mothering, or that their babies can read their feelings. Such ideas imply that the first rule of parenting is to be true to oneself, yet so many of us are unsure of who we are, or what we want in life.

One quality that a child seeks from his mother is spontaneity, in the sense of acting on one's own free will. Playworker Alison Stallibrass believes spontaneity is essential to full personal growth:

> Becoming oneself consists of: . . . 3. Developing spontaneity – by which I mean the ability to respond in a manner that is true to oneself as an integrated whole so that, instead of reacting compulsively to this or that force or mechanically to this or that irritation or being stuck in the railway lines of habit, one has free will.
>
> This is a tall order, or seems so at first sight. Does anyone ever develop all these qualities and powers? Yet, from a biological point of view, they are merely what one should expect in a wholly healthy member of the human species; they are the birthright, the potentiality of everyone. So one should rather ask, why do people *not* possess them?[21]

Babies are born, as we have seen, with a series of reflexes that allows them to indicate their needs. Once these reflexes, or half-sentences, have been filled in by the responses of his carers, they are programmed into the brain. And once a baby is capable of building on his early experiences, he can begin to make choices. He may, for instance, at any given time choose to suckle, kick, smile or cry. Whatever choice he makes, he acts spontaneously. Stallibrass describes this as the beginning of being himself.

The spontaneity of a baby can be taken for granted, and children who are allowed to interact with the world as they need to do will also develop spontaneously. This is what Reich meant by self-regulation.

In my first book I wrote about a baby's suckling at the breast as an act of hope[22]. We could also call it an act of self-realisation. The healthy being, however small, does not wait passively for the world to deal him his fate: he takes what he needs to the best of his ability. As the twentieth century Austrian psychotherapist Bruno Bettelheim put it:

> What humanises the infant is not being fed, changed or picked up when he feels the need for it . . . It is rather the experience that *his* crying for food brings about *his* satiation by others according to *his* timing that makes it a socialising and humanising experience. It is that *his* smile, when it is an invitation to play, results in being played with.[23]

A baby does not need to cry to make his demands clear. His gestures might be minute, just so long as they are recognisable to his care-giver. In many rural societies, mothers know from the feel of their babies' bodies when they are about to defecate or urinate, to the extent that their babies do not need nappies. Few Western mothers can claim to know their babies this well.

It is only possible to notice and respond to the subtlety of a baby's communication if our babies are close to us. If the baby is being cared for by someone who does not recognise his signals, then he will surely abandon subtlety for unmistakeable distress. And the more self-absorbed, anxious or dogmatic we are in our approach, the harder the baby has to work to be heard. A baby's communication is gently honed by the attentive carer. He does not have to raise his voice to be heard, nor she to him. Joseph Chilton Pearce states that

> . . . the fully conscious parent encompasses the psychological state of the child. They participate in shared functions that need no articulation, that simply call for spontaneous response, a mutual meeting of needs and a mutual fulfilment on emotional-intuitive levels.[24]

Notice the word 'spontaneous' again, this time applied to the parent. This is not the impulsive behaviour of one who *reacts* to circumstances, whether nervously, compulsively or violently. It is free will developed out of self-knowledge, and the feeling that caring for a small baby brings its own immeasurable rewards. (All of which presupposes that the baby-carer is well supported by an interested and child-friendly community. For more on this, see Chapter 10: A Time and Place for Us.)

The truly spontaneous parent perceives harmony, not hostility, in her world. She responds to her baby's ups and downs with calm. She sees beyond her child's tantrum to his deep feelings of frustration and anger. Many of us feel as strong, wise and responsive as this on occasions. On such days, the world seems to reflect back to us a sense of harmony, and no matter what irritations arise, nothing ruffles us. On other days, it can seem as if the world is conspiring against us, and our children can do no right.

A spontaneous conversation between a mother and her child is a highly potent thing. In the symbiotic[25] relationship, a mother is aware that she is everything to her child, and he in turn feeds her sense of well-being. Health professionals sense the power of a relationship in which the mother knows she can meet all her baby's needs and mend her own mistakes. This can present a challenge to some professionals, who try to find some way of being 'useful' to the mother and baby. They intervene with unasked-for advice. It is one reason why women are so often urged to wean their babies from the breast, or to embark on regimes that would never otherwise have occurred to them. A mother who is responding to her baby *according to her senses* does not plan too far ahead.

YOU GOT RHYTHM?

Regulating a baby's life by the clock is one way to stifle our spontaneous impulses. Such clock-watching has usually been justified by child care experts on the basis that babies need order and consistency in their lives. But waiting for a clock to tell you when to eat or sleep is a sophistication only adults can manage (and many of *us* still prefer to eat when we are hungry and sleep when we are tired). The kind of order and consistency that a baby needs was outlined many years ago by Maria Montessori, the Italian professor whose teaching methods for small children revolutionised education at the beginning of the twentieth century. Montessori's ideas are explained here by American physician Dr Herbert Ratner:

> Dr Montessori feels that orderliness is built into the infant – an orderliness that is co-natural with nature's intended prepared environment, the mammalian mother. When the baby has an urge to suck, there is a breast to suck on. When the baby has hunger, milk comes out of the breast. When the baby looks up from the breast, a smiling face shines upon him. When the infant is cold, a pair of loving arms envelop him with love. When wet, he is changed. When he cries, somebody picks him up and comforts him. This is a wonderful, orderly world. For every question of need, there is a responsive answer.[26]

When parents falls out of rhythm with their baby, his half-posed questions are greeted with an inconsistent reply. Sometimes, their desire to feed and hold him will coincide with his need to be suckled and held. More often, it will not. There is no order in his world; no foundation for trust; no basis for applying his infant logic. The effects of unresponsive or ambivalent mothering have been the subject of twenty years of attachment research.

American developmental psychologist Mary Ainsworth, working closely with British child psychiatrist John Bowlby, originated a technique called Strange Situation to research the effects of mother and baby separation. She observed distinct patterns in children's behaviour, according to the way their mothers responded to them over a long period, finding that responsive mothering generally created 'securely attached' children; that anxious mothering generally produced 'anxiously attached' children; and that mothers who were 'out of sync' raised 'avoidant' children.

The avoidant child is the one who, when left by himself in a strange situation, does not seem to need his mother at all, and avoids her when she returns. Many adults, including some playgroup leaders and infant school teachers, regard this as mature and desirable behaviour in an under-five. Mary Ainsworth's research exposed the child's apparent nonchalance as part of a sophisticated bluff:

'The thing that blew my mind was the avoidant response.' [Ainsworth] The avoidant children, who seemed indifferent to their mothers' comings and goings, even to the point of snubbing them on reunion – who looked so extraordinarily independent – had appeared quite insecure at home. They had cried and showed more separation distress than the secure babies. And they turned out to have mothers whom the observers rated as interfering, rejecting, or neglectful.[27]

Interfering in this context means 'untimely'. Although these mothers held their babies as often as mothers of babies classed as securely attached, they did so when the babies did not wish to be held:

[Ainsworth] has one scale called Cooperation and Interference. On the cooperative end the parents fit what they do to the child. They do things in a timely manner, they do things when the child is open to them, they don't do things at cross-purposes to the child. On the other end, interfering, the parent is coming in doing things when the child isn't ready. Ainsworth showed that mothers of babies who are later avoidant hold their babies as much as mothers of babies who later are secure. So if you just measure frequency of holding you get no difference. But there's one circumstance in which mothers of babies who are later avoidant do not hold them, and that's when the baby signals that it wants to be held.[28]

So it is possible to be an interfering parent, even though your child may be only a few weeks old. Babies require their carers to be spontaneous and responsive, not dogmatic and interfering.

A cooperative parent does not interfere with her child's natural sense of rhythm and order by imposing on him her preconceived ideas. She does not expect him to suppress his needs, or separate from her before he is ready. After all, if a baby has to eat, sleep and play to an *adult* timetable, what opportunity does he have for being himself?

THE AMAZING NEWBORN

The development of initiative and self-confidence begin at the earliest possible age. Even a tiny baby may be relied on to use his own judgement regarding those issues on which he is an expert: his feelings and his immediate needs.

A baby knows better than anyone when he is hungry, or miserable, or in need of his mother. Instead of trying to shut him up because she does not like the sound of his crying, the responsive adult attempts, to the best of her ability, to answer him. She will not always succeed, but she will try. Soon the baby learns to rely on his own body messages as reliable, acceptable and reasonable. He requests, and the universe responds. He learns that his environment is bountiful, and his infant logic will go on assuming bounty and harmony all around him. He is eager to practise the skills of self-realisation, when given the chance.

Maria Montessori was keen that parents should not dominate their children, even their young babies. She talked of the dangers of 'substituting' adult personalities for those of the young and vulnerable. A parent's interference is like a one-way conversation, in which the child is thwarted at every turn:

. . . adults look upon a child as *something empty* that is to be filled through their own efforts, as *something inert and helpless* for which they must do everything, as *something lacking an inner guide* and in constant need of direction. In conclusion we may say that the adult looks upon himself as the child's creator and judges the child's actions as good or bad from the viewpoint of his own relations with the child. The adult makes himself the touchstone of what is good and evil in the child. He is infallible, the model upon which the child must be moulded. Any deviation on the child's part from adult ways is regarded as an evil which the adult hastens to correct.

An adult who acts in this way, even though he may be convinced that he is filled with zeal, love, and a spirit of sacrifice on behalf of his child, unconsciously suppresses the development of *the child's own personality*.[29]

Letting go of a baby has nothing to do with putting him down, or training him to accept a certain level of separation from his mother. To 'let go' in this sense implies an alert respect for the baby's needs, stemming from a healthy awareness of one's own. Counsellors use the term in training, with explanatory notes such as these:

To 'let go' is not to cut myself off, it's the realisation I can't control another.
To 'let go' is not to deny, but to accept.
To 'let go' is not to adjust everything to my desires, but to take each day as it comes and cherish myself in it.
To 'let go' is to fear less and love more.[30]

This list was compiled with adults and adolescents in mind, but the letting-go process does not have to wait until the rebellious teenager explodes with anger and frustration. It does not even have to wait for a two-year-old to become 'terrible'. We can let our children go from the moment they are born by trusting in the processes of nature and responding to their needs as they become apparent.

A SENSITIVE DANCE

Close-contact nurture of infants, coupled with calm acceptance of their needs – this is the style of parenting which evolved with humankind and which is still practised in most parts of the developing world today. Parents in traditional cultures strive for an early and healthy intimacy with their babies which allows them to separate fully later on. By contrast, the recent Western model of parenting involves training programmes which attempt to limit and control babies' demands. It is often not until the child is two or three years old that he starts to crawl into his parents' bed, regress into his parents' arms and make his needs known.

While the traditional parent rarely has to consider how she is managing her child, the westernised mother may be in an almost constant state of self-doubt. There are a number of reasons for maternal confidence in some cultures, for instance: life-long practical experience in childcare; an unquestioned system of taboos; the support of the entire community. But another reason is that, simply by holding her baby all day, the mother swiftly learns his delights and dislikes in a very deep, physical way. This body-knowing, which creates a huge increase in parental confidence, is one of the best arguments for bonding in the twenty-first century.

In the 1970s, bonding researchers Marshall Klaus and John Kennell caused a sensation with their study into infant bonding. They broke with decades of Western tradition when they suggested that the habitual separation of mother and baby in hospital might be having a long-term detrimental effect on maternal relationships. Even an hour of skin-to-skin contact after birth could, they claimed, improve babies' ability to relax and relate.

The bonding bandwagon was followed by the almost inevitable backlash, and critics uncovered fatal flaws in Klaus and Kennell's research. The idea that there was only one window for bonding lost credence[31] and, in the end, did not make complete sense. The verb 'to bond', active, implies something ongoing and human. The noun 'bonding' felt far too absolute and perfect – as if bonding were some unattainable state like nirvana or baby heaven. As British sociologist Frank Furedi points out, the very concept of bonding became a burden for some new mothers, who were anxious that they wouldn't be able to 'do it' and that without it their children might be permanently damaged.[32]

Yet despite the flurries of accusation and protestations of guilt, some good did come out of this phase of research. The realisation that mothers and babies needed time together was a wake-up call for modern hospitals, who now began to allow women early access to their newborns. This helped breastfeeding, reduced postnatal depression and restored the privacy of the newly-delivered pair, as practised throughout the world in the ancient tradition of 'lying in'.

Looking back through the original data, Klaus and Kennell had characterised bonding as a sensitive dance, spontaneously choreographed between each unique mother and child. This image powerfully conveys an ongoing relationship, flowing in rhythmical interaction. Bonding may not be a perfect science, but it can be a useful metaphor to begin with.

Although some may feel that 'bonding' is an ideal they cannot live up to, in reality it is no more terrifying than marital love or friendship. Learning to love your baby is not so much a goal as a process – one which occurs naturally and takes on the special characteristics of the people involved. All researchers say that ordinary, loving parenting is enough for ordinary babies. Human infants are extraordinarily resilient beings, who persistently seek the comfort they need, prompting their carers into an appropriate response. Even when things go wrong and long separations occur, it is possible to start all over again.

Bonding is usually characterised as something only for babies: a complete and fulfilling attachment to one person, after which they become able to form lasting relationships of their own. But bonding has a function for mothers and fathers, too. Breastfeeding and carrying operate on a sensual and hormonal level to make parents more in tune with their babies. They enhance receptivity to the baby's signals. They begin a subtle and open dialogue that has the potential for change.

Mothers who embark on such a dialogue with their new babies are then surprised to find it hard to separate from them in order to return to work. This newspaper article describes the 'growing pains of separation':

> Sonia, 28, is suffering from what she calls 'separation anxiety', a term more commonly used to describe the condition suffered by babies deprived of their mothers. But research in the United States suggests that the suffering is not one-sided. Anxiety, guilt and difficulties with maternal bonding are an increasing problem for women who must spend time away from their babies, especially those under one year old. Anecdotal evidence here suggests that many women suffer in silence.[33]

This is why it is so important that breastfeeding and carrying are done with feeling, *not* mechanically and *not* according to a pre-set regime. Eye contact, holding, baby talk and breastfeeding are all expressions of love. No method arrived at by an 'expert' can describe the way a parent communicates with her child. What the baby needs is not formula mothering, but the experience of the unique and intimate conversation that is teaching him what it is to be human. The baby reaches out with 'love me . . .', and his parents show him what it is to be loved.

Analysts' waiting rooms are full of people whose infantile needs are unresolved, and whose struggle to be heard met with early defeat. Yet we also know that most babies find a receptive audience in the mothers and fathers to whom they are born. As D. W. Winnicott put it, we should maintain a firm belief in the ability of the 'ordinary devoted mother' to listen to her baby's side of the conversation. In fact, Winnicott understood that small failures are what mothering is all about, and that the mother should not expect, unrealistically, to get it all right:

> Is it not true that the mother has communicated with the baby? She has said: 'I am reliable – not because I am a machine, but because I want to provide what you need.

This is what I call love at your stage of development.'

But this kind of communication is silent. The baby does not hear or register the communication, only the effects of the reliability; this is registered in terms of on-going development. The baby does not know about the communication except from the effects of *failure* of reliability. This is where the difference comes in between mechanical perfection and human love. Human beings fail and fail; and in the course of ordinary care a mother is all the time mending her failures.[34]

Western parents are prone to feel they have failed their children, even when the children have grown up and gone on to fend for themselves. Strict ideas on how things might have been, or should be, appeal to the notion that we are not 'good enough' parents. But guilt interferes with our spontaneity. When we wallow in what might have been, we cannot be fully responsive to what *is*.

Mothering and fathering are not perfectible skills. A parent is forced to relearn the ropes with each child, and in doing so, she will sometimes fail that child. But failure is human, and a baby soon learns that his 'good enough' guardians will try to make things right: in this way his negative experiences are transformed.

I believe the quality of 'good enough' mothering can be found everywhere, from the tribal communities of Africa, to the isolated bedsits of inner-city London. It is only by follow-ing their own baby that parents can determine his needs, and the pattern of intimate communication can develop. And before they know it, he will be ready to move on.

Letting go as children grow: babies

- The beginning of life requires intimacy. In order to 'let go', our babies first require a healthy, human attachment
- A newborn child is not merely a blank sheet for parents to write on. He is aware of his own needs and is equipped to communicate them
- By noticing and meeting our babies' needs, we answer the reflexive, open-ended questions which are programmed into the newborn brain. Our accumulated answers convey the nature of the baby's environment, his culture, the relationship he can expect with us
- Parents' responses help to form the baby's personality, while the baby's questions (his crying, his smiles) help to shape the parents. So begins the subtle conversation which lasts for the rest of their lives. When it's going well, the conversation often falls into its own, unique rhythm
- Babies' cries are neither a reproach, nor merely an irritating side-effect of infancy. The baby does not want us to withdraw, nor to become over-involved. He does appreciate a loving embrace
- Babycare is best provided by concerned communities, not stressed individuals. Parents need physical and emotional support to help them love, accept and nurture their young

2

THE SAFETY GATE –

DEMONSTRATING TRUST IN TODDLERS' BODY SKILLS

> Thy father's pride and hope!
> (He'll break the mirror with that skipping rope!)
> With pure heart newly stamped from Nature's mint –
> (Where *did* he learn that squint?)
> Thou young domestic dove!
> (He'll have that jug off, with another shove!)
> Dear nursling of the hymeneal nest!
> (Are those torn clothes his best?)
> Little epitome of man!
> (He'll climb upon the table, that's his plan!)
> Touch'd with the beauteous tints of dawning life –
> (He's got a knife!) . . .
>
> Thomas Hood (1799–1845), 'Parental Ode
> to My Son, Aged 3 Years and 5 Months'

'You wait,' the experienced mother nods wisely, 'he'll soon be into everything.' About a year has passed since your baby was born. He is no longer a helpless infant, but a confident child who has started to take control of his legs, his life and your environment.

Crawling or walking, he'll move out of your arms and into the wide world. Once he knew only the feel of your skin and soft clothing, now he cavorts with corners, plug sockets and carpet fluff.

This can be a time of great stress, not so much for the baby, as for the modern parent. She is used to being her baby's protector, but how can she protect him in the domestic jungle? Her child crawls towards the stairs: 'No!' she might shriek, fearing a disastrous tumble. He makes for the kitchen and is instantly whisked away from the threat of boiling pans, sharp knives and delicate china. The lounge then; but he is barely halfway through programming the video when his mother runs in and smacks him on his outstretched arm. What, the child might wonder, is going on?

We have only to read the newspapers to know what is making his parents so anxious. Headlines such as 'Deadly Waters', 'Dish-washer Warning', 'Gate Death Riddle' all lead to tales of dread and disaster.[1] A survey of accident statistics is equally alarming. In Britain, around 150 children under fourteen die each year from accidents around the home, of which approximately 100 are under five. Another 950,000 children a year are treated in hospital for non-fatal accidents occurring at home.[2]

The larger the country, the more alarming the figures sound. More than 7,000 American children are killed each year in accidents around the home – another 50,000 are 'seriously injured.'[3] And when you add in details such as: the largest number of accidents to children under fourteen happen in the living/dining room, but the most serious accidents take place on the stairs[2], it becomes completely understandable that some parents are fearful for their own under-14s, who usually live at home and must negotiate the stairs and living room every day.

THE CHILD VS. THE LANDSCAPE

So the parent believes it is her job to protect her child from the environment. She also wants to protect the environment from the child. In a house full of precious objects, even the most precious object of them all (the baby) cannot roam free. If it's a case of survival of the fittest, baby will surely survive, but in the process books may be torn, Chippendale chairs chipped, and cassette tapes painstakingly unwound. The infant explorer cannot evaluate the material worth of his surroundings, and is unlikely (in the early days, at least) to treat inanimate objects with the kind of respect adults give to their belongings.

An encounter between a baby and a delicate chair does not offer much in the way of educational opportunity. As the educational pioneer Maria Montessori wrote:

> An adult environment is not a suitable environment for children, but rather an aggregate of obstacles that strengthen their defenses, warp their attitudes, and expose them to adult suggestions.[4]

In a culture without furniture, most activity occurs at the child's level: mother squatting while she prepares the vegetables; the family sleeping on the floor; games played in the earth and dirt. Some cultures, like the Japanese, traditionally designed their furniture in a way that did not interfere with natural body usage.

In contrast, most developing cultures have gone up in the world: into high, soft beds, comfortable chairs and tall, elegant tables. This not only means that we have lost the art of working and playing on the ground, but that our children have to strain and struggle to join in a world they can barely see. No wonder they are so desperate to grow up and leave childhood behind like the second-class citizenship it really is.

But furniture is not in itself a source of great danger to children. There is, after all, the natural furniture of nature – mountains, rivers, holes in the ground, sheer cliffs – that all animals have to contend with. Imagine a sheep who was scared of heights, or a mountain goat who couldn't climb mountains. The child who lives in a clearing in the jungle has to move out of the clearing and into the jungle one day. Rural peoples take their landscape in their stride. Only in the urban West have we learnt to fear the physical world. Many of us would share the opinion of Michael Cowdy of London's National Gallery, who, when asked why 'dozens of visitors' had fallen down the stairs of the new Sainsbury Wing, replied, 'Stairs are inherently dangerous.'[5]

This is akin to saying 'alcohol is a dangerous substance', a commonly held view in our culture. But alcohol is only dangerous in the wrong hands. It is not threatening to someone who is not prepared to abuse it. Anticipating the worst, we behave as if the worst will happen. In the words of John Holt, the American teacher-turned-homeschool-campaigner:

Many people seem to think that the way to take care of children is to ask in any situation what is the most stupid and dangerous thing the child could possibly do, and then act as if they were sure to do it. One warm April morning I sat playing my cello at the edge of the swan boat pond in the Boston Public Garden. At its edge, the pond is perhaps a foot deep, maybe less. Around it is a broad granite curbing. During the hour and a half I was there, four mothers came by, each with a small child in tow. The youngest of these was about a year and a half old, the oldest close to three. Each of these four children was interested in the water and wanted to go look at it. Each of these four mothers assumed that if the child got anywhere near the water's edge he or she would fall in. They did not shout at their children or threaten them, but each mother rushed about trying to stand between the child and the water, or trying to distract him from the water, or turn him in another direction. Naturally, the more they tried to keep the children away from the water, the more the children struggled to see it, despite the mothers' ever more frantic cries of 'No, no, you'll fall in, you'll fall in!'

But all these children were good steady walkers, well past the tottering and falling stage. The odds against their falling into the water, if they had not been harrassed and rushed into carelessness and recklessness, would have been, for the youngest over a hundred to one, and for the older children a million to one.

If these mothers are 'careful' this way long enough, they are likely to get just the behaviour they don't want.[6]

Children are all the time passing into new realms of experience, many of which could be frightening and painful. But the likelihood is that their experiences will confirm their trust in the world, that reason and harmony prevail, and that, on the whole, inanimate objects behave as you expect them to. Only if we teach our children anxiety do they begin to move fearfully through life. And once we make them fearful, we have disturbed the complex process of growing up.

A CLIMATE OF MISTRUST

The standard reaction of modern parents who have themselves been raised to believe they are their children's first line of defence, is to rush in when danger looms. After a few mishaps, parents learn to rush in before danger has even had a chance to get its coat on. Knowing that accidents are *possible*, we react as if they are probable. Parents start to alarm their children as crawling commences, and they may never stop.

In a book devoted to correcting fearful inclinations, Susan Jeffers urges us all to 'Feel the Fear and Do It Anyway.' Not an easy task, when we have been programmed like this:

> In all my life I have never heard a mother call out to her child as he or she goes off to school, 'Take a lot of risks today, darling.' She is more likely to convey to her child, 'Be careful, darling.' This 'Be careful' carries with it a double message: 'The world is really dangerous out there' . . . *and* . . . 'you won't be able to handle it.' What Mom is really saying, of course, is, 'If something happens to you, *I* won't be able to handle it.' You see she is only passing on her lack of trust in *her* ability to handle what comes your way.
>
> . . . [My] overprotective mother . . . was recently in intensive care after serious surgery, with tubes down her nose and her throat. When I was told it was time for me to leave, I whispered in her ear – not knowing if she could hear me – that I loved her and would be back later. As I was walking toward the door, I heard a small, weak voice

43

behind me saying – you guessed it – 'Be careful.' Even in her anesthetic stupor, she was sending me admonitions of doom and gloom. And I know she typifies the great percentage of mothers out there. Considering how many 'be careful's' our parents bombarded us with, it is amazing we even manage to walk out the front door![7]

What is so awful in saying 'be careful'? Nothing, if used sparingly in the right circumstances. But as a repeated message from a parent to a child, it ceases to be a useful warning and becomes instead a chronic picture of doom. In typically irreverent style, the British radio show *Steve Wright in the Afternoon* once gave a parody of fearful farewells to its young listeners: 'Don't get lost or killed!' said Sid the 'mad' telephone voice cheerily, as he signed off.[8] This extreme reflects the sentiment behind many parents' fears. 'The dread of losing your child is universal, and part of being a parent,' says journalist Kirsty McLeod. But she does not believe this deep-rooted anxiety justifies the over-protection of our children:

> What sort of adults will they grow into, these children, so watched over and protected, taught to mistrust strangers, ferried from safe house to safe house in the locked capsules of their parents' cars?
> In my own childhood, when I wailed in fright at the tall dark stranger about to get me, my mother replied tartly: 'He would only drop you at the first lamp-post.' Perhaps it was the sheer repetition of it, but there was security in that phrase. Nor did police come to our school showing videos and handing out badges for their Never Never ('Say No! Never Go!') and Danger Stranger campaigns.
> . . . What a fine line we tread between protecting the young and destroying their childlike trust in the world![9]

Stranger-danger is a pertinent example for this British writer to choose. If she lives in England, she enjoys one of the lowest homicide rates of all industrialised countries (1.1 people murdered a year out of every 100,000, compared with 20.1 in the USA.)[10] The chances of a child aged one to four being killed by a stranger in the UK are one in a million and the risk for five-to-fifteen-year-olds is even less.[11] While the public perception is that risks to children are increasing, the reality is often the opposite – stranger-murders in Britain have fallen by one third since 1988.

In retrospect, it looks as though Ms McLeod's mother was putting an extremely sensible spin on her child's qualms. And as writer Angela Phillips points out, society's misplaced fears are an enormous stumbling block to the creation of a child-friendly society:

> The growing epidemic of fear doesn't only stop people from asking for help, it also stops them from offering it. They are worried that others will see in them the monster they fear in others . . . Every man who decides not to rescue a lost child because he is afraid that he might be accused of being a pervert is increasing the risk that the child really will be picked up by someone wishing to do harm . . .
>
> If the safety of those children who are on the street is not the responsibility of passing adults then whose re-sponsibility is it?[12]

The child raised in a traditional rural village in Asia or Africa receives the daily concern and protection of almost every adult he meets. It's an ancient kind of Neighbour Watch system, where all women may be addressed as 'auntie', or 'granny', all men as 'grandfather' or 'uncle'. By contrast, the twenty-first century British, American or Australian child may be taught to trust almost no one, (but especially men and those who look in any way different.)

A recent innovation, in response to the perceived risk of child abduction, following the highly publicised murder of toddler Jamie Bulger from a Merseyside shopping mall, is the Infant Tagging System. As used on criminals, electronic tags set off an alarm when the child wanders out of range. However, as Susan Pinckney of the Child Accident Prevention Trust rightly points out, tagging

> gives parents a false sense of security. An alarm may go off when the child is 30 feet away but 30 feet could be in the middle of the road. Parents should be teaching their children about safety not relying on alarms.[13]

Connected to his parents via reins or radio tags, the urban child is more isolated and more vulnerable than his rural cousin. His inability to trust teaches him an astonishing lesson about the culture into which he is born – apparently, he has washed up on a continent and in a century where children are not habitually protected and nurtured by those in a position to protect and nurture them. Yet most adults *are* trustworthy and love to exercise their sense of responsibility towards children. When we teach our children to mistrust, we are feeding them a falsehood, one that (sadly) may not even save them from the dangers we most fear.

PUSHING AND PROTECTING

Protection clearly is an important part of a parent's role. Our children depend on us for their safety and look for our guidance when encountering anything new. There are some dangers, such as electricity, medicines, poisons and fast cars that the small child is not equipped to deal with. I do not know any parent who would wish her child to learn about electrical currents by poking his fingers into an open socket. A socket-cover easily solves the problem. Poisons, drugs and bleach may look like sweets or talcum powder, and we do not want our children to taste lethal substances to find out their effect, so we keep them away from inquisitive hands.

But most physical obstacles in our environment carry no hidden powers. A steep step, a nasty corner, a slippery floor, are all there to be noticed and acted on. The trouble with modern conditioning is that before our children get to learn about their world from experience, we block their exploration. We over-protect them.

From the moment we furnish our infants with scratch mittens, we are protecting them unnecessarily from themselves. (Cutting or biting their nails for them leaves them free to feel with their fingers, while removing any sharp edges. Allowing a baby no opportunity to feel with his fingers is a form of sensory deprivation.) Reins that restrain without the subtle contact of a parent's hand; straps that restrict movement; gadgets that 'educate' the child into an artificial state of walking or bouncing – all these devices interfere with the small steps a child could be making by himself.

Boys as well as girls are treated as incompetents by their over-anxious parents, but there is a long history of cossetting girls in particular. In many societies, women are not traditionally expected to challenge the world, but conform to it. American author Nancy Friday describes how stereotyping has influenced the way we deal with our daughters:

A little boy will crawl away, try to maneuver the stairs, even push his mama away when she interferes because the impulse to grow is so strong. She is afraid for him but knows she must train him in courage . . . 'Don't baby him,' her husband says. 'Let him go,' the culture warns. The boy is emerging from symbiosis into the pleasures of separation. The world opens before him. Through experience, practice, and repetition the boy learns that accidents happen but are not fatal, rejections are lived through, the self goes on.

Little girls, on the other hand, get the opposite training. The great, crippling imperative is Nothing Must Ever Hurt My Little Girl. She is denied any but the most wrapped-in-cellophane experiences. When a little girl ventures into the backyard and hurts herself, mother doesn't encourage her daughter to try again, as she would her son. She holds the girl tighter, fearing for them both because she's been there; she has been hurt, anxious and afraid much of her life. 'I knew this would

47

happen,' mother says, repeating to her daughter a life-long warning to herself, implanting the notion that women are tender, fragile, easily and irremediably hurt by life.[14]

It would be a generalisation to say that boys have it better, but there is nevertheless a cultural tendency to shield girls from experience and push boys towards it. This tendency is more pronounced in some cultures than in others. Gender-specific conditioning is still considered an important part of child-rearing in many societies around the world.

I believe 'pushing' is just as inappropriate as 'shielding', and that both spring from parents' fears. I remember witnessing some quite painful child programming at a Manchester gym that Frances, my first daughter, used to attend. Mothers would hover around as their children balanced on this, rolled on that, issuing warnings about taking care and urging them forward with praise and promise of rewards. Sometimes fathers came along with their sons, and then the tension rose. It appeared that fathers who brought their sons to the gym were more goal-oriented than mothers with either sex of child.

One day a small boy (this was an under-fives group) had fallen off a piece of equipment, despite being closely guarded by a posse of vigilant parents, and had started to wail. His father was furious. If girls are not expected to venture too far, boys are not allowed to fail. The father did not attempt to suppress his rage and, having pleaded with his child to 'stop crying and grow up', he roughly pushed the boy outside. The boy, in his humiliation and fear, was hysterical. His first crime was in falling (failing) and his second in being a 'cissy' for crying.

The danger in pushing is that we force the child to take risks that he is not ready to take, and thereby deprive him of the chance to exercise his own judgement. We also hurt our boys when we teach them not to appear vulnerable, and prevent them from expressing their fears. At least girls and women are usually allowed to express themselves through tears. Take, for instance, the story of Dr Brian Roet, a general practitioner and author who has written about the importance of crying. He reminds us that tears are a natural form of expression, conveying a multitude of emotions. Yet, having being conditioned as an average westernised adult male, he is unable to shed tears to express his deepest feelings:

> The only safe place for me to cry is in the cinema where the tears well up and flood over at the most trivial of situations. I have spent much time and effort attempting to release these tears in appropriate situations, to no avail. My enquiries have led me to believe I was admonished as a child with the dictum 'Boys don't cry' and that this imprint has sealed my tear ducts, except out of sight in the darkness of the make-believe cinema world.[15]

Deprived of this outlet, boys are not allowed fully to experience and accept their failures, much less express any feelings of weakness. In fact, author Joseph Chilton Pearce argues that male children may be inherently *more* nervous than female, due to the difficulty that nature has producing boys. He describes the study which supports this thesis:

> Movies were shown to eight- and nine-year-old boys and girls. At moments of tension, when terrible things were about to happen on the screen, the little boys jumped up in agitation and thrust their arms out as if to fend off disaster. The little girls sank quietly back into their chairs, grew very still and waited. From the beginning, the female, being of the base-line genetic structuring of life, is able to flow with, bide her time, and survive. From the beginning, the male is anxious, tries to fight against, dominate, pit himself against the odds.[16]

When a toddler prowls around his living room, it is a rehearsal for his entry into the wider world. When his parents place themselves, bodily or verbally, in the way of physical obstacles, they are erecting the first line of defence between the child and experience. They remove his opportunity for taking risks.

They know he is unstable on his little feet, and to that instability, they add their own fear.

READY OR NOT, HERE HE COMES

Bio-energetic therapist Alexander Lowen does not believe it is easy to conquer inner fears that have been learnt from infancy and throughout childhood. In his book, *Fear of Life*, he describes the origins of our neurotic society. Neurosis is fear in its chronic form, affecting our ability to change, and to trust in life's processes. The small child, as yet only partially programmed by the neurotic culture (through his parents) is not fearful of the future:

> Why is change for the better so difficult and frightening? We know that in every process of change there is an element of insecurity. The move from a known to an unknown position entails a period of instability. The child learning to stand up and walk is insecure but not frightened. He is not afraid to fall. We cling to the old because we believe it to be safer. We believe the new is dangerous.[17]

A baby has no such belief. He is programmed for change, both expecting and welcoming it, despite the instability it brings. As every parent knows, a child shows signs of relief when he finally begins to attempt new skills like walking, talking and doing small tasks for himself. This is what he was born for.

In Joseph Chilton Pearce's terminology, the crawling baby has moved into a new 'matrix'. Matrix is Latin for womb: 'a source of possibility, a source of energy to explore that possibility, and a safe place within which that exploration can take place.'[18] A child moves through five matrices towards maturity. The first matrix of human life is the womb itself, and the first 'matrix shift' is birth, when the baby moves out of the womb and into his mother's arms. Mother (or another reliable, mother-like figure) is his second matrix: 'The mother,' says Chilton Pearce, '*is* the infant's world, hologram, the content for his intent; she is the infant's power, possibility and safe place.'

When a baby crawls away, the mother's role changes: she is no longer *everything* to her child, but she is his safe harbour, the place to which he will return for refuelling. Although he starts to explore the strange world beyond his mother's orbit, his ability to do so depends greatly on his connectedness to this one person: his mother-figure. In *Oneness and Separateness* American psychologist Louise J. Kaplan charts the progress of the child from infant to individual, and makes these remarks about the eight-month-old baby:

> Between wonderment and panic is a wide range of possible reactions to strangers. But all babies are wary. As soon as a baby has a special attachment to a special mother, the sight of a strange face will sober him. By the time he is seven or eight months old, the baby's sobriety is heightened with at least a tinge of worry. Even the bravest of explorers will eventually slide into the safety of home base. Wariness of strangers works two ways, the 'more obvious being the flight of the baby *away* from the stranger. The path of flight, however, is not without direction or orientation. It is *toward* someone the baby can count on.[19]

The crawling child is exploring his third matrix, the earth itself, a task that takes him until he is around seven years of age. He gets to know his immediate environment until he is ready to leave his mother's side for wider experience. It is a recent idea that a child is ready for full-time education before he is six or seven, and indeed, most children in Europe do not begin their formal education before this age.

Between the ages of seven and fourteen, the child learns independence and survival in the larger world, the fourth matrix. The final matrix shift, adolescence, is the transition to maturity: the whole person is his own matrix, number five. If all has gone well, he will be sufficient to himself, a successful synthesis of 'mind-brain and body' and able to draw on his own resources for all his needs.

Ready or not, we all undergo these shifts and changes. The

baby who has not had enough mother-love to satisfy his own needs will still move on to explore the earth and all he finds in it. But he will be considerably weakened in his endeavours. Since 'the biological plan provides that the child remain squarely rooted to the mother while he explores and structures a knowledge of the earth matrix'[17], the child who has not bonded well to at least one person cannot move out with certainty:

> If the child's security with parents is unquestioned, then his concern over survival will never become an issue. The child is designed to enter into experience freely, without pre-judgement, and evaluate that experience after it has taken place. Concern over survival, safety, or well-being immediately forces an evaluation of experience before the experience can take place . . .
>   Anxiety over survival causes a screening of information through the question: Am I safe? The bonded child does not formulate this question. The bonded child asks only, Where am I?, and moves to interact accordingly.[20]

Each matrix shift brings a period of instability. But it seems that the older we get, the harder it is to 'shift' or change. Compare the qualitative experience of an early matrix shift to a late one. The baby who crawls out of infancy greets his new world with curiosity and joy: he is uncertain, but not frightened. The average Western teenager, however, may suffer doubt, depression and emotional turmoil at the changes that come over him. The emotional intensity and instability that characterise puberty become a dangerous cocktail when mixed with deep-set fears.

Do we need to become increasingly anxious as we get older? Anxiety seems to stop us moving forward. Our old, safe ways become our jail-keepers, and we are often unable to break through the walls we build around ourselves. Much of today's assertiveness training is aimed at combating the fears that prevent us taking the necessary risks for life and growth. In the words of the early twentieth century Chicago businessman

John Shedd, 'Ships in harbour are safe, but that's not what ships are built for.'[21] Yet it would seem that some fear is both necessary and useful. The fisherman who stays in harbour may not catch any fish, but neither will the one who sets out in the storm.

True awareness moderates our behaviour, so that we take some risks and avoid others. The skill is in knowing which ones to take. Of course, a child lacks experience when starting to use his own judgement. He does not know the fire is hot, and most adults would not want him to burn himself in order to find out. So we rush in to stop him when he first meets fire. What else could we possibly do?

Well, we could begin by moderating our responses. If we are always panicking we do not set a useful example in the ways of dealing with the world. We can be aware of dangers long before our children encounter them, which gives us an opportunity to prepare.

THE INTREPID EXPLORER

Were we to trust in the child's process, we might find that he does not need to burn himself to find out about the quality we call 'hot'. A real fire throws off its heat in such a way that would prevent a curious, but slowly approaching toddler from getting burnt. A few inches away, the smoke and heat are already unbearable. He backs off. Similarly a child will not be burned by a radiator, unless it is allowed to become dangerously overheated. He notices its heat, and does not leave his hand where it will burn. We may tell him the radiator is hot, but we need not overstate the fact. Sometimes parents inform bewildered children that a radiator is hot when, in fact, it is switched off. They are assuming that the child will not be able to cope with the possibility of a thing being hot one minute and cold the next. But a young child has no problem with this: he soon learns that radiators are *likely* to be hot, and approaches them with care.

A hot ring on a stove is more dangerous than either of these two, for its inviting glow is no indicator of its extreme heat. A toddler could be introduced to the cooker by his parent before he climbs up to discover the danger on his own. She might hold his hand near the element to let him feel the heat, so offering him direct experience as well as protection, and allowing him to gather the information he needs to protect himself.

In his book *Human Aggression*, Anthony Storr argues that a child's first forays into the real world are aggressive acts, a part of the natural drive to explore and learn. He believes that, as modern Western parents,

> . . . We are forced to over-protect our children psycho-logically, because we live in an artificial environment; and, because small children are ill-equipped to look after themselves when surrounded by the dangerous trappings of civilization, we tend to guard them too carefully in situations where this is not necessary.
>
> In a recent experiment, Eleanor Gibson constructed a 'visual cliff'; that is, a floor which appears to end in a sheer drop, but which is actually safe since the floor continues as a sheet of tough glass. Babies crawl to the apparent edge, but will not venture on to the glass even if encouraged to do so, since they are already aware of the danger of the drop.[22]

We do our children a disservice when we habitually stop them from using their own judgement. It is through experience and the exercise of judgement that a child grows in intelligence and becomes himself. Take, for instance, climbing, an activity that allows a goal-free aquisition of skills, based entirely on the child's own initiative. Many adults actively prevent children from climbing, and few see the point in it. Alison Stallibrass, who had many years' experience of running a free-choice playgroup, regarded climbing as an essential pre-school activity:

> There is one situation in which the youngest toddler can be completely autonomous, because he can be at the same time independent and successful, and that is when

he is climbing upon some suitable object or surface. ('Climbing', for a very small child, includes scrambling and sliding on sloping surfaces, swinging from his hands, jumping or stepping down from boxes, crawling upstairs and easing himself down from one step to another.) As we have seen, he can be relied upon to use his judgement successfully when he is in a situation in which he can depend entirely upon the information concerning that situation that his sensory-motor system is giving him from moment to moment. This is the case when he is 'climbing'. He is deciding for himself where to place his hands and feet and how to hold his body in order to balance, and he is deciding how far and exactly where to climb; moreover he is deciding what he will do with his whole body and not only with his hands and eyes. He feels self-respectingly responsible for himself. It is probable that, at the toddler stage, 'climbing' enhances a child's self-respect and self-confidence more than any other sensory-motor activity.[23]

Falling is always a possibility, but it is a risk we must take if we are to attain new heights. A child teaches himself to climb by moving in small stages at his own pace; he does fall occasionally, but he does not view falling with the same horror and shame that adults do. A child whose body is relaxed falls easily and softly, and is unlikely to do himself serious damage. He knows that falling is not a sign of incompetence, but of having ventured a little too far. Like the entrepreneur who bounces back despite the inevitable setbacks along the way, a child, once mended, wants to know when he can go back for more. While teaching mathematics in America in the late 1950s, John Holt made these observations:

The point I now want to make is that 'success', as much as 'failure', are adult ideas which we impose on children. The two ideas go together, are opposite sides of the same coin. It is nonsense to think that we can give children a love of 'succeeding' without at the same time giving them an equal dread of 'failing'.

Babies learning to walk, and falling down as they try, or healthy six- or seven-year-olds learning to ride a bike, do not think, each time they fall, 'I failed again.' Healthy babies or children, tackling difficult projects of their own choosing, think only when they fall down or off, 'Oops, not yet, try again.' Nor do they think, when finally they begin to walk or ride, 'Oh boy, I'm succeeding!' They think, 'Now I'm walking! Now I'm riding!' The joy is in the act itself, the walking or the riding, not in some idea of success.[24]

WHEN'S THE BEST TIME TO PANIC?

A child has a healthy appetite for activity and no suicidal tendencies. All children are motivated to explore their world in their own way and at their own pace. They are also, however, highly susceptible to adult suggestion about the way the world is. If we panic about their cuts, bruises and any other failures in life, they learn to panic, too.

We react in haste when our children hurt themselves, because we feel powerless to heal their hurt. Health professionals have a valuable role to play in saving lives and repairing broken limbs, but their position has been so elevated in our society that we rarely approach them as our equals. Instead we 'rush' to them fearfully hoping for dispensations of reassurance and a little modern magic. Joseph Chilton Pearce is convinced that we abdicate our power unnecessarily, and gives an astounding example of healing between a father and his eight-year-old son:

A man came to a magical child seminar as the result of an experience that had unnerved him and threatened his academic and rational world view. His eight-year-old son was whittling with a knife, slipped and severed the arteries in his left wrist. Following an instant's panic at the sight of the spurting blood, the father, as if in a dream, seized his screaming son's face, looked into his eyes, and commanded, 'Son, let's stop that blood.' The screaming stopped, the boy beamed back, said 'Okay', and together they stared at the gushing blood and shouted, 'Blood, you stop that.' And the blood stopped.[25]

Chilton Pearce adds that, 'Stopping bleeding has a long history; yoga adepts can do this, and it can be done through hypnosis.' The saying 'mind over matter' reminds us that psychology and physiology are closely interlinked. We can call on the power of the mind to help us deal with physical matters. The same conviction and sense of trust in the child's own healing processes can be applied in any area of communication. We do not have to wait until they are physically hurt.

When I first read *The Continuum Concept* by Jean Liedloff, I had the impression that, if left well alone, my children would have no accidents. Jean interprets the rarity of accidents amongst the Yequana (a remote tribe in the Venezuelan jungle) as a sign of adults' trust in children's competence, which seems entirely reasonable. But she also argues that children only fall and hurt themselves, cut or burn themselves, to fulfil their parents' deepest expectations. As a result, some 'continuum'-following parents blame themselves whenever their child takes a tumble.

However, day-to-day experience with young children teaches us that accidents cannot be entirely avoided. (According to Liedloff, Yequana children also suffered accidents of varying severity.) Close observation has taught me that my children's accidents are usually a consequence of their finding new limits, and exceeding them in some way. There will always be accidents, and I do not believe we need to look for an underlying psychology unless there is a chronic pattern.

If we are to respond humanely to our children, it is vital that we see them as individuals. It is not enough simply to apply a theory and hope for the best. For example there is more than one way for a child to learn that ponds are deep: some children may do this through questions and a cautious approach, while others prefer to tackle life head-on. A parent may inform her child that the pond is deep, but we cannot expect our toddlers to understand this until they experience the sensation of 'deep' for themselves in some way. 'Little the child cares about the knowledge of others;' said Maria Montessori, 'he wants to acquire knowledge of his own . . . to experience the world through his unaided efforts . . .'[26]

Yet, if we detach ourselves from the situation and watch carefully, we soon see that many accidents are caused when an adult offers interference, rather than information. A word out of place, or a guiding hand that interrupts the child's own halting efforts, may be enough to send him toppling onto the sharp corner from which he was being protected.

Prison psychiatrist Dr Bob Johnson uses this very image when describing how parents need to hand over responsibility to their small children. He draws a parallel between letting go in childhood and empowering prisoners to make them want to behave:

> Let's take something as elementary as learning to walk. At first you grip the infant's hand so tightly that she cannot fall. You guide her through the rough patches, and settle her safely down where you know she cannot come to harm. So far, so good. Life's risks and hazards are circumvented by your superior physical prowess and overriding control. But the time [comes] when you must let go that tiny hand.
>
> You know the sharp edges against which the infant skull can crash – but if you never let go, the child will never learn to walk for herself. Maximum control strategy must give way to devolved responsibility. This can be a crucifying moment for any parent – but if you don't do it, the child will never walk tall.[27]

While the adult focuses on sharp corners, the child may not even appear to see the dangers in his path. He does not dwell on obstacles, but steers his way through them, concentrating on the good progress he is making. Like a karate expert who chops his way mentally and manually through a pile of wood, he imagines the positive outcome. However, despite his apparent nonchalance, the toddling child *does take obstacles into account*. He quickly learns what not to bump into, what not to touch and where not to go, from the point of view of his own safety.

EVEN INTREPID EXPLORERS NEED TO REFUEL

Good body awareness starts with the intimate parent-baby relationship. The parent expresses her feelings of inner well-being to her child as she holds him, in the way she rocks and carries him, and in the timeliness of her approaches towards him. Once a child is securely attached to his mother (and/or the other carers who make themselves readily available), he will eventually be ready to move on to the next stage. He feels good, he knows where he feels good, and though he has little or no experience of the world, he is not about to shatter those good feelings with unpleasant experiences. He will protect himself.

When a child starts to move by himself, he first has the chance to learn self-control. Alison Stallibrass believes that such a lesson is best learnt in the early years:

> If children are able to realize their potentiality for general sensory-motor judgement while their centre of gravity is still low, they will continue to respond to opportunities to develop it as they grow taller and heavier. If they fail to acquire it early on, there may come a time when the gap in the sequence of development becomes unbridgeable. As a result, the quality of their behaviour in any activity entailing movement – even moving through a room containing a number of people and pieces of furniture – will be poor for the rest of their lives. They will suffer, at least during their childhood, from a sense of inadequacy and an inhibiting fear of being proved unable to respond effectively to the challenges of their environment.[28]

Now is the time a child must practise his new skills. A crawler needs space in which to crawl, and a groper-of-furniture needs to be allowed to pull himself up into a standing position whenever he feels the urge. This does not mean that a parent has to put a child endlessly through the paces of walking in order to bring on that particular skill more quickly. The child will indicate his needs, as he has done throughout infancy. Constantly urging him to perform new tricks may bring him on faster, but it can also interfere with the delicate process of spontaneous learning. The child's aim is not to learn to walk as quickly as possible, but simply to keep on acquiring body knowledge. Whatever state of maturity you are looking for, the average baby will reach it in the end.

I used to imagine that once Frances had achieved a certain state of independence, she would never look back. It took me a while to accept that my two-year-old was capable of talking in sentences, choosing her own clothes and chopping vegetables, yet in an instant she would run to my arms, suckle contentedly at the breast and act for all the world like a baby again. She even looked like a baby, and felt as soft and yielding as a baby while she fed. Moments later, having taken her fill, she would be off exploring once more. I eventually learnt to see the 'baby' and the 'big girl' as one person. She was able to feel her way through the day and let me know her needs.

The American psychiatrist Dr Ross Campbell talks of the need to replenish a child's 'emotional tank' through love and understanding.[29] Children of all ages return to their parents for refuelling. Their 'babyish' needs are just as valid as their moves towards independence. So although he can now crawl, the newly mobile child does not stray too far from his mother at first. As Jean Liedloff describes, he is preparing to exercise his skill of self-preservation, and does not want to over-stretch it at the start:

> With the commencement of crawling, the baby begins to cash in the powers accumulated passively through his previous experience combined with the physiological development that renders the powers usable. In general, his first expeditions are short and cautious and there is

almost no need for his mother or caretaker to take a hand in his activities. Like all little animals, he has a keen talent for self-preservation and a realistic sense of his capabilities. If his mother suggests to his social instincts that he is expected to leave his safe conduct to her, he will co-operatively do so. If he is constantly watched and steered into moving where his mother thinks he ought to go, stopped and run after when self-motivated, he soon learns to stop being responsible for himself as she shows him what she expects.

One of the deepest impulses in the very social human animal is to do what he perceives is expected of him. (This is not at all the same as doing what he is told.)[30]

The attitudes of adults become vitally important as a child starts to move out on his own. His crawling or shuffling away signifies the shift from complete to partial dependency: will his parents allow him to use his own judgement?

FEARFUL AND FEARLESS

A child soon learns to hand over his sense of self-awareness when invited implicitly to do so. He knows from his parents' manner, their agitation, the way they flash looks at him, whether or not they really trust him to look after himself. If the parents are not undermining him, in our culture strangers often oblige.

In no time at all, the curious, adept, yet self-protecting little human being is at odds with his own environment. Adults' over-protectiveness confuses his innate sense of judgement, and he may react in one of two main ways.

Some small children, when undermined, become excessively fearful for their own safety, to the point where they do not feel able to explore a playgroup or join in with the rough-and-tumble games of their peers. Children absorb the idea of their own incompetence with a vengeance. It saddens me to hear a child say 'I mustn't or I'll hurt myself', in a clearly identifiable adult tone, because a premature fear of failure has stunted his approach to new experience. Alison Stallibrass encountered such children in her playground:

> [A child] . . . needs to encounter all sorts of hazards, obstacles and challenges to his skill, and to be able to decide for himself which to overcome and which to circumvent, and to be entirely responsible for where and how he moves . . .
>
> A small child can become fettered by a consciousness of his lack of general sensory-motor judgement. No matter how permissive the environment in which he finds himself, if he has lacked opportunity to learn to move with precision, speed, balance and agility, he might as well be dragging a ball and chain. We may say to him: 'Here you are; go ahead and play!' But if he has no confidence in his ability to enjoy active play, he is not free to play . . .[31]

While some children under-react to the world, others overdo it. They are not cowed by their parents' hold on them, but are sent into a frenzy by it. They become kamikaze in their approach to their environment, hurling themselves around without regard for their own or others' safety. At a playgroup I helped to organise in Manchester, we encountered the occasional child like this. On entering the room, one such child was not satisfied until he had upturned every toy in sight. He would arrive in a pushchair, from which he was unleashed like a whirling dervish. Whether he was strapped in because he was deemed uncontrollable, or whether his actions were a revolt against being strapped in, was not entirely clear.

Maria Montessori believed that every child longed to respect his environment and his place within it. The 'deviations' of violence, disorder and over-fearfulness that she identified in children disappeared in the free, but fearfully prepared Montessori environment. She called this 'normalisation':

> Anything that enables a child to come into contact with reality and to experience and understand his environ-

ment will help to free him from this disturbing state of fear . . .

A 'state of fear' is different from that dread aroused by the instinct of self-preservation in the face of danger . . .

None of the children in our schools have performed any heroic feats, though they have on occasion expressed some truly noble desires. As a rule our children develop a kind of 'prudence', which enables them to avoid dangers and consequently to live with them. They can handle knives at a table and even in the kitchen, use matches for lighting a fire or even sparklers, stand alone near pools of water, and cross city streets. Our children have learned how to control their actions and avoid rashness . . . Normalisation, therefore, does not consist in hurling oneself into the midst of dangers, but in acquiring a prudence which permits one to recognise and dominate dangers and thus be in a position to live in the midst of them.[32]

We all do, and must, live with danger. Whether the danger consists of jungle beasts, flights of stairs or steaming hot kettles, we need to learn to know and respect our enemy. With the right approach, we can make the enemy our friend. This is what Montessori meant by 'dominating danger'.

The pursuit of safety, on the other hand, is relentless.

THE SAFETY CATCH

Safety campaigns that are designed to scare or bully us into taking better care of our lives, do not take into account the importance of risk for human happiness. If we are prevented from taking the small, well-planned risks that lead to growth, then many of us are driven to take bigger, unplanned risks that carry greater dangers.

Risk Homeostasis Theory, which explains why, after a certain point, safety measures do not actually improve safety, is explained in full in John Adams's book *Risk and Freedom*. Dangerous-looking roads with fast-flowing traffic often have low accident records: 'the road looks dangerous and so people respect it,' says Adams. He goes on:

> there are considerably fewer children under the age of fifteen killed in road accidents now than there were in 1927. This does not mean that the roads have become safer. Traffic has increased enormously since 1927 and the roads have become much more dangerous. If children played in the streets today with the same heedlessness to traffic that characterised their behaviour fifty years ago there would be slaughter on an unimaginable scale. The reduction in the juvenile road death rate has been brought about mainly by changes in the behaviour of juvenile road users. Safety for children has been purchased at the cost of their freedom.
>
> . . . the low priority accorded to the rights of children is betrayed by the language used to discuss the accidents in which they are involved. A category commonly used in the safety literature for the classification of pedestrian accidents is 'dartouts'. Haight and Olsen note that a more appropriate label might be 'children'.[33]

In 2002, British politicians announced they were considering a proposal from Holland to make road junctions safer. This involved doing away with existing safety measures and replacing them with a simple box painted in the road. The Dutch had found this was a more reliable way of reducing accidents. Instead of relying on external signs and mechanisms, drivers were forced to make eye-to-eye contact with each other and negotiate their way through the junction.[34] This is the essential paradox of living safely: the more we try to protect ourselves from danger, the more responsibility we abdicate and the less we rely on our own sensing to get us out of trouble. Relying on safety systems may be less safe than relying on ourselves.

When children's (and adults') freedom is restricted, and with it the opportunity for measured risk-taking, we are forced to look elsewhere for our kicks. In an article entitled 'The doctor prescribes white-knuckle terror', British psychologist David Lewis explains the current popularity of theme parks like Alton Towers in Staffordshire:

> The white-knuckle ride is a way of getting your thrills in a more communal way. There's a sense of having been through an experience together. The screams and the rattle of the machinery are part of it, along with the G-force on your body, the effect on your balance mechanism and the zapping of your vision. Your whole sensory mechanism is being disturbed, but deep down you know that you're safe, because you see others getting off and going back time and time again.[35]

In a theme park, despite the simulation of risk, safety is actually taken care of. The child does not have to exercise his judgement, only strap himself in. This is how he is expected to satisfy his need for risk and exploration. In one way, it works – the child receives the physical jolts (or disturbance of his sensory mechanism) which deliciously remind him that he is only human after all. But minimal risk or exploration has taken place. Back in the real world, real dangers remain untamed. They lie in wait like wild animals, sometimes causing a disproportionate level of fear.

If the child grows up without having learnt to master any so-called 'dangerous' skills, for example, swimming, balancing or handling sharp objects, then he may grow up to be clumsy or accident-prone. His fearful actions make the danger precisely as dangerous as he fears it to be. Instead of the child dominating the danger, the danger dominates the child.

SCISSOR HAPPY

Let us consider the first encounter between a small child and a pair of sharp scissors. Most parents take care to keep such an item out of the child's way, but we all make mistakes. One day, the scissors are left within reach of a curious toddler. We will presume that he has not yet been taught to mistrust his own senses. He picks up the scissors and starts to examine them, slowly turning them over in his small hands. They feel cold and heavy. Shiny, too: he can see his face in them. He is attracted by the sharp point at one end – he has already encountered some sharp points in his short lifetime. He puts his finger tentatively to the tip, and retracts it again. Ow!

Now he knows a lot about the scissors, and he runs to Mummy to show her what he has found. Mummy screams, snatches the scissors from his grasp, and shouts at him for handling them. She feels guilty for having left scissors lying around, and that makes her shout a little louder than she intended. The child screams, frightened and bewildered at her outburst.

In fact, the boy's sensory awareness was still well-tuned and he would have been quite safe in a situation like this. He might have cut into his mother's favourite curtain fabric, because he would not know any better, but he would not deliberately poke the scissors in his eye, because he already knows that his eye is a highly sensitive organ.

He had thought he was beginning to understand scissors, but his mother's reaction makes him believe otherwise. Scissors now hold a special allure, becoming something he either fears or longs to get hold of: what hidden potency do they contain? Why is his mother frightened of them? There must be more to scissors than meets the eye.

But there isn't, of course. Scissors are just about as dangerous as they appear, to anyone with eyes to see and hands to feel them. If mother had used this opportunity to show her child what scissors are made for, perhaps even allowed him to 'have a go', then he would have even more information to enable him to understand them. She could perhaps, without any sense of panic, put a word, 'sharp', to his experience of the point. She could, depending on his age, show him a way of walking with scissors or where they are kept. She could at least take them from him gently, calmly and with interest in his discovery. She might then invest in a set of small, plastic scissors for his little fingers to use, if it makes her feel happier.

The well-equipped child can be trusted in most instances to

be full of care. Any approach that comes naturally from the care-giver as an expression of her trust in him empowers him to look after himself. The empowering of our children, so that they will grow up trusting in their own inner resources, is the best protection a parent can give her child.

FALLING DOWN STAIRS

It is not easy to let a baby crawl out of our protective arms and into the great unknown. With first children, Western parents are often as inexperienced as the child himself: it isn't until your toddler has pulled down the first cup of coffee all over himself that you realise the coffee table is something of a liability.

The answer is to prepare the environment in such a way that a child can feel his freedom, and we can relax. I spoke to one mother who said she had brought up her children (now teenagers) almost entirely in the family lounge, having installed stair-gates in every doorway. This sounds quite restrictive, but in fact she did this because she never wanted to nag her children, and she never had to. She asserted that they have grown up to be 'wonderful, caring, responsible' adults. The stair-gates gave her freedom from worry, and she did not have to focus on her children's safety. But like any other gadget employed to restrict a child's freedom, the stair-gate carries its own risks. It draws attention to itself, and makes the carpet on the other side look very tempting. The day the stair-gate is mistakenly left open, the frustrated child is impelled to explore the terrain that has for so long been denied to him.

No chance to sit and contemplate the dangers, pottering around its lower steps, or judging distances from the top. No opportunity for practice. He jumps straight in; and falls straight down. The distraught parent may then conclude: a) that she is an inadequate parent for having left the gate open, and b) that her child truly is incapable of coping with the stairs. She increases the pressure on herself to be her child's perfect guardian, and continues to underestimate her child's ability to cope in the real world.

When making our decision about stair-gates and other protective devices around the home, parents must consider their own home and inclinations. Not all of us would have the nerves of steel required to deliver this idyllic scene from the South American rainforest:

When he goes about on his hands and knees, a baby can travel at a fair speed. Among the Yequana, I watched uneasily as one creeper rushed up and stopped at the edge of a pit five feet deep that had been dug for mud to make walls. In his progress about the compound, he did this several times a day. With the inattentiveness of an animal grazing at the edge of a cliff, he would tumble to a sitting position, as often as not facing away from the pit. Occupied with a stick or stone or his fingers or toes, he played and rolled about in every direction, seemingly heedless of the pit, until one realized he landed everywhere but in the danger zone. The non-intellect-directed mechanisms of self-preservation worked unfailingly . . . he took charge of his own relationships with all the surrounding possibilities. The only suggestion from the members of his family and society was that they expected him to be able to look after himself.[36]

On the assumption that a young mammal is equipped to deal with his physical world, we decided to try to give Frances this level of freedom. But the first time she pulled herself up the stairs, I lagged nervously behind, not daring to trust in her instincts to make it to the top. Three quarters of the way up, she turned and saw me anxiously following her. She jumped – after all, mummy had made her mistrust emminently clear. I couldn't quite reach. She was not really hurt, but we were both shocked. It is the only time she has ever done anything daft from a great height.

I soon realised that my child's natural mechanisms of self-protection were not going to work as long as I was in the way. I sat myself in the lounge, biting my nails, while Frances heaved herself up the stairs. Gradually, over the next few days, I learnt to relax, and she mastered the ups and downs. Our second daughter, Alice, was allowed complete freedom to explore the stairs. I had realised that children are constantly living on the edge, taking small risks, and that therefore there would be falls. Writing now, at a distance of more than a decade, I can't remember even one. And that also goes for my son, Joe, who began his stair-climbing career some four years later.

The following quotation from Maria Montessori reminds me of the reason that children struggle to attain ever new heights:

> 'Staircases have the greatest appeal because children have in themselves an innate tendency to go upwards . . .'[37]

Children are programmed for experience, not self-destruction. I try to remember this every time my children break the safety barrier and my heart misses a beat. As Joseph Chilton Pearce put it:

> The mother risks her child because she knows that she has no choice except to trust the life process.[38]

Without any sense of perspective on the matter, a child knows how to grow up. He is programmed to follow his own instincts, which propel him to equip himself for life. He knows that he has many different needs – sometimes to be like a baby, sometimes to be allowed to 'do it himself' – but it does not occur to him that these needs are contradictory unless an adult tells him so.

Only when his judgement is called into question does he doubt himself. When parents over-protect a child, his natural steering begins to go off course.

We need to trust our children, if they are ever to trust themselves.

Letting go as children grow: safety

- Small children are generally able to protect themselves from visible dangers, such as stairs, slopes, furniture, scissors and pointy corners
- They are not able to protect themselves from dangers which are invisible or difficult-to-judge, such as speeding cars, medicines or cleaning fluids
- The best way to nurture a child's innate safety mechanisms is repeatedly to demonstrate trust in his own body sensing and to give him the chance to practice physical skills
- Climbing is a supremely useful activity for all children, as it hones their confidence and self-assurance. The climbing child progresses very much at his own pace
- We may not be able to prevent our feelings of panic rising when children attempt new tricks, but we would do well to hide them if we can

3

A CHILD REALISES HIMSELF –

WAYS THAT SMALL CHILDREN EXPLORE THEIR WORLD

> But I, being poor, have only my dreams;
> I have spread my dreams under your feet;
> Tread softly because you tread on my dreams.
>
> W.B. Yeats, 'He Wishes for
> the Cloths of Heaven'

'Busy, busy,' my parents-in-law would say as they watched their grand-children playing. Our children, like most small children, were on the go from the moment they opened their eyes in the morning to the minute their heads hit the pillow at night. Climbing, prodding, dismantling, mending, questioning, loving, jumping, pulling, pleading – the action never stops. A trained athlete was once set the task of following a two-year-old around for the day, and copying every movement the toddler made. The athlete gave up long before the toddler.

The natural exuberance of a small child is wonderful to see, yet it is a source of irritation to many grown-ups. Just stand in any long queue in a bank or store, and watch the annoyed faces of adults as two-year-olds run rings around their legs, threatening to pull over the rope barriers and squealing with evident delight. Public bars bear notices announcing we can bring our children in so long as they don't make a noise. Yet there are few restrictions on adults laughing, shouting or becoming rowdy under the effects of alcohol.

A healthy, alert toddler is capable of making his presence felt in any company. He likes to reach, to explore, to run and jump and climb. Only a sick, exhausted or shy child sits limply on his mother's knee and does not move or shout or interrupt. Yet this is the model of childhood society has chosen as its ideal: the child who is seen but not heard. And it is the quiet, the unadventurous, the placid child who is most likely to receive the label of 'good'.

So if you take your child to the supermarket, and present him with shelves of brightly coloured packages and expect him not to touch or make any demands, there is an evident conflict of interests. When trouble occurs, you will be judged for your ability to suppress your child's natural means of expression and exploration.

This is not a recommendation for children to create havoc, but it is a plea for tolerance. The following extract by gardening columnist (and father of three) Stephen Anderton neatly sums up a very British attitude. He proposes that, since there is little for them to do 'except run and shout', children should be banned from public gardens:

> Gardeners who have their loving work stomped on by children speak with bitter frustration. Many would like to double the adult entry fee for children. To these gardeners, thoughtless minor damage has a cumulative effect: a small branch of a magnificent rhododendron pulled off to dip in a pond, a fern frond stripped to its spine by a passing hand, plants trodden down to climb up a wall. If a deer or rabbit did this, it would be shot.[1]

Listen carefully – you can almost hear the gardeners cheering behind the hedge as their rights are playfully asserted. And as a fair-weather gardener myself, I have some sympathy with the frustration of the serious plant-person. However, this argument belongs to a particularly vicious circle which creates its own problems. In Britain, we ban children on the basis that they can't behave; in South America, children are welcome everywhere on the basis that they can. Who is right? It seems to me that in each continent, we get the children we expect and deserve.

One 1990s survey on 'dining out' revealed that children were welcome and usually indulged in Spain, Japan, Sweden (where 'it would be unheard of to restrict access'[2]), France, Italy, Hungary and America. In most countries, Reasonable Infant Behaviour is achieved, not by loading all the responsibility onto harassed parents, but by all adults assuming some of the joys and responsibilities of having children around. In Britain, the two-fold belief that 'our kids are brats'[2] and that their parents are to blame, has created an atmosphere of zero tolerance:

> 'I *certainly* won't be applying for a [children's] certificate,' [allowing pubs to admit clients of any age] says David Meredith, landlord of The Swan at Denham, Buckinghamshire. 'Children are so badly behaved, often completely out of parental control – and the parents are oblivious to what their kids are doing. I would lose my regulars.'[2]

The way out of the maze requires a brand new map. In order to create a child-friendly society, we have to start by acting as if we *are* child-friendly – that means supporting parents and taking some of the responsibility for other people's children when they are out and about. Spanish parents do not forever have to chase after their babies or hush them in a visit to a late-night café – the children are fondly attended by waiters and kind strangers; they are played with and cared for by bigger children who know how to behave.

Of course it is important that small children are supervised and taught good manners; of course it is inappropriate for them to disturb the atmosphere with yelling and screaming; but paradoxically, when tolerance levels are generally higher, children are less likely to step seriously out of line.

JUMPING FOR JOY

It's the unfettered exuberance of childhood which seems to grate on many adult nerves. As the American play therapist Virginia Axline wrote, the child expresses his whole self through his body:

> One need only to observe the physical response of a child to realize that, when happy, he is happy all over. His eyes dance and sparkle. His step is light and carefree. His laugh is free and quick to come bubbling to the surface. When he feels loved and secure and successful, he goes forth courageously about this business of living, and life is a gay adventure that he rushes out eagerly to meet.
> . . . when a child is sad and depressed, his figure droops, his movements are slow and heavy, his eyes mirror the unhappiness that is in his being. He is unhappy from the top of his head to the bottom of his feet.[3]

When we ask our children to control their excited bodies, we might as well ask them not to be quite so happy. 'Children are known to be so excited they literally jump'[4], says bio-energetic therapist Alexander Lowen. When a small child is prevented from jumping, he misses out on some of life's excitement. Many adults have long ago learnt to suppress their bodily responses. Alexander Technique teacher and author Glen Park says the physical letting-go experienced by her students is often accompanied by waves of emotional release. She contrasts adults' restricted movements with those of a child:

> I remember seeing a short film which concentrated on the movements of human beings. It showed speeded-up scenes of children and of adults. It was fascinating to notice how the adult movements were quite clearly the same movements as the children were making, but cut off short, so where a young child would fling out an arm, an adult might move the arm outwards just an inch or two and then halt the movement and hold it within very tight

74

parameters, covering only about 5 per cent of the child's movement. Our civilizing process seems to necessitate this kind of repression at all levels of our being, physically, emotionally, mentally and spiritually.[5]

It is commonplace to tell children to shut up and keep still. Many people regard this as an essential part of the socialisation process. I have often found myself begging the children to 'calm down' or 'take it easy', although it is not healthy, boisterous, open-air kind of behaviour that bothers me, but late-in-the-day tiredness that results from us all being cooped up indoors, or from being 'wound up' or tense.

The same kind of wound-up feeling is sometimes induced by adult visitors, typically the young-at-heart avuncular types, who breeze in occasionally and do a star turn, and get a kick out of winding children up to a pitch of excitement. The children's squeals of anticipation and delight, drawn out to a frenzy, often end in tears.

Neither over-stimulation nor suppression is what the child seeks. As children get older and gain more control over their bodies, they may feel they have to suppress their urge for self-expression and sensual gratification. A few learn to hide their feelings from the world by wearing an all-body mask. Eventually they may stop knowing what it is they feel at all. There is a danger of conveying to our children that only quiet, peaceful, non-interruptive behaviour is welcome.

Thérèse Bertherat, a body-awareness therapist working with adults in France, believes many of us have become alienated from our bodies. She says it is as though we live in houses 'on a dead-end street'. We have been conditioned into stiffness, lifelessness and muscular deficiency:

Without realizing it, from the first months of your life you have reacted to family, social, and moral pressures. 'Stand like this, like that. Don't touch things. Don't touch yourself. Be nice. Defend yourself. Hurry up. Don't run . . .' Confused, you bent your will and your body as much as you could. To conform, you have deformed yourself. In place of your real body, naturally harmonious and dynamic, a foreign body has been substituted.

You have trouble accepting it. In your innermost self, you reject it.[6]

If adults reject themselves, then they are likely also to reject their children. Children's aliveness, their bounciness and their expressiveness make us feel uncomfortable at times, for we have long denied ourselves the possibility of expressing our feelings in so overt a manner.

LEARNING THROUGH TOUCH

Body learning begins long before verbal conditioning. The baby in his mother's arms responds to the way he is held. Born so soft and malleable, a baby's body will, if left alone for long periods, become stiff and unyielding. If his carer always holds him anxiously, he will feel ill at ease in himself. But if held lightly, with sensitivity whenever he needs it, the baby's senses will be vibrant, his body energy undisturbed. Alexander Lowen describes how the quality of touch can help build her child's body image:

Since the child's identity in early life is mainly a body identity, the quality of the physical contact between mother and child will determine its feeling for its body and the nature of its responses to life. Warm, tender, and supporting arms give the child a pleasurable feeling in its own body and reinforce its desire for further contact with the world . . .[7]

A tiny baby reaches out with his mouth for the breast. As she feeds her child, a mother feeds his natural optimism, letting him know that it is good to make his needs known, and that if he uses his initiative he will make things happen. If his infantile requests are not denied in the early days, he will continue to greet the world with an interactive curiosity that feeds his intelligence.

76

However, as a child matures, plenty of opportunities arise to thwart his attempts at self-realisation. Parents and teachers habitually try to curb a child's activity, until his capacity for learning in small steps, following his own intuition and driven by his lust for life, is gradually diminished. As Thérèse Bertherat says,

> Since a stationary image would be most convenient for us, we're forever telling our children to 'be still'. But for a child, to move is as basic a need as to eat or sleep. His physical and also his intellectual development depend on it . . . A child's 'agitation' is his way of investigating not only the external world but his own possibilities.
>
> When we scold a child for his physical activity, we reduce his field of experience, we impede the development of his intelligence, and we encourage him to repress the natural expression of his emotions. By giving the child, who has a natural gift for imitating, the example of skimpy or stiff movements, we teach him to deaden his feelings and we set him a trap of awkwardness and lack of confidence from which he'll have difficulty escaping once he's an adult.[8]

Educator Maria Montessori, who saw the cot as a cage, and spent her life creating an environment where children could be 'free', recognised the signs of chronic frustration in children who were cooped up in restrictive environments: 'A child often cries when he is confined in a small space which offers nothing but frustration to the exercise of his powers . . .'[9], she wrote. She also realised the damage done when a child was prevented from exercising all his senses, especially his powers of touch.

When only a few months old, before speech or independent mobility, the child begins to reach out with his hands. The need to experience the world through touch is fundamental and yet, as Maria Montessori recognised, we fear a child's hands as much as we fear all his other excited movements and out-reachings:

The human hand, so delicate and so complicated, not only allows the mind to reveal itself but it enables the whole being to enter into special relationships with its environment. We might even say that man 'takes possession of his environment with his hands.' His hands under the guidance of his intellect transform this environment and thus enable him to fulfil his mission in the world . . .

The first intelligent moving of these tiny hands, the first thrust of that movement which represents the effort of the ego to penetrate the world should fill an adult's mind with admiration. But instead he is *afraid* of those tiny hands stretching out for things that are of no value or importance in themselves, and he strives to keep them from the child. He is constantly saying 'Don't touch!' just as he constantly repeats, 'Be still! Keep quiet!'[10]

Reading this, I am reminded of scene from my own childhood. I must be seven or eight and I am standing in the corner shop, which has a new owner. They have a new range of children's toys: metal cars, a few plastic dolls. Intrigued, I pick up the first toy to hand. From around the shelf comes the shopkeeper, a woman with a surprisingly loud voice. 'What do you think *you're* doing, Miss Fiddlefingers?' she says sharply. 'Put that down at once!' I put the toy down and everyone turns to look at me. Utterly humiliated, I do not go back into the shop for years.

It's all right for adults. We have long moved out of the stage where we need to feel things, to taste them, to *experience* them before consigning them to the mental catalogue of the brain. We don't need to eat wallpaper paste because, somewhere in our memory, we ate something similar many years ago and decided it tasted foul. We don't need to poke our fingers into frog spawn because we've been there before.

It is not uncommon for children to have phobias about death, and I believe this is in part due to the way they are shielded from it. A child who witnesses illness and dying for himself, approaches it with the matter-of-fact attitude with which he approaches all things. I know this from seeing

Frances around my father as he was dying in hospital. She understood the seriousness of his condition, and talked freely about it, but was never fearful or hysterical. Her first-hand experience taught her that loved ones may die, but she can cope. At four years old, she was not old enough fully to 'understand' death – which of us does? – but she *could* cope with reality, whatever form it took.

Rather than allow our children to have a hands-on approach to life, we may decide to protect them 'for their own good'. Sometimes we tell children they are naughty for having explored the world and caused a mess. Even if we don't, they soon pick up on our subconscious attitudes to their creative endeavours. ('Look Mummy!' said Frances aged three, sitting with her scissors in a pile of paper pieces, 'I made a damage.') Sometimes we remove them from the scene of the 'crime' ('before something gets broken.'). At other times, we simply butt in with our opinion: 'Oh, don't eat that, you won't like it.'

WORDS AND DREAMS

It is almost inevitable that the child's immature view will eventually be replaced by the views of his parents, his school, his friends – his culture. Children try to teach themselves about the world, but people swiftly intercept with their impressions and opinions. This is an unavoidable and natural process, but it does involve some loss on the child's side. Before long, he realises that he cannot rely merely on his own experiences and beliefs. Everything he does is glossed by cultural interpretation. In *Diary of a Baby*, developmental psychologist Dr Daniel Stern describes how the worlds of adults and children collide as a mother offers her interpretation of the world to twenty-month-old Joey. Joey is exploring a patch of sunlight in his own special way, when mum walks in:

. . . Joey is standing in his own room waiting to be dressed. His mother will be back in a minute. He sees the sunlight on his wall and floor. He walks over to a sunpatch lying on the dark wooden floor. Absorbed, he drops to his hands and knees. He looks at it. He touches it with his hand. He lowers his face and touches the sunpatch with his lips.

At that moment, his mother returns and sees him. She is both surprised and a little disgusted. She shouts, 'Don't do that! Joey, what are you doing?' Joey stops abruptly. He stares at the spot of sunlight, then looks up at his mother. She walks over to him, bends down, puts her arm around him, and says reassuringly, even with a smile, 'That's just sunshine, honey. It's just to look at. It's only light on the floor. You can't eat this sunshine. It's dirty.'

Joey looks at her a long while and then back at the sunpatch on the floor. He disengages himself from her arm and walks out of the room.[11]

Joey's version of this incident is expressed for him by Dr Stern. Joey tries to comprehend the pool of sunlight by comparing it with other experiences in his memory. He loves the sunshine, and while his reactions to it are scientific (sifting through the data without judging it), they are also poetic and full of awe. But before he can fully log this harmonious experience in his brain, mother steps in:

The morning glow is there again, with its slow dance on the wall. And on the floor it is a pool, bright and beautiful and deep. It is like looking down long stairs. It is warm, like a blanket. It vibrates like music, glows like honey. And it tastes like –

Mommy's voice slaps me. At once it freezes my bright space. It chills the warmth, stops the music, douses the glow. Why?

I search her face. I can see it get all pinched around the nose. It turns quickly into anger. Then both expressions flow out together, and loving rushes in. I am still stunned. She holds me and says soft, lilting words. Yet each of her words is a muffled blow that cracks my space into pieces.

'Just sunshine' – but it was my pool, a special pool!

'It's just to look at' – I heard it. I felt it, too!
'Only light on the floor' – How?
'It's dirty' – I was in it.
When she stops, the pieces lie all around. That world is
gone. I feel naked and sad. I'm all by myself.[11]

Parents destroy their children's dreams in a thousand ways. They cannot help it, for they intrude on the small child's non-verbal world with words. Words analyse, explain, justify, but they cannot capture the multi-sensual experience of the small child.

Keith Johnstone, author of *Impro*, the classic handbook on theatrical improvisation, describes how schools may disturb a child's creativity. More and more adults achieve literacy in the modern world, he says, but there has been no corresponding boom in the number of poets, playwrights or artists . . .

You can get a glimmer of the damage done when you watch people trying out pens in stationers' shops. They make feeble little scribbles for fear of giving something away. If an Aborigine asked us for a sample of Nordic art we'd have to direct him to an art gallery. No Aborigine ever told an anthropologist, 'Sorry Baas, I can't draw.' Two of my students said they couldn't draw and I asked, 'Why?' One said her teacher had been sarcastic because she'd painted a blue snowman (every child's painting was pinned up on the walls except hers). The other girl had drawn trees up the sides of her paintings (like Paul Klee), and the teacher drew a 'correct' tree on top of hers. She remembered thinking 'I'll never draw for you again!'[12]

Many a child learns to withdraw his hand after it has been scorched by an adult wishing to elevate herself to the role of judge. The play therapist Virginia Axline described the defences a child is forced to erect in order to protect his inner world from outside criticism:

Too many people are tempted to exploit his personality, and so he defends his identity. He keeps himself apart, revelling in the things that to him are so vastly important and interesting.

Bent intently over some simple thing, the child indulges his insatiable curiosity and sensory interests, and the adult is prone to laugh or belittle him when he announces, with the thrill of a true discoverer in his voice, 'Why this sand is gritty and sharp and it tastes like nothing. Is *this* what nothing tastes like?'[13]

Dr Richard Lansdowne, Chief Psychologist at Great Ormond Street, the Hospital for Sick Children in London, once told me there's no faster way to send someone mad than to laugh at them. Keith Johnstone describes sanity as 'a pretence, a way we *learn* to behave.'[14] He says, 'Most people I meet are secretly convinced that they're a little crazier than the average person', but they keep their crazy ideas quiet.

THE CRAZY CHILD

Society has historically felt so threatened by people's psychotic or heretical ideas that individuals were locked away for expressing them. Likewise, when children overstep the boundaries of acceptable behaviour, they are liable to be sent to their room, and even locked in there. The irony is that incarceration is liable to drive a person crazy, as it deprives him of the freedom to express himself to anybody who cares.

Take, for instance, the story of Dibs. A highly intelligent young boy (he was eventually tested to have an IQ of 168), Dibs appeared to his early teachers to be mentally retarded. Today, we would say he had 'special needs'. He spent his school day lying prone on the floor or hiding under tables, and yet had temper tantrums when it was time to go home.

The school paediatrician thought Dibs might be brain-damaged or psychotic (crazy), but could not get close enough to test him. Dibs went for play therapy with Virginia Axline, and the result of their encounter over many months is described in her book *Dibs: In Search of Self*. Here Miss Axline visits the family home:

I opened the wrought iron gate, walked up the steps, and rang the door chimes. Through the closed door I could hear muffled screams, 'No lock door! No lock door! No! No! No!' The voiced trailed off into silence. Apparently, Dibs was not going to join us for tea. A uniformed maid opened the door . . . The maid was a very trim, serious woman who looked as though she could have been with the family for many years. She was remote, precise, formal. I wondered if she ever smiled . . .

The house was beautifully and precisely furnished. The drawing room didn't look as though a child had ever spent five minutes there. In fact, there were no signs that anyone really *lived* in the house . . .

[Dibs' mother said]: 'It is very kind of you to undertake this assignment. And I want you to know that we do not expect any miracle. We have accepted the tragedy of Dibs.'[15]

Dibs and 'Miss A.' develop a friendship and mutual respect, and soon the highly sensitive little boy begins to reveal his feelings. In this episode Dibs is sitting cross-legged in the sandbox of the play therapy room:

He took a deep breath. Then he started to sing . . . His expression was serious. He looked like a little choir boy. The words, though, were not choir-boy words.

'Oh, I hate – hate – hate,' he sang. 'I hate the walls and the doors that lock and the people who shove you in. I hate the tears and the angry words and I'll kill them all with my little hatchet and hammer their bones and spit on them.' He reached down in the sand, picked up a toy soldier, pounded it with the rubber hatchet, spat on it. 'I spit in your face. I spit in your eye. I gouge your head down deep in the sand,' he sang. His voice rang out, sweetly and clearly. 'And the birds do fly from the east to the west and it is a bird that I want to be. Then I'll fly away over the walls, out the door, away, away, away from all my enemies. I'll fly and fly around the world and

I'll come back to the sand, to the playroom, to my friend.
I'll dig in the sand. I'll bury in the sand. I'll throw in the
sand. I'll play in the sand. I'll count all the grains of the
sand and I'll be a baby again.'

He sucked on the nursing bottle again. He grinned at
me. 'How did you like my song?' he asked.

'That was quite a song,' I replied.[16]

Dibs was suffering from severe emotional neglect. He was used
to being confined to his room and shut out in many other ways
by his parents. Whether we restrain our children physically or
psychologically, we may put a bar on their growth. Dibs needed
complete acceptance in order to grow, and the atmosphere of
tolerance provided by his play therapist was enough to make him
feel worthwhile. But, being the intelligent, sensitive child that he
was, Dibs put Miss Axline's tolerance thoroughly to the test.
Complete acceptance is difficult even for a therapist, and this
therapist could not help herself shouting out when Dibs tried to
taste scouring powder from a high shelf. Imagine the difficulty
for the average parent, who copes on a daily basis without
training or support. If parents sometimes find themselves shouting, interfering and prodding unnecessarily in their children's
lives, they need not feel guilty – they are in the company of
parents struggling all over the world to get things right.

Play therapy offers an oasis of calm for the beleaguered
child, an hour-long session during which he can do as he
pleases within a few well-defined limitations. He can shout,
throw things, paint blue snowmen or *do nothing*, and his
therapist keeps her ego out of the way. He will not be
criticised, praised, hurried, cajoled or directed in his play.

Genuine respect, backed up by non-interfering behaviour, is
what a child needs to discover his own strength. Parents, of
course, have the added task of delivering discipline (see
Chapter 7: The Roots of Discipline).

The therapist's premise, that she does not know as much
about the child's inner world as does the child himself, is the
basis of their relationship. *She allows the child to reveal
himself.* This is a hard task for parents, who do not have

the training, the support or the luxury of an hour's play therapy in which to accept all a child's emotions and outbursts. However, we can at least try to apply the principle of letting the child realise his own dreams. This might mean letting him paint blue snowmen, but not letting him throw paint all over the room. It might mean letting him express his wildest ideas and deepest fears without fear of rejection or scorn. It would *not* include expressing his anger by (for instance) hitting his mother, or hurting another child.

Although I believe parents are more informed than the experts about their own children, I also feel we have to relinquish our 'knowing' with every day that passes. I may feel I know my children *now*, the way they are today, but my memory of them last week or last year is hazy at best. I also have no idea how their lives will turn out. Nor does anyone else. You simply cannot get an overview on your own child. So why do we insist on labelling them? 'You don't like broccoli,' a father tells his daughter who has only tried it once. 'You'll never be a librarian,' a grandmother warns, an oracle of ignorance and doom. Labelling is just another way of putting children down, of keeping them pidgeon-holed and ensuring that they turn out as we expect.

CONSTANT INTERRUPTIONS

When we let our children be, they slowly begin to realise their own potential, to create themselves. Some years ago I went with a friend to visit a local Montessori school. She found it 'weird' to see a small room full of children all busily engrossed in their activities, some waiting patiently for their turn with a certain piece of equipment. It certainly would have been unnatural for the children to have been so quiet, ordered and still if the orders had come from the teacher, or were being somehow imposed on them. But as Axline said, and Montessori understood, 'responsible freedom grows and develops from inside the person.'

Children long to be allowed to reach out to find themselves. Montessori's schools provide the activities their eager hands are seeking, and it is up to the child himself to take what he needs. When we give children the opportunity to do things for themselves, they become open to learning.

The work of children is not to produce an artifact, but to make small steps towards self-realisation. For this reason, it is crucial that they be allowed to make mistakes and gather their own experiences. A child knows he has to push himself towards new realms of experience, and is therefore attracted to activities that challenge his present capabilities without crippling them. Alison Stallibrass observes the way this is done:

> . . . an infant tends to select for investigation things which are different but not too different from those with which he is already familiar, things that have a quality of . . . 'difference-in-sameness'; the baby's curiosity is aroused by the slightly strange and the mildly frightening, his desire to master by the slightly difficult and the mildly frustrating.[17]

A child approaches a new object with all his senses alert. He must discover what place this object occupies in his world, what opportunities it affords for honing his personal skills. Unlike the modern adult who may try to distract himself from work, because it makes him feel alienated from himself, children are drawn towards useful experience. A child who is absorbed with his hands is never merely 'messing around', but realising himself. We do our children a great disservice by interrupting their spontaneous play, as Maria Montessori believed:

> If a child is to develop his interior life, he must not only be allowed to touch various objects and work with them but he must do this in a rational and consistent fashion . . .
> . . . but he is never allowed to lay out a continuous course of action. If a child is playing, an adult interrupts him, thinking that it is time for a walk. The child is dressed and taken out. Or a child may be working at a

task such as filling a pail with stones when a friend of his mother calls. The child is then interrupted in his work and shown to the visitor. An adult is constantly interrupting the child and breaking into his environment. This powerful being directs the child's life without ever consulting the child himself. And this lack of consideration makes the child think that his own activities are of no value.[18]

Interruptions come in many guises. Sometimes a parent treats his child as inferior to herself, someone who must drop everything when she calls. Sometimes she interrupts his play with a negative attitude, shattering a promising experience. To understand how this must feel to the child, consider what it feels like to have *our* new experiences ruined by an intrusive and negative opinion.

In *Considering Children*, progressive British teacher David Gribble reminds us of the many ways in which children are bullied by adults. In the simplest and smallest ways we treat them as our social inferiors:

> Manners were invented as a form of self-defence. They were for the defence of the refined against the boorish. In the relation between grown-ups and children, however, they have too often become offensive weapons as well, with good manners usually a one-way business. It is the children who have to abandon their games to say goodbye to their parents' visitors, the children who have to open doors for teachers, the children who must never contradict. With many adults even the words 'please' and 'thank you' become condescending or facetious when used towards children. It is the children who have to stand up when a visitor comes into the room, the children who have to remain at table until everyone has finished, the children who have to sit in the back seat of the car.
>
> I grant that all such behaviour can be pleasant and attractive. My point is that there is no expectation that the adults will be equally pleasant to the children.[19]

Adults have a vested interest in keeping children dependent on them in all sorts of ways. We ensure that they 'need' us for our opinions, our permission, our organisational skills, our approval, our authority. The independently-minded, self-respecting child won't stand inequality for long. Nor will he keep quiet in company. When he is feeling happy and creative, his feelings bubble over in excitement, and he will not relish ridicule. He will not like to be interrupted in the middle of his work. Sometimes, he will shout back. In other words, he will have a mind of his own. This can be hard for parents to accept, as the following anecdote from the play therapist's casebook shows.

Virginia Axline tells the story of Jerry, a weak, inept four-year-old who could not talk, walk properly or do any of the things a healthy four-year-old would do. He was rapidly transformed through therapy into a self-motivated, increasingly competent individual. In only two months of weekly one-hour sessions, Jerry learnt to say his first words: 'trucks, streetcar, ducks and cow'. He started to take off his socks and shoes and almost put them on again by himself. His eating problem faded along with his phobias. His co-ordination improved.

This case illustrates the power within the individual to become more mature *if* given an opportunity. And yet the empowerment of Jerry presented a challenge for his mother:

> The mother gained a certain amount of insight into the problem of her relationship with Jerry. This influenced her attitude and her actions towards Jerry. She commented at one time that Jerry *was much harder to handle now, because he seemed to be developing a mind of his own*, but she guessed that that was all for the good and she should welcome the change.[20] [my italics]

When we give our children the chance to discover themselves, they grow *into* themselves, and, inevitably, apart from us. A healthy child forces us to accept his individuality. Daily, he claims the freedom that he senses to be his. A compliant child is easy by comparison, he does not upset our world views or challenge our authority.

CREATIVE ACTS

Child psychiatrist D. W. Winnicott wrote that a baby suckling at the breast is 'gathering stuff for dreaming'[21]. This act, which a baby is able to initiate, enjoy without interruption and finish when he chooses, is supremely creative. Winnicott contrasted a child's creativity with his compliance. This is the barely perceptible yet crucial difference between acting out of free will, and acting according to the will of someone else:

> In making further reference to the baby's communication with the mother I suggest that this can be summed up in terms of creativeness and compliance. About this it must be said that in health the creative communication has priority over compliance. On the basis of seeing and reaching to the world creatively the baby can become able to comply without losing face. When the pattern is the other way round and compliance dominates then we think of ill-health and we see a bad basis for the development of the individual.[22]

Many of us tend to think of creativity as art: painting and pasting and making models. But while all these activities may be done creatively, we need to broaden our definition. A child's creativity is the realisation of his dreams. It is the expression of *himself* that matters, an act that need not be confined to art or music, though these are, of course, supremely expressive media.

A child may be creative in his speech, in his play or in his sense of humour, even in his manner of asserting himself. What matters is that the process is personal, and respected by those around him. And yet we continually disturb our children's means of expression.

Peter Dixon, once a senior lecturer in education, now a full-time painter and poet, has some magnificent ideas about the collision between a child's abundant inner world and adult expectations. As a budding playgroup leader, I attended his Under Fives Study Day in Manchester in July 1991. These are some of the things he had to say:

> When it comes to creative work people become paranoid with misery – because children can't make a Father Christmas look like a Father Christmas . . . Parents can't bear this. They even draw the pictures for children and children colour them in. I have seen playworkers say to children: 'Press this, stick that, stamp this and then take it home!' Parents say, 'If they did it themselves it would be all jerky and blobby.' Yes, of course it would, because they are at the jerky and blobby stage.
>
> Children live in a different dimension from you and me – they behave, perform, act, live in a different way from us. To a child, this gate *is* a castle, that stair *is* a mountain . . .

Dixon echoes the French philosopher Jean Jacques Rousseau, who said 'Childhood has its own ways of seeing, thinking and feeling'. Creativity comes from spontaneity. It is an expression of the inner self. If someone else draws the outline, or guides the child's hand, then it can only be an expression of *their* inner self. Evidently, Peter Dixon went on to express *his* inner self with a new career in performance poetry. There is a pattern here. The radical thinker and maths teacher John Holt decided his time would be better spent writing books and teaching himself to play cello than failing to teach schoolchildren the maths syllabus. The logic step when you've decided not to push, cajole, test and suppress children may be to get on with your own creative life.

We struggled with the problem of parental attitudes at our playgroup: some mothers were displeased when their children brought home art-table offerings that looked like nothing on earth. They wanted Father Christmases cut out by playgroup leaders, and stuck down by playgroup leaders, so they could pretend to themselves that their children had done it.

It is worth noting that at Alison Stallibrass's free-play nursery, children did not take artwork home for adult inspection (i.e. approval) at all, until a temporary staff member introduced the practice. The value of art was seen to be in the process, not in a product to please the parents.

When we invade our children's activities with our own expertise, we 'spoil' their work just as much as if they were to scribble all over ours. It is quite common for parents to rewrite school essays, finish off children's puzzles, and even to 'perfect' their children's artwork.

Children do not paint, or write, or play as we do: with a product or a performance in mind. They are simply painting, or writing, or whatever, and dislike to be interrupted in the process. They are often aware that the choices of words or colours they make have more to do with their dreams than with reality.

Peter Dixon described a small girl who painted her elephant fantastic colours, and was told that it should be grey. 'I know they are grey,' she replied, 'but grey is not a good enough colour for an elephant.' 'Children,' says Dixon, 'paint what they feel.'

ALL KINDS OF ACTIVITY

A child with a vivid imagination of his own will find himself bombarded with images dreamt up by adults for him to inhabit. Commercial images invade the space where a child's own imaginings should be. Theme parks are one of the big success stories of our times. In massive, expensively designed stage sets, someone else's imagination has worked overtime to provide bigger, scarier, noiser experiences to overwhelm us. Here, one observer questions the effect:

'When you send your children to these,' says Terry Veitch, who runs her own leisure consultancy, 'you're putting them into someone else's dream, not giving them their own fantasy, not crediting them with any imagination.'

... We don't, or daren't, look upon childhood as a time of self-exploration and freedom any more ... Children are no longer allowed to use their creativity. Some are valued as little adults, junior shoppers, yuppi-kins. But they are the lucky ones. For too many children without access to a fat parental wallet, play means Tarmac, broken glass, dog shit and no ball games.[23]

Freedom to move, freedom to initiate, freedom to express his immature thoughts and make his dreams come true, these are some of the elements that allow a child to be himself. When we tell children how to play, providing all the pre-moulded shapes we think he needs, we show little respect for his own capacity to create. We are asking him to step into someone else's dream.

A child's natural love of hoarding shells, pebbles or shiny objects is easily abducted by the allure of an advertising campaign. But the joy for the child is in the collecting more than the possessing. In our society, possessions may become a way of enhancing status before a child has even gone to school. Parents who splash out on artefacts of the collective commercial imagination should prepare themselves for hours spent begging their children to tidy up the clutter.

When my children were small, I noticed the difference in their mood following certain types of activity. Like most children, they enjoyed playing 'mummies and daddies', a fantasy that they constructed themselves. A fair amount of time would be spent deciding who should play which role. Even at two, Alice was more than capable of asserting herself. '*No*,' she would insist to her five-year-old sister, '*Me* the mummy and *you* the baby.' One game might then last up to an hour, as they went for walks, to the shops, to the doctor's, and so on, encountering the occasional robber or monster along the way. Their bodies were lively and involved, as they role-played their way around a familiar or invented domestic scene.

But sit them in front of the television for the same amount of time, and, despite the wonderful world of Disney, or some semi-violent cartoon intended for their age group, their bodies began to droop, and they would eventually slink towards the kitchen, bored and looking for some stimulation (crisps/a drink/an argument?).

Certainly, the television itself has this effect, and the whirlwind adventures of various superheroes do nothing to ease children's sense of alienation and passivity. A child cannot be involved in this world, only amazed by it, and eventually, perhaps, addicted to it.

But the category of activity that seemed (and still seems) most to satisfy my children is handwork. Making pastry, chopping vegetables, moulding playdough or real dough, sorting buttons . . . anything that allows construction and destruction, and minimal parental involvement. As Montessori remarks:

> An adult who does not understand that a child needs to use his hands and does not recognise this as the first manifestation of an instinct for work can be an obstacle to the child's development. This is not always due to a defensive attitude on the part of the adult. There can be other causes as well. One of these is the fact that an adult looks to the external finality of his actions and determines the means which he employs according to his own mental outlook. For him there is a kind of natural law, 'the law of minimal effort', which induces him to employ the most direct means that will enable him to attain his goal in the least possible time. When he sees a child making great efforts to perform some seemingly fruitless action which he himself could do in an instant and much more perfectly, he is pained and attempts to assist the child.
>
> . . . Who would ever imagine that the needless assistance given to a child is the first of the various *repressions* which he will experience and one which will have serious consequences in later life?[24]

When we stop children in the middle of their chosen activity simply because we can't see the point in it, we are forgetting what it feels like to be a child. Peter Dixon asks us to tread carefully, in order not to tread on their dreams:

Creativity is: environmental awareness; making new things out of old ones; being able to work for long periods uninterrupted; persistence . . . Children have all these attributes at two or three, and then they gradually disappear.

The process is what goes through your mind to get there. It's the skill of seeking; trying to find. Like the little boy who spent all day looking for the right gold paper to make the dragon's eye. Most parents don't see the process.

A child who carefully dismantles his toys is embarking on the first, crucial stage towards dicovering how they are constructed. Parents may see nothing constructive in his actions, and many would stop him, assuming him to be wilfully 'naughty'. But the child is not vandalising his environment. He is not acting wildly, or without restraint, but deliberately pursuing his own driven intent to uncover the secrets of his world. While his hands are deconstructing, his mind is building a picture of the way life is. Just like the breastfeeding baby, he is gathering stuff for dreaming. Grethe Laub, an Alexander Technique teacher and former nursery school teacher, expands this point:

Children love to experiment. When they pull their toys apart, it is not in order to destroy, but in order to find out what is inside. They discover how much easier it is to destroy, but they regret when they cannot put the bits together again. The child will gradually learn the lesson about destruction if it sees that it must be without its toy unless it mends it, and the grown-ups must help the child, when necessary, to find out how to put it together.[25]

Every day in minute ways, we trample on our children's dreams. We catch them doing something we wouldn't do, something we were once stopped from doing by our own parents, and we swoop down. Using whatever excuses come first to hand, we interrupt that which we cannot understand,

94

claiming it to be destructive, inappropriate, time-wasting or mess-making. For, along with Making Noise and Running Around A Lot, Making A Mess seems to be one of the great sins of infancy.

A FINE MESS YOU'VE GOT ME INTO

Of all the childhood virtues, cleanliness is probably the most overrated, and yet the need to keep clean is impressed on children from an early age. The desire to keep children (and their surroundings) pristine is directly at odds with the child's impulse to locate dirt and move it around. On visits to Magna, a hands-on science museum in Rotherham, north-east England, I noticed that the very longest queues in the building were for the chance to handle a real dumper truck and shift some real dirt. Here, *Magical Child* author Joseph Chilton Pearce tells the story of perfectly-presented Sam, a toddler 'ready for the photographer or grandmother'. Sam meets a mud puddle:

> . . . interesting stuff, this – and down he goes, as dutifully prompted by his intent. Nice, squashy texture, oozing between fingers . . . Sam interacts with all available tools and eventually makes the taste test . . . leaving a wide swath of the stuff across his face, his two pearly front teeth now quite brown. He . . . decides that this is not a pudding, in spite of appearances; he . . . notices all its other possibilities – or starts to. For here comes mother. Horrors! Her little dear eating the mud. All those germs! And his nice clothes. Suppose mother-in-law should come in right now and see him. What would she think? What would she say? What kind of mother would mother-in-law take daughter-in-law to be?
>
> Sam's mother is conscientious. She does try to keep him clean. She has seen, with a cringe, those pictures of little children with flies crawling on them, dirty, unkempt, in Bangladesh or wherever . . . Now here he is, wallowing in mud, even *eating* it. What perversity. What

has she done wrong? She must ask her pediatrician. 'No, no, *no*! Dirty, dirty, *dirty*! Bad, bad boy!' she wails, chanting rhythmic trinities as she snatches him up and rushes off to the bathroom for a general purification.

Consider what happens to Sam's concept of mud . . . The whirlwind of action resulting is one long, sensory-overloaded blur, but out of it emerges one clear thing: Mud means trouble, Mud is *bad* . . . He likes the experience, yet his mother's reaction was so negative.[26]

It is through educative experiences of this kind that many of us got to be where we are today.

Most parents have long ago forgotten what it felt like to be curious and unprejudiced about the world and all that's in it. Most of us were scolded for getting dirty when we were young, and so the unnacceptability of mess and dirt is passed on through the generations. If young children get dirty, it is as a result of their thirst for knowledge and natural lust for life. If we never allow them the chance to get mucky, we teach them the lesson that by exploring the world or taking risks, they might make a mess. We teach them that the costs of creativity are too high. Professional artists, laboratory scientists and business entrepreneurs would not succeed if they were afraid of making a little mess along the way. We should not make our children afraid of getting dirty – or afraid of life.

PLAYGROUNDS OF THE IMAGINATION

If a parent should stop and observe – on the sidelines, of course, so as not to disturb the action – she will start to see the child's process at work. Sam's foray into the mud begins to look like creative exploration, instead of an alarming aberration. A child balancing in the gutter might not merely be trying to irritate his mother, he might be learning a new skill:

No toddler wants to stop short at the achievement of the useful art of walking; he proceeds – often in defiance of authority – to discover how to make increasingly complicated, subtle and gravity-defying movements. Groos [Karl Groos, the German psychologist and play researcher] noticed this: 'Almost as soon as a child has learned to preserve his equilibrium in ordinary walking, he proceeds to complicate the problem by trying to walk on curbstones, in a rut, on a beam, on a balustrade or narrow wall.'[27]

I believe we have become more sceptical about a child's capacity to amuse himself, and realise his own dreams, than ever before. I have a cutting (circa 1960) from a Birmingham newspaper, that reveals how subtly different attitudes were only one generation ago. The full-page feature shows pictures of children playing on a wasteland-cum-building site. In one photograph a boy is launching himself out of the ground-floor window of a derelict house. He is watched by two delighted little girls. This is the report by journalist Diana Hutchinson:

> The demolition belt around Birmingham makes a wonderful playground for a city child.
>
> Cramped by living in a small flat or an over-crowded villa in decaying suburbs, the garden-less children spill out into the streets looking for a television-type adventure.
>
> They find it in the derelict houses and flattened slums that make the area a vast rubble tip. Recently the 'Crowbar Kids' pulled down two empty buildings and blocked a street.
>
> Now the children have been promised a new deal by Parks Committee chairman, Alderman Frank Price.
>
> He says: 'I want them to have a better childhood than I had. I was brought up in the "Styx" and roamed the most notorious streets.
>
> 'It is natural for children to play on building sites, but we are going to give them something better. Children today are more intelligent and need creative play shapes to weave into their games . . .'

Even the picture caption is not judgemental:

> Adults have abandoned this crumbling shell of blackened
> brick – with a kind of fearsome joy, the children move in.
> The window has gone. The floorboards are unsafe. The
> door creaks on one hinge. To the children it is the
> threshold of adventure.
>
> Children in the suburb of Ladywood ignore the orga-
> nised playgrounds and swarm over devastated ground
> that is pock-marked by slum clearance . . . The feeble soil
> swoops down to an old cellar and heaves up again above
> road level in a rash of obstacles and mystic shapes. The
> girls play King of the Castle. The boys, jackdaw-eyed,
> look for riches in the rubble.

What a wonderful portrait of childhood ingenuity. The
children of Birmingham abandon the carefully prepared
playgrounds that will be the lot of future generations, for
a terrain that leaves something to their own imagination. It
is unlikely such a piece would appear in a local newspaper
today, given the ultra safety-conscious, censorious mood
that grown-ups are currently in. Even Alderman Frank Price,
who is quoted as wanting to build children a 'better' environment, realises that it is natural for children to want to
play on the building site.

Peter Dixon tells his own story of a council-built 'Mecca for
children', a play park packed with all the educational equipment children could dream of (at least, all that the adults
could imagine the children could dream of). But this wasn't
good enough for the children. When asked what they had
liked best at the end of the first day, their excitement spilled
over. 'It was great!' they said, 'We've been playing in the
toilets!'

So the next time your child plays with the wrapping paper
instead of the present, you might breathe a sigh of relief. His
imagination is alive and well, and taking care of itself.

Letting go as children grow: early learning

- Babies and small children learn through touch: first from being held, and later, by holding and exploring with their own hands
- The more involved in an activity a child can be, the more it will absorb him and hone his capacity for learning
- What looks like mess and destruction to the adult eye, is often an important by-product of the child's creative process
- We cannot know as much about the child's inner world as he does himself. Respect for his creativity helps nurture his sense of discovery
- A child's ideas and behaviours may appear mad or heretical – there is a little madness and heresy in all creativity
- Ordinary words cannot begin to describe the imaginings of the young child. When using words, we might be careful not to judge, prescribe, label, or ridicule their experiences
- Snowmen, elephants and trees can be any colour, any colour at all

4

BALANCING ACTS –

THE EVERYDAY PLAY THAT IS A CHILD'S WORK

All experience is an arch, to build upon.

Henry Adams

You cannot teach a man anything; you can only help him find it within himself.

Galileo Galilei, sixteenth century Italian astronomer

Frances was given a two-wheel bicycle with stabilisers for her fourth birthday. When we moved to Bath, she wanted to be like the other children in our street who rode *without* stabilisers. She asked us to take them off for her, but was then unable to ride her bike. She would sit astride her two-wheeler, unmoving, as her pavement-wise friends sped past.

Two frustrating months later, Frances woke up with great excitement. As she opened her eyes she exclaimed, 'Mummy! Guess what I dreamt! I went on my bike with you holding on the back, and then you let go and I could ride all by myself!' 'Well, we'd better try it out and see,' I said.

The same afternoon, we took the bicycle over to the field opposite our house. I held on the back, Frances cycled off, I let go, and she was away. She was jubilant. Through her own efforts, she had made a wish come true. She did not falter, or take it slowly; she was acting out her dream of free, unlimited motion and sped around the field for more than an hour by herself.

Learning to ride a bicycle is not always as dramatic as this, but it is often a poignant moment for both child and parent. It is something that most children learn to do and, once learnt, the skill is apparently never forgotten. As he grows up, a child uses his bicycle to increase his independence. For American psychologist Susan Jeffers, not being allowed to have a bicycle was a sign of her parents' lack of trust:

> I can remember wanting desperately to have a two-wheel bicycle and my mother's refusal to buy me one. Her answer to my pleas was always the same: 'I love you too much. I don't want anything to happen to you.' I translated this to mean: 'You are not competent enough to handle a two-wheel bike.' Having become older and wiser, I realize now that she was really saying: 'If anything happens to you, I will fall apart.'[1]

Part of the process of letting go of our children is allowing them to take risks; to move out of our sphere of influence and protection. Independence is what our children crave. They take it for themselves, we don't need to arrange for it to happen, or worry about its outcome. The parent who can stand back when she is no longer needed will see her child wobble off into the distance, and eventually find his own balance.

My friend's children taught themselves to ride two-wheel bicycles when they were each two-and-a-half years old. This is extraordinarily young. She might have stood in their way, and insisted they were 'too young' to ride a bike. Instead, she allowed herself to trust in her children's intuition and put aside her own fears. This does not, however, mean that we should all be aiming to have two-year-olds on two-wheelers. Had the mother insisted that her children learn to ride, she would have been ignoring their own readiness for risk-taking. And, as the American childcare authors Win and Bill Sweet have pointed out[2], a child's readiness is everything. We need only to trust that, given the opportunity, children learn what they need to learn.

This principle can be applied to any area of parenting. In fact, even the verb 'to parent' is over-active, for it implies that parents have to *do* something in order for their children to be educated. We do not. We do not even need to have aims for our children: our children are best equipped to aim for themselves.

WHAT'S MY JOB, THEN?

The parent's job is to equip the child's environment, not merely with 'things', but with love, acceptance and direction. Direction is provided through example and the setting of personal limits. A parent who attempts to do everything for her child gets in the way of his natural growth. Yes, we should be on call for the times when a child signals his need for help, but that is all. As Israeli child psychologist Dr Haim Ginnott said, 'The measure of a good parent is what he is willing *not* to do for his child.'[3]

When we get in the way of a child's learning processes, we can really mess things up, like the time I tried to 'teach' Frances to swim (see Introduction). No child should ever have to squirm or complain while he learns a skill – this is a sure sign that he is being pressurised, and that a grown-up is probably over-involved. Play researcher Alison Stallibrass describes a more useful role for caring adults:

> We must try and make it possible for them to find things to do which they are at the time capable of doing. We must provide the opportunities and then sit back, for we cannot digest the experience for them, and in any case we do not know exactly which bit of knowledge they are at any moment ready to digest. Only the child himself knows this. We can trust a child to recognize what experiences will nourish his general sensory-motor judgement at any time, if the latter is already well-nourished and therefore healthy and capable of digestion.[4]

Alison Stallibrass believes that bicycles offer a superb opportunity for honing balancing skills. Children naturally seek out ways of perfecting their co-ordination, and many are eager to try riding a bike from the age of three. Some parents prefer young children to ride tricycles, as they are under the impression that a tricycle is a safer riding machine for a child than a two-wheel bike. Not so, says Stallibrass:

> It would be interesting to compare the use made of bicycles and tricycles in a playgroup where there is adequate and suitable space for both. Tricycles are useful for various make-believe games and for learning a certain amount of balancing skill, but are not so good for the latter as bicycles. However, they are much more dangerous because it is possible to mount them and make them move at some speed before one has learnt to control them and particularly how to take corners on them. It is impossible to have them in our playgroup because of the very small area of level ground and the number of steep little banks.[5]

It is difficult to describe how little one has to do in terms of skill-training when children are in harmony with themselves, and feel safe to explore their world. Yet it is commonplace for experts to offer parents new ways of becoming involved in their children's education, however young they may be.

The recommended curriculum for the pre-schooler includes reading, writing, maths, history, geography, science, music, dance, art and practical skills, all of which a child would be picking up anyway in the daily round, but today are given the gloss of scholastic respectability. Attitudes to children have not always been so intense. Recalling her 1940s Yorkshire childhood, actress Dame Judi Dench says education at home was a self-initiated series of explorations in the local environment:

> We were *always* outside. Riding our bikes, usually in someone else's garden. The only interiors I remember are when I was sitting on the stairs at night, listening.[6]

Nowadays, perhaps owing to a greater alienation from our children, because both parents work, and an increasing sense of guilt, parents are expected to involve themselves in every aspect of their child's life, whenever they *are* around. The modern middle-class child has less free time than any child before him.

School-age children are ferried by car to adult-led activities, like Scouts and music lessons. Or they are expected to sweat over homework after a day spent in school. There is less and less opportunity for children to play and direct their own growth. Even their quiet, 'coming-together' moments tend to happen in front of a television set.

PARENTS AS PART OF THE WALLPAPER

Our attempts to orchestrate our children's waking moments begin at the cradle. Babies move from one controlled environment to another, from 'quality time' with mother, to a perfectly designed nursery. British author and broadcaster Libby Purves questions the wisdom of Western ways:

> After all, where would you rather be put, if you were a baby? In a neat, sterile crib, alone in a neat designer bedroom with a plastic activity centre as your only companion? Or would you rather live hugger-mugger with nine brothers and sisters, crawling around in the maize harvest? Babies are creatures of cuddle and impulse and an uproarious instinct for making whoopee: tell me honestly, which lifestyle sounds more fun?[7]

Spontaneous movement, which is essential for the development of intelligence, can only be achieved in an environment in which the child feels loved and yet not over-protected. As soon as the play is led by an adult, especially one who demands compliance with his own set of rules, then a child is not exercising his full capacities. Teacher David Gribble believes that:

Young children need to chase, and hide, and splash, and build camps, and climb trees, and pretend to be things that they are not. So do adolescents. If they are *organised* to do these things, however, the point is lost. They must have time to choose the kind of play they need. It is a stage of growing-up that can only be by-passed at a cost. Children who miss it become cautious, unsociable, inhibited or tense . . .[8]

Children tend to accept whatever system is imposed them, says Gribble, but it does not follow that we should take advantage of their eagerness to please adults. Many grown-ups feel a sense of satisfaction when they have controlled the activities of a group of children, and organisation is the key to running a school. But it is vital that children have the chance to do their own thing, too. Providing a free-choice atmosphere was Alison Stallibrass's aim at her playgroup:

Small children will, on entering an entirely new environment, quickly sense whether the adults in charge expect them to act on their own initiative or to wait to be told what to do. On the whole they will quite easily accept either situation. In my group the children soon became accustomed to acting spontaneously and, after a bit, expected it as their right. They treated me more and more like a piece of equipment – there only to be made use of when necessary; and they ignored me for much of the time. Sometimes, when in sole charge of ten or twelve children, I would keep a piece of very simple knitting handy in order to give the impression that I too was busy, and also to keep my hands occupied while my eyes and ears and mind were alive to everything that was going on around me, for it is easy to become involved in an activity with a few children instead of keeping oneself free to observe what is going on in the whole group.[9]

Observing children rather than organising them can teach us a lot about the way children work. It was through observations of this kind – noting, without judgement, which activities children preferred or rejected – that enabled Maria Montessori to design the Casa dei Bambini, her first school.

But even observation can be overdone. It's fine if parents can contrive to become part of the wallpaper: peeking occasionally over the newspaper or even a row of stocking stitch. But a child who is watched too intently becomes unable to expand his unconscious activity. 'It is well established,' says John Adams, a British geography professor and risk theorist, 'that people behave differently if they think they are being watched.'[10] A child may show off, or he may become self-conscious and take fewer risks. He interprets the adult's solicitous gaze as a sign that he is not to be trusted by himself, or realises that the adult is experiencing the world vicariously through him.

Growing up is not a spectator sport. When a child becomes bound up in his parents' gaze, he may find himself unable to 'let go' enough to master skills, enjoy himself fully, or be creative. Children do not consciously set out to achieve a sense of balance, it has to be allowed to happen. But in watching and hanging over our children, we may get in the way of that process. Perhaps we should remember the words of the Austrian psychotherapist Bruno Bettelheim, that: 'Talent is nurtured in solitude.'

YOUNG, GIFTED AND LONELY

Whether or not we mean to, we convey our desires for our children through our body language. When they were small, my children could sense when I wanted them to 'perform': to behave in a certain way, or to be sociable with strangers, though I may have said nothing specific. Their reaction, more often than not, was to tease me. Parents often refer to this as 'acting up', 'showing off', or 'being silly'. Our hopes, if felt too intensely, can get in the way of children's own aspirations.

Why, after all, are we so desperate for our children to achieve? When they are babies, we realise how ridiculous it is to long for them to walk, because, all being well, they will walk one day. Yet as they become older, we may feel anxious for them to succeed in various pre-set ways. Recalling our own feelings about failure as children, we are not satisfied until our offspring have overcome the hurdles we once faced; until they 'succeed', often in areas in which we ourselves have 'failed'.

When we act like this, we are forgetting that children are motivated to learn for the sake of learning. Regardless of the end result, children enjoy spontaneous activity. They derive great pleasure from the exercising of skills that enhance their equilibrium and sense of self. In fact, as children are motivated to feel pleasure, they are attracted towards activities that enhance their self-fulfilment. Alexander Lowen believes that:

> In situations where one can be freely spontaneous without giving any conscious thought to the expression, the experience of pleasure is very high. Children's play has this quality. In most of our actions there is a mixture of spontaneity and control, the control serving to give our actions a sharper focus and a greater effect. When control and spontaneity are harmonized so that each supplements rather than hinders the other, the pleasure is greatest. In such actions the ego and body work together to produce a degree of co-ordination in movement that can only be characterised as graceful.[11]

It's fun to learn, and the product of self-motivated learning is a well-balanced child. The product of learning that is motivated by others is, more often than not, *im*balance. The child genius who moves awkwardly and who does not play with friends of his own age is an extreme example of this. He has been encouraged to develop one aspect of himself at the expense of another. No child, even one born a genius, would choose to neglect himself in this way. Here, the leader of the UK International Mathematical Olympiad Team argues that bright children should not be condemned to social isolation:

There are those like Michael [Tan, the maths student who began his university studies aged seven], or our own Ruth Lawrence [who graduated from Oxford with first-class honours at the age of thirteen], whose precocity is such that it becomes difficult simply to leave them in their peer group. These instances are exciting and challenging; but they are also extremely rare . . .

In contrast, there is a surprisingly large group of adolescents who are perfectly capable of doing GCSE maths slightly early . . . Indeed, good students can find GCSE maths so uninspiring that it may be tempting to get it over and done with as quickly as possible. The major drawback is that the child may then be condemned to working in isolation – either in the library or at the back of the class – for the rest of his school career. This sometimes solves the 'problem' in an unfortunate way, with social isolation slowly undermining the child's appetite for mathematics altogether.

. . . Before embarking on any course of action those involved have to ask themselves what their proposed 'solution' is likely to achieve in the long term. The goal must be to produce an eighteen- or twenty-one-year-old who is firing on all cylinders, and ready to take full advantage of whatever talents he or she may possess.[12]

The gifted child does have special educational needs, but he does not need treatment so special that it robs him of a normal childhood. The danger is that, once a child has been identified as 'gifted', adults take him terribly seriously.

The label of 'gifted' can be an enormous burden for any child to bear, as was evident in a longitudinal study from Middlesex University.[13] The research, spanning thirty years so far and begun in 1974, interviewed seventy children, all members of the National Association for Gifted Children, as they grew up. Each 'gifted' child was matched with a child of identical IQ.

By their early thirties, many in the 'gifted' group said their biggest regret was ever being labelled as such. The study found they were less likely to fit in at school and had fewer friends. There were more likely to suffer from poor coordination and insomnia. Later, the 'gifted' girls were more likely to leave their careers, while boys were likely to choose careers in science or computing which required little social contact. Apparently, many of their parents had assumed that their children's social isolation and lack of grace were somehow part of the gifted condition. They were convinced that gifted children were bound to be 'odd'. Well-behaved, conforming pupils were less likely to be classed as gifted in the first place.

The perilous route to becoming a special child is recounted here by mother Cridge McCullogh, whose son Sam could read and write at the age of four. Ms McCullogh was persuaded to test his talent at a school for gifted children:

> Other mothers would stop me to comment on how 'remarkable' Sam was. Apparently our son would approach his schoolmates' parents to ask them whether he had spelt 'Paraguay' or 'hexagonal' correctly. One mother, a former Montessori teacher, repeatedly urged me to investigate a new school for bright children. Other mothers could not believe I was serious about consigning 'such a clever boy' to the wastelands of state education. The implication was that we were being cavalier about the future of our child.
>
> It is hard to convey the isolating impact of this sort of interest in one's offspring . . . Resisting my husband's opposition, I determined to do the rounds of certain private schools. Just in case . . .
>
> In order to get into the school, the children had to undergo an aptitude test . . . The session started well. Sam sat at a table opposite a pleasant woman who explained the rules of each game in a kindly manner. There were word exercises and puzzles, which became increasingly tricky. Sam happily moved pieces around until they fitted. But as the minutes passed, he sensed this was something more serious than fun. Built into the exercises was the inevitability of failure because they

were constructed to reveal a rising scale of intelligence. As the woman turned the pages of the book, the expression on Sam's face became more solemn and his voice dropped to a whisper. He seemed crestfallen when he was unable to get the 'game' right. The test lasted forty-five minutes. I was later informed that Sam was 'a very bright little fellow who would probably get into university.' He was clearly no Einstein, but he did have the reading and writing ability of a seven-year-old. He was offered a place at the school. We were sent a bill for £50.

I still suffer pangs of remorse that I subjected him to an experience he quite obviously found unpleasant and which, in the event, only confirmed what we already knew. I am not proud of the fact that I pursued such a course partly because I felt pressurised by the comments of other parents. This autumn term will be Sam's first taste of state education. I will be keeping a watchful but judicious eye on his progress.[14]

As soon as a child's talents become apparent to the adults around him, he may be hijacked from more 'normal' activities in order to pursue his specialisation. This tendency to organise and teach children invades even a toddler's free time. A child might be honing his skill of balancing on the furniture, but someone entices him away to the more 'worthwhile' activity of learning to read instead. We even interpose one play activity for another, supposing that *our* choice of game will be more fun than just messing around. Although children are open to our suggestions, they don't necessarily need bought games and adult organisation to have fun. It is the misplaced atmosphere of enforced jollity which turns many a family game of Monopoly into a ritual of misery.

We want our children to be healthy and strong and have fun, but *we* cannot provide the laughter and the good appetite and the zest for life and learning. Our influence tends only to introduce an inappropriate air of seriousness and tension to the process of growing up. Instead of desperately trying to be everything, or provide everything for her child, a parent might do better to let herself off the hook. As she stands back, she might see that her child is everything to himself.

PRACTICE MAKES PEOPLE

Marion Pears, a teacher and home educator from Australia, bravely allowed her children to follow their own instincts. They only went to school when they wanted to go (admittedly a freedom not all parents can afford). They did not, according to their mother, grow to be social outcasts, or academically stunted, but, through a programme of self-development, emerged as rounded, well-balanced adults:

> They are more individual; the individual personalities have been preserved. They seem very active, have many interests in which they are deeply involved. They are capable of enormously concentrated intense and absorbed concentration for long periods of time. In general, they do not believe in the superiority of experts, and therefore try many things which others might deem impossible. They are very ingenious in their thinking and tend to be divergent thinkers.[15]

Children who are not sent to school, where the regime is predetermined, often concentrate on one skill for weeks or months, until they have honed it to their satisfaction. They get their fun from *practice*: many repetitions that enhance their physical or mental co-ordination and develop their experience. This is the kind of dedication that creates teenage snooker stars, super skate-boarders and computer whiz-kids. You will note these are all fields in which adult input is minimal.

Piano practice, on the other hand, imposed as it is by adults on children, is the scourge of many a young life. If classes were to be given in skate-boarding, and practice demanded every night, you could bet that teenagers would be selling their boards as fast as their parents would allow. Conversely, if pianos were played by older children and adults for fun, and no one mentioned it again, the younger ones would soon start practising by themselves. This seems a good time to mention the Suzuki approach, which encourages children to learn through listening and copying. Parents come along to lessons and help coach children during the week. I have had years of Suzuki experience with all my children – and the atmosphere of our practice times were like a heightened version of my relationship with each child. *Nurtured by Love*, Suzuki's creed, requires just that – a great deal of love and patience from the involved parent, and a respect for the child's 'rhythm of readiness'. It is entirely possible to ruin the method – and the relationship with one's child – if parents are not sensitive to their children's rhythm of learning.

Australian-born composer Alison Bauld, who has published a method for learning to play music creatively, believes that pushing children does a lot to destroy their natural love of learning. In her words:

The idea is that the child should experiment individually, taking however long they need, and not be panicked. As soon as you set the concept of time-bound goals, you've introduced the concept of failure.[16]

Individual experimentation, with no time limit? This sounds amazingly like play. But play is inadequate as an educational method if we believe certain commentators:

The problem with learning the 'play way' is that it happens in a largely unconscious and wholly inarticulate manner, and is often quite accidental and random. To translate such a hit or miss way of learning to the infant or junior classroom is to leave far too much to chance and to waste much valuable time. It must inevitably slow down the process of learning at that point in their development when children are particularly keen to learn and are unusually receptive. What is more, such intellectually difficult and demanding skills as reading and writing cannot be acquired accidentally, as if children were plants who absorbed such skills as naturally as the air they breathe. If they did, we wouldn't need schools.[17]

This particular case for schools is not a good one, however, as many children *do* teach themselves to read and write. Children who need help are able to signal their need for adult assistance. Those who show no interest are, on the whole, not ready to learn. Given a relaxed and joyful literate environment, they will come round. Reading and writing are no more intellectually difficult than learning to talk.

The fact is that many schools are in a tremendous hurry to teach particular subjects, and as a result play is in danger of becoming an after-school activity. Teacher David Gribble points out that P.E., music and art are referred to as 'release' subjects, 'which presumably means that everything else is a kind of imprisonment . . .' He says that:

> Schools tend to disapprove of play because of the desperate need they feel to cram far too much into the first sixteen or eighteen years of a person's life. They make the extraordinary assumption that by the time you leave school you should be in some miraculous way ready for anything . . . If schools were not so intent on teaching the impossible – *all* spelling, *all* moral behaviour, *all* the A-level syllabus – they would be able to give children more time for more important things.[18]

Despite the evidence that spontaneous play develops a strong, true personality, enhances self-respect, skill-learning and a social conscience, many parents still regard it with suspicion. 'Play,' said Peter Dixon, 'is seen by parents as a side dish, a recreation, not the stuff of life'. The government, he says, has institutionalised this view:

> The government doesn't like the word 'play'. It's dangerous, it's offensive, it's anti-social. They prefer to class play by activities: 'The children are sorting sand.'
> Educator Margaret Donaldson said that children learn

in meaningful contexts, by trial and error, and the work must be intrinsically rewarding . . . Play is not 'playing about'. The government likes to pretend this is what's happening, but it's not. Hang on to the play, hang on to it and use it.[19]

AMAZING GRACE

A child who is playing freely in his own space, with no pressure to perform, uses all his body. He is alert, eager, exploratory, expressive. Contrast this with his behaviour a moment later when he is forced to sit and 'learn' something for which he has no inclination. He goes into a slump. His body manifests the boredom and depression that he feels with his whole being. By the time the child reaches adolescence, his boredom may have become chronic. So unused is he to directing himself in his own environment, that he can no longer think of 'anything to do'. The challenge for educators is to engage the child's natural curiosity without disturbing his lust for life. When teachers cannot manage this, a child would do better to educate himself.

Bio-energetic therapist Alexander Lowen describes the grace-ful movement of the person who is truly healthy in mind, spirit and body. Grace is the outward sign of balance that is evident in someone who has found (or retained) their inner equilibrium. Hunter-gatherers following the ancient human lifestyle can be described as 'graceful', but natural grace and poise have been sacrificed over millennia for a goal-oriented way of life. Speed, stress and pressure are all enemies of graceful living.

We have a vague notion that grace is worth teaching to models and rich young women by asking them to walk around rooms with books on their heads. We order schoolchildren to 'stand up straight', and we teach baby ballerinas to adopt a string of forced positions. All these examples are parodies of true grace, which cannot be learned consciously. When we interfere with the way our children move, we introduce more tension, and may consign them to a lifetime of inner disorder and dis-ease.

Francis Matthias Alexander, the Australian actor whose famous Technique was developed at the begining of the twentieth century, realised that it was virtually impossible *consciously* to undo the bad habits of a lifetime. Only by inhibiting old responses, he said, can 'use of the self' be improved. An Alexander pupil discovers his inner equilibrium as he regains the natural grace that is his birthright. He unravels layers of interference to reveal, in part at least, the primal state of 'freedom-from' stress. This gives him more 'freedom-to' achieve the things in life he really wants.

A child who is allowed to take responsibility for himself in small ways from the beginning is not struggling against his natural balancing mechanisms. He does not perceive his body as separate from himself; he is merely doing the next thing, and so bringing himself to his full potential. He moves literally and figuratively through the world with ease.

Joy Morris, a mother from Wigtownshire in Scotland, wrote to tell me of some of the early experiences of her third child, David, who was carried (by Joy and other family members) for his first eight months. Like many children who are given their fill of parental contact, David's suppleness and natural balance were undisturbed. At nine months, he began to walk:

His muscle tone and balance were excellent – due we think to the constant bracing of himself as I moved – leant over – down etc. His extraordinarily good sense of balance has been a striking feature – teaching himself to ride a two-wheeler at about his fourth birthday – we didn't do anything. He practised himself till he had mastered it – then he said 'Come and see!'

While abroad [in Nepal] he joined the local children in their games running along the tops of walls – he never had an accident. I stayed away from this activity as I might have made him fall by my anxiety. I checked from our flat windows. The children of the culture we were in at that time were sure of themselves, not being competitive or having any overbearing cruel tendencies towards young children so I knew he was safe with them. They also had had their fill of 'in-arms' experience.

David later taught himself to read, as often happens in literate families in which a nurturing atmosphere prevails. While Joy 'risked' her child, as Joseph Chilton Pearce puts it, she also allowed him to fulfil his needs for dependency, breastfeeding him until he was four years old. Given opportunity for growth and a stable base from which to explore, David was busy making himself. The dependent and independent parts of him were slowly balancing themselves out.

Many of us spend our adult lives struggling to find a balance: to achieve the inner harmony that will make all our activities run together seamlessly. We strive to greet the world, the people we meet and life's fortunes with an inner calm. I believe the balancing acts performed by a small child represent the initial stages in a process that eventually applies to all aspects of our life.

KIDS IN SPACE

During the 1940s, Alison Stallibrass took part in a free-play experiment at the Pioneer Health Centre in Peckham, London. School-age children and their families were allowed open access to sports facilities, but no classes were provided for the 200–300 children who used the centre every day, and few restrictions were placed on their movement around the building. In this safe environment, it soon became evident that children were highly motivated to learn and hone new skills, and that they would spend many hours working on one area before moving on to the next.

For Stallibrass, a researcher on the project, the gymnasium was one of the most fascinating areas of the Peckham experiment. She describes the set-up:

> An extremely interesting phenomenon was the behaviour of the children in the gymnasium. The latter was conventionally equipped, with ropes . . . ribstalls . . . a

'window frame' . . . booms, vaulting-horses, balancing forms, parallel bars, a punch-ball, coconut-matting etc., and a beautifully-sprung cork-covered floor. The one rule enforced was 'bare feet'.

The gym was, however, used in a very unconventional manner: there were sometimes as many as thirty children in it at one time, but no instructor . . .

. . . at the same time as some children were swinging on ropes, others might be chasing each other – playing 'off-ground' or some similar game – or running after balls; and yet collisions were very rare. (Incidentally, there was only one instance in four and a half years of a child breaking a bone in the gym. This, I am told, would have been considered an exceptionally good record in a gymnasium used for the same number of children for organized classes.) The children not only exercised judgement in moving in relation to the apparatus, but also in moving in relation to the movements of the other children. They threaded their way with accuracy and at speed among their constantly moving companions, and in order to do this they had to be aware of what all the children in their vicinity were doing and to anticipate what they were likely to do in the next few seconds.[20]

These children, allowed to play in a crowded room full of equipment and yet without a presiding adult (observers could watch the room from on high), were learning inter-personal as well as personal skills. Essential for the functioning of such a gym is that a child's sense of balance be relatively intact. Thus he is able to exercise, and feel, the harmony of co-existence. His every movement, swift though it may be, is enacted in consideration of others.

This can only be achieved in an environment where children know themselves to be in control. At the Peckham Centre, responsibility for safety and social awareness lay with the children. Progressive educationalists John Holt and David Gribble each report cases of children looking after themselves when given freedom from parental interference. John Holt describes a parent-free playground in London, where children learnt to deal with danger, and find their own balanced approach:

Years ago I visited an adventure playground in Holland Park in London. The playground was full of trees to climb, ropes to swing on, and other 'dangerous' stuff. I asked the young people in charge whether many children got hurt there. They said, 'No, not since we told the adults that they couldn't come in.' When the mothers *could* come in, they were constantly saying 'Don't do this, don't do that, it's too dangerous.' The children would be so angry and humiliated by this kind of talk that in a spirit of 'I'll show you' they would rush to climb a too tall tree or use a too difficult piece of apparatus. Once in danger, with their mothers' 'You'll fall, you'll fall' in their ears, they would soon get rattled, and down they would come in a crash. So the people in charge of the playground built a little waiting area where mothers could sit and talk *but could not see their children* while the children used the playground. Since then, they told me, their most serious injury had been one mildly sprained ankle. Left alone, the children made very prudent choices about what kind of risks they would run – for being adventurous, of course they wanted to run *some* risks. At the same time, they learnt to be cool and collected in risky situations.[21]

POWER GAMES

I like the image of children weaving in and out of each other, playing together, and yet separately, as they develop their own skills. Many schools and after-school associations promote the importance of team-work as part of the greater lesson of loyalty. But children who have not yet fully developed their sense of self do not naturally team together (unless there is a crisis). Even in groups, children play alongside each other, each developing his independence within the group.

This may be contrasted with 'gang' play, in which one gang is motivated by competition against another gang. It usually entails a leader on each side: the most popular child picks the teams, decides who may and who may not belong, and makes most of the rules. All gang members must demonstrate loyalty to their designated leader.

Gangs are actually a form of role-play, an enactment of the power games played in classrooms and other areas of a child's life, where authority, responsibility and decision-making are invested in a single adult. Schools' inter-house games are often run along these lines. Some school playgrounds and housing estates are dominated by gangs, many of which use peer pressure to wreak havoc on the neighbourhood, or to perpetrate bullying. The weakest members trail along in subservience and a desperate desire to be liked by the strongest members of their team. David Gribble takes this further:

> It seems to be an assumption of those who favour group-centred education that children, if not combined, will scatter in irresponsible individuality. In fact children *want* to be together, *want* to share interests, *enjoy* organising themselves into large-scale games. They may need practice in working together, but they do not need artificial grouping systems to make them want to do so . . .
>
> It is such group identifications and abdications of personal responsibility that result in religious and ideological wars, concentration camps, torture and genocide. The selfish impulses are harmless by comparison.[22]

My favourite childhood recollection of group play was when I was second flautist in our school orchestra. The orchestra was an expression of harmony (sometimes!) that did not require anyone to surrender their identity. No one instrument was any more important than another, all made a distinct contribution to the whole, and I remember it as an uplifting experience.

CHILDREN AT WORK

When we give a child the chance to play, all those activities that appear so rambling and undirected and *slow* start to look more and more rewarding. Your child runs in to you triumphantly and says, 'Mum, I can skip all by myself!' Copying your actions, he wants to chop vegetables, play the piano, sweep the floor, dig with a spade . . . Montessori called this 'the work'. Such work is quite different from that of an adult. In fact, Montessori's 'work' sounds remarkably like Alison Stallibrass's 'spontaneous play'. It adds to his grace and self-awareness. It does not force him into boredom or specialisation:

> When a child works, he does not do so to attain some further goal. His objective in working is the work itself, and when he has repeated an exercise and brought his own activities to an end, this end is independent of external factors. As far as the child's personal reactions are concerned, his cessation from work is not connected with weariness since it is characteristic of a child to leave his work completely refreshed and full of energy.
>
> . . . A child does not follow the law of minimum effort, but rather the very opposite. He consumes a great deal of energy in working for no ulterior end and employs all his potentialities in the execution of each detail.[23]

Work for a small child may take the shape of learning a new skill with a ball, or perfecting balancing or climbing techniques. It may also, incidentally, take the form of an activity that contributes to the running of the home. Here are two different examples of a child at 'work'. Firstly, an American mother watches as her child aquires a new skill:

> How could I explain to a casual observer, for instance, what was really going on while I watched my son run down a steep hill and run exultantly back to the top? How can I recapture just what it was like, watching him slowly

overcome his initial fear? How long would another person sit and listen to me recount each experience with that hill – how at first, he wouldn't even go to the edge, then he'd go down a little bit and run back, then down a little more . . . Who's going to sit and listen to that?[24]

Some adults see a child's running about as aimless and hugely irritating. Perhaps they might be more approving, or at least more tolerant, if they thought of it as: A Child Learns to Run Down a Steep Hill. Goals are often more readily appreciated than the process required to reach them.

Such adults might be even more appreciative of Jean Liedloff's account of a little girl taking her first lessons in cookery, a task that is easily classifiable as 'useful':

> I was present at the first moments of one little girl's working life. She was about two years old. I had seen her with the women and girls, playing as they grated manioc into a trough. Now she was taking a piece of manioc from the pile and rubbing it against the grater of a girl near her. The chunk was too big; she dropped it several times trying to draw it across the rough board. An affectionate smile and a smaller piece of manioc came from her neighbour, and her mother, ready for the inevitable impulse to show itself, handed her a tiny grating board of her own . . .[25]

Although Jean Liedloff felt she had attended the first moments of the girl's working life, no doubt the work had begun long before, when the girl was still a baby in her mother's arms, observing and sensing her mother's activity. She had perhaps already held manioc, and spent hours quietly watching, in preparation for her own attempts. An outsider can log the moments in a child's life when something first *appears* to happen, but the process begins unseen, in the dark. It is worth remembering that no one knows another person as well as he knows himself. Least of all do we fully know a child, whose processes are so different from our own.

Liedloff's last sentence is important. The mother had ready a small grater to hand to her child, having anticipated her desire to join in. One of Montessori's great contributions to the modern nursery was the introduction of child-sized furniture, including small tools for use around the classroom. The children could help to care for their own environment and appreciate the result of their endeavours.

Marion Pears describes how she allowed her children to make small decisions for themselves, before they moved on to greater responsibility:

> I had great trust in them – trust that they would explore the world carefully, joyously and safely; trust that they would learn all they needed to know; trust that they could find suitable clothes to wear, and eat a nourishing well-balanced diet.
>
> Thus the children were allowed to do things and use things that many others were not. When Arnold picked up a very sharp knife, I showed him how to cut safely with it. When Bryn (at two) picked up a blunt axe and 'chopped' little sticks with it, I supervised without comment. When Omi (at eighteen months) discovered the automatic lighter on the stove, I asked her to light it for me to cook. Careful supervision and explanation, rather than prohibition, seemed to be the answer.[15]

Juliet Solomon, mother, environmentalist and author of *Green Parenting*, catalogues the kinds of activities that many toddlers enjoy:

> Very small children can learn to wash up, to load and unload the washing machine (which will take them ages as they enjoy doing it so much), to handwash clothes and other items, to clean (a two-year-old with a couple of cloths will sometimes leave a basin looking as if it had been French-polished), to begin to cook – a blunt knife will cut a mushroom . . . We ate a lot of fresh peas when

our children were small because they loved shelling them as their contribution.[26]

It may come as a surprise (or a shock) to many adults to think that a small child can be as responsible for himself as this. Even those regularly in charge of children may be unaware of the capabilities of the age group they tend. This may be because they approach the children with a method, and their prejudices well-set.

Some adults offer the argument that making a child undertake caretaking duties (of himself, his environment, or other children, depending on his age) is forcing him to grow up too soon. The point is that none of this activity is forced. Were it to be imposed upon the child, he would be likely to react, and to do the job unwillingly and badly. He would experience none of the joy that comes from spontaneous involvement. The first task of responsibility is to work out how much responsibility you want to take.

RESPONSE AND RESPONSIBILITY

While teaching maths in an American state school, John Holt began to re-examine teaching methods and the effect they had on children. His observations were not confined to the classroom. Holt discovered a lack of trust in children throughout the institutional system:

At this school children were not allowed to be waiters at lunch tables until fifth grade. The adults who ran the school – many of them psychologists – felt that until children were ten they could not be trusted to carry dishes of food around a room without dropping them, or maybe even throwing them. When children went from one class or building to another, they had to be guided by an adult, in carefully straight lines – one child was always appointed line leader, to help the children do this. Without some such system, everyone assumed, the children would never get to where they were going.

As fond of children as we were, Bill [Holt's colleague] and I shared enough of these prejudices so that when, a few years later, we saw in public schools in Leicestershire, England, six-year-olds carrying dishes of food from kitchen counters to lunch tables, or going from classrooms to assemblies and back again without adult supervision, we were absolutely astonished. When we came home and told people of these marvels, they said, 'Well, English kids must be different, you could never get American kids to do that.'[27]

Children have a natural balance that, with practice, becomes their key to coping in the real world. A child trusted to carry his own tray will, provided he has not been negatively programmed thus far, be able to carry his own tray. The occasional accident should not be used as an excuse for making our children entirely dependent on us. The sooner we let go of our children, the more balanced they will be.

As John Holt began to believe more fully in the capabilities of children, his views became increasingly radical. He came to feel, quite passionately, that many schools were unsuitable for the education of children. The more Holt opened his eyes to the potential of the child, the more examples of capability he discovered. In his preface to Stallibrass's *The Self-Respecting Child*, Holt describes a two-year-old cooking on a hot stove. This puts his earlier story about six-year-olds carrying trays, rather in the shade:

In recent months I have come to know . . . two mothers of children who, *since before they were two*, have been cooking, on a real stove, real food that they and their parents then ate. To do this, these tiny children had to move chairs to the sink or stove, and then climb on them to put water in a pot or do the cooking itself. For all my deep respect for the seriousness and ability of children, I would not have thought this possible for children much under five. Such examples, of which there are probably many others, show clearly not only that children are able

124

to be far more competent and careful than we think, but also that they need far more opportunities than we give them not just for adventurous play *but for serious work*.[28]

Before Frances' third birthday, I wrote down some of the things she liked to do, or had attempted to do, as part of her spontaneous play. These included: washing the car – her first word was 'pla' (splash) while doing this with me; dressing herself, including fastening buckles and zips; blow-drying her own hair and mine; chopping vegetables; taking photographs on a real camera with film in it; pegging out washing, taking it in and folding it when dry; opening tin cans; making up songs with words; making her own breakfast; hopping on one leg; ordering a drink in a restaurant (politely); polishing shoes; pouring glasses of water for herself; cutting with scissors; posting letters (when she could reach); cleaning her own teeth; and mending things, like broken toys, or the bath plug.

I am sure most parents could add to a list like this with the surprising things their children are capable of. It is quite a good exercise when you are feeling low about yourself or your child, because it's a reminder of his capabilities and his growing independence. I do not believe my daughter was exceptional to perform these tasks – Alice and Joe had their own, quite different lists, although (of course) I never found the time to write them out. All three were given the opportunity to try new things whenever they showed an interest. Conversely, if they asked me kindly to do things for them, I didn't usually refuse. I knew they were equally happy to lend a hand when I needed it.

At two years old, Alice had started to dress and undress herself. She was quite slow about it, and sometimes got in quite a muddle. It required an effort on my part not to jump in with both hands to assist her before she had asked for assistance. Her sister, too, was only too eager to play the 'little mother' and help her out of her difficulties. But Alice was capable of deciding when to announce 'I can't'. Each day, Alice got a little further than before. Alison Stallibrass describes the spontaneous development of ability:

. . . a baby's ability grows like a tree whose branches multiply by the growth along their twigs of new buds, which themselves grow into twigs, and so on. A child's faculties (1) require regular nourishment if they are not to wither and die; (2) can only grow in due season; (3) are capable, through the digestion of suitable nourishment, of sprouting new shoots; and (4) one bit of growth makes the next bit possible – a bud cannot grow on a non-existent twig. When a baby elects, entirely of his own free will, to learn something new, he does so because his body (or tree) of knowledge is ready to put out new shoots in that particular direction.[29]

Like a sapling plant, the self-directed child grows from strength to strength, to become a healthy, vigorous adult. Marion Pears gives a list of accomplishments of her son, now fully grown. There is nothing weak about his self-directed development:

. . . the point being that if we leave our children in the real world, instead of taking them out of it, they will be more capable (not less!). If I start to jot down the skills and experiences of my twenty-two-year-old son, it looks like this: metal work, forging skills, makes knives, swords and imitation mediaeval armour; brass work, bowls, enamelling; leather-work, makes bags, hats, key-rings; lettering, Gothic lettering and illuminated manuscripts; designs and sews own costumes for fancy dress functions; cooks good plain meals and understands nutrition; can clean a house; ride a horse; build a shed; build a forge; play the violin; make a Celtic harp; shoot a gun; fire a bow; swim; plant a vegetable garden; sing in a choir; drive and repair a car; operate and programme a computer and use a word processor; takes part in the sport of fencing (with foils); sat on the school council and was convenor of the building and grounds committee; can ice-skate; can roller-skate; mediaeval dancing; mechanical skills – can fix things that break down . . .

And lest people fear that he has been neglecting study and the things of the mind, let me hasten to add that he is in the last year of a math/computing degree, and an A student. The purpose of these lists is simply to illustrate how much more exciting it can be, to be an inner-directed, continuum person, out in the real world![13]

And all this, from allowing a child to find his own balance.

Letting go as children grow: self-motivation

- A child's play is his work. However meaningless, rambling or slow it may appear to us, it is the thing he was born for
- Children who are allowed to play/work at their own rate, following their own passions, are equipping themselves for a self-directed life
- When handing over responsibility to children, we might ask them to tell us how much responsibility they are ready to take on. Imposed chores do not have the same quality as elected tasks
- Children rarely benefit from the labels we impose on them. The best gift for any child, whatever his special needs, is to be allowed time to learn through play, to socialise and to explore his own passions

---

5

HURRY UP, HARRY –
PARENTING IN A PRESSURISED WORLD

Our patience will achieve more than our force.

Edmund Burke, *Reflections on the Revolution in France*

The sign on the revolving glass doors at our local superstore said: 'Automatic Doors – Please Do Not Push, Except In An Emergency.' One by one, shoppers ignored the advice and tried to force their way in with their trolleys. This caused the doors to grind to a halt, with the shoppers trapped inside. Voluble sighing and swearing indicated what people thought of the revolving doors, but eventually they calmed down, read the notice, stopped pushing and allowed the doors to twirl gently (and automatically) on their round.

As I watched the Saturday-morning shoppers, it occurred to me that children are like automatic doors, programmed to move forward at their own pace. Push them too fast, and they are liable to misfunction. Perhaps children should go round with stickers on their foreheads, to remind over-anxious adults: 'These items grow up automatically. No need to push.'

For we do push our children a great deal, and this is usually because we are in such a hurry ourselves. The clock dictates where we have to be and when, and as a result we cram as much into our days as we can. 'Time out' is often a luxury we hope to be able to afford one day. The effect of our haste is to make us feel tired and ineffective. We jump into cars, speed along to each event, and while there, we mentally prepare for the next item on our agenda.

When children come along, it is soon evident that they respond to a quite different beat, they just don't know the meaning of the word 'hurry'. They dawdle, they stop and stare, they ruminate, they infuriate, they don't seem to understand the importance of arriving on time, and they take forever to do things that you could do in a flash. They also fail to appreciate that you are usually hurrying *on their behalf* to ballet, Brownies or football training, or whatever activity you have organised for them. If it weren't for us, parents reason, they'd just sit at home and twiddle their thumbs.

Time is on a child's side, and yet it soon becomes his enemy, just as once, somewhere in our growing-up, it became ours. Play therapist Virginia Axline considers haste to be the menace of the modern child:

> The child lives in a hustle-bustle world. Things spin by him with bewildering speed. He is rushed here and there. By nature he is slow. This world is a big place, and he needs time to take it all in. Everyone is familiar with the adults who cannot let the child do things for himself because 'it takes *forever*!' For example, the very common exasperation adults sometimes show at the fumblings of little children who cannot button up their coats 'in a hurry' or who cannot tie up their shoestrings 'in a hurry' – who can't, in fact, do much of anything 'in a hurry'. The adults swoop down and do it for them. Tensions and frustrations are multiplied.[1]

When a child is habitually hurried along, or feels he must hurry in order to be effective, he may grow up to be too speedy for his own good. Amy and Thomas Harris, founders of the Institute for Transactional Analysis in California, offer this check list of types of self-defeating speedy behaviour:

> You *always* move, walk, and eat rapidly.
>   You feel *impatience* with the rate at which most events

take place, hurrying the speech of others, head nodding, yes, yes, yes . . . and finishing other people's sentences for them.

You do two or more things at once. Do you always automatically grab for something to read when you sit down to eat a sandwich? People can go through their whole lives not *experiencing* eating . . .

You feel guilty when you relax.

You don't observe well, and because you are preoccupied, you don't see a sunset or a garden or the dimpled hands of the little child . . .

You schedule more and more in less and less time.

Your body language includes a clenched jaw, grinding teeth and tight muscles.

You are afraid to stop doing everything faster and faster.[2]

Many of us will recognise the types of behaviour in this list, for they are the symptoms of modern living. I remember attending a case history class by Janet Snowdon, an experienced homeopath based in Bath. One student described a case where a woman complained of feeling rushed and never having enough time in the day. 'I'm afraid that's not an indicator for a particular remedy,' said Janet. 'Feeling rushed is the complaint of nearly everyone I see these days.'

When I became pregnant for the first time, the world continued to spin around me, but I no longer wanted to spin with it. I left a responsible and hectic job in journalism to sit at home and stare out of the window. I had never felt so content in my life as when I gave up commuting into London and began expanding into pregnancy. My inner clock was already honing in to the rhythms of the growing baby inside me.

This feeling of being in time and tune with my baby lasted for as long as I was breastfeeding, but as Frances entered her third year, conflicts began to arise. It was an education for me to live with a small child who did not have the same sense of urgency as myself, nor the need to prove herself by being overactive. It is an education I have yet to complete, as I struggle to manage the extra-curricular lives of three highly-motivated children. Regular reminders to them that they don't have to have so many hobbies are greeted with despair: 'But I don't know what to give up!' sighed Joe, who, at eight, was devoted to his tennis, his gym, his dancing, his violin. By encouraging their self-motivation, I have set myself up for a second career in activity management. But the extra-curricular itinerary of the average middle-class child is also a modern cultural phenomenon and children want to be part of it. They are used to a packed diary and – since they can't stroll over to the park to meet their friends these days – the gym class and the tennis lesson become an important feature of their social life. As British novelist Maeve Haran puts it,

> We've managed to brainwash kids so successfully with the twin bogeys of road accidents and stranger danger, they daren't go anywhere alone. Instead, we've organised their lives so totally that, in the same, way that prisoners start to love the bars of their jail, they actually expect their lives to be planned in advance. . . . modern children have us over a barrel. Refuse them a swimming trip and they threaten you with days glued to computer games. 'I need exercise,' they taunt . . . A look of total derision greets any suggestion that they might play in the garden or, God forbid, read a book. Going for a walk is for the uncool or brain dead.[3]

In 1991, a house move from Manchester to Bath allowed us to take stock of the extra-curricular scene and wind it right down. Ten years later, by the time we moved again, there was hardly a day in the week when one or other child was not trampolining or tap dancing. Luckily, the new house was nearer to the hobbies, a feature which must, in itself, have palpably reduced exhaust emissions in the Bath area. If the children wanted to follow every creative urge that occurred to them, I reasoned, at least they could walk there. Now they could dash or dawdle, just as they chose . . .

DASHING AND DAWDLING

Given time and space, children are capable of a great deal more than we might imagine. In our hurry to get places, we may bundle small children into car seats or pushchairs, and consequently imagine that they are unable to walk very far. But the educational pioneer Maria Montessori reminds us that even small children can walk long distances by themselves:

> The child under two is well able to walk for a mile or so, and also to climb. Our impression that a long walk is beyond her comes from making her walk at our pace. But the child is not trying to 'get there' – all she wants is to walk. And because her legs are shorter than ours it is we who must go at her pace . . . [4]

The point Montessori uncovers here is crucial to an understanding of a child's concept of time. There is no goal-orientation, no fixing on the future, or the result of his actions. There is only now, and what-he-happens-to-be-doing. The adult hurries because she wants to complete a task, and to achieve this within a certain time limit. The child is engrossed in the moment, and will not respond to pleas of 'Hurry up!' They mean nothing to him. If he does learn to hurry, he is merely mimicking a form of adult behaviour in order to please his parent. This behaviour will soon become ingrained as his way of interacting with the world. The timeless quality of childhood is thus easily destroyed.

Play researcher Alison Stallibrass found that parental haste was a cause of instability in the occasional child who came to her playgroup. Such a child had been forced always to move at his mother's tempo, but had not assimilated his mother's speed with any confidence. Rather, he was unsure of his own safety, and moved clumsily. Children are not born bad movers. They learn their lack of co-ordination from being pushed or dragged along:

> . . . Another four-year-old, with whom I had a fleeting acquaintance, neither walked nor ran but always pro-

ceeded at a shambling kind of jog-trot – perhaps acquired through having to keep up with his mother as she pushed his baby brother's pram on hurried expeditions to the shops. He would not attempt to climb the easiest part of the climbing frame, designed for – and normally used by – two-year-olds, 'because I might hurt myself.'[5]

Of course, small children can run around at break-neck speeds, but at times of their own choosing, not of ours. And they run for running's sake, not in order to 'be there' more quickly.

By the age of about four, a child may be persuaded to run for a short stretch in order to meet a deadline, but will usually collapse in mock exhaustion along the way: 'I'm tired!' he will cry, when his mother knows he is capable of running much further. This same child will burst into life ten seconds later at the sight of a friend down the road, and suddenly prove himself capable of the four-minute mile. It's motivation that matters, and that's something a child has to work out for himself.

I had a friend in Manchester who was happy to adapt to the pace of her small children. Because she did not drive a car, she had to walk everywhere, and so did not make distant plans. Instead she spent hours walking around her local streets, which proved to be a great source of education for her children, who were, of course, excellent walkers. Dawdling is a 'green' activity, says environmentalist Juliet Solomon:

Finding the balance between your interests and the child's can be trying, but less so if life can be slowed down a bit. The toddler seems to be either racing around or dawdling, and dawdling conflicts with the modern ethos of speed and productivity with which we are all imbued. If the child wants to stop and look at every tree and every garden gate on the way to the shops, it may be very irritating, but provided you allow enough time to get to the shops, it can be incredibly enlightening. Looking with her at details in the local environment may open your eyes to much that you have never previously had time to notice.[6]

CHILD TIME OR REAL TIME?

An extreme example of child-paced living is to be found in a book entitled *The Children on the Hill*. The true story of 'Maria' (not her real name) and her family has both inspired and exasperated readers since it was published in the early 1970s.

Maria, a devotee of Montessori ideas, set herself the task of providing an ideal environment in which to raise her children; one with no outside pressures, and in which she and her husband 'Martin' would be entirely immersed. In a remote Welsh mountain farmhouse, Maria took absolute responsibility for the children's education. Photo-journalist Michael Deakin reports on what he saw there:

> Usually she reacts to situations which other mothers would hardly consider as impinging on the area of child-rearing, by ignoring the pressures and conventions of everyday life to an almost comical extent. For example, if Paul, on the way to the bus stop, becomes absorbed with the goods on display in the greengrocers, she will refuse to hurry him up until she is satisfied that what seems to her his very reasonable interest has been slaked. The fact of missing the bus is a very minor consideration. But such an attitude has its own rewards. If catching the bus is really important – if it is the last one, or one which is being met – Paul, without any loss of serenity, can be persuaded to come on.[7]

This is a lovely example of how a child's preoccupations operate at odds with 'real' time. It is certainly rare for a child to be accorded more respect than the bus timetable. In Maria's world, the children are not merely respected as equals, but – if the account is accurate – they are treated by their parents as superiors. Maria rises like a servant at dawn to complete her housework before the children wake, so that she can focus on their needs and demands for the rest of the day. The children's 'process' is not even allowed the interruption of an incoming telephone call. When four-year-old Paul wants to play the same record over and over again (despite being asked not to) he does so for two whole days.

The result of tiptoeing around the children is, in this case, to create four young geniuses. Christian, Adam, Paul and Ruth shine at their chosen subjects, whether maths or music, but are apparently egocentric and at odds with children of their own age. While their intellectual capacities are impressive, other aspects of their development appear less advanced. The boys are described as 'gawky and restrained'[8], (see *Young, Gifted and Lonely* in Chapter 4), and many anecdotes reveal them to be lacking in any discernable sense of humour.

Michael Deakin, who tells Maria's story, offers a fascinating study of the possibilities of controlling the child's environment. But for every parent who wonders whether she should become more involved in her child's world, Maria's story stands as a warning.

Maria's life is a model of self-sacrifice. Her attempts to control her children's education involve her every waking minute, and test her patience to the limit. She organises all their activities, and though she does not do the work for them, is utterly available to meet their needs. She takes on the responsibility of anticipating the things they need to learn next, in order to maximise their stimulation. She even, for instance, monitors and orchestrates language learning when her children are still babies:

The prepared environment is equally important in the next stage, when the baby has first learned to talk. Then there will be scope for an endless exchange of words between the mother and child, but if this is allowed to happen in an entirely random fashion, a lot of the child's creative energies will be expended in pursuing unnecessary diversion of vocabulary and meaning. To avoid this Maria set about deliberately classifying the vocabulary she felt the children should learn, trying to make use of their exploratory instincts, hoping to harness their innate sense of orderliness to the development of their vocabulary. After she and Martin had discussed it, the father put shelves around the babies' cots. On these Maria arranged all the child's possessions in a rigid order – soap, baby powder, nappies, toys, clothes and so on, always in exactly the same place and every time she or Martin picked something up they would name it out loud before replacing it in the same spot. Soon Christian was repeating the words after, and then before, his parents.[9]

It seems terribly intense to be discussing in the dead of night which words a baby will learn the next day. Not only does this remove much of the spontaneity from a child's life, it smacks of repression and fear – fear that without mother's guidance, the children would grow up in unacceptable ways.

On the one hand, there is a sense of Maria's enormous respect for the powers of her children, yet on the other is the belief that, were they left to their own devices, their learning would be random and would therefore include the 'unnecessary'.

According to the twentieth century developmental psychologist Jean Piaget, the child's mind, whether 'playing' or 'doing maths' is not making random connections, but is busy constructing its own logic. The child attempts to connect with whatever he finds in his immediate world, but if we put too many workbooks in front of him, he may learn more about adult interference than about the content of the books. There is an important difference between encouraging and forcing a child to read.

A huge amount of parental effort goes into maintaining the hot-house atmosphere, in which little seedlings may grow to perfection. Taking so much responsibility upon themselves for their children's time, Maria and Martin sacrifice their own. It amazes me that children should be reared without ever seeing their mother devote time to herself.

THE MYTH OF QUALITY TIME

Some parents are over-involved with their children without necessarily spending much time with them. To be intrusive in a child's life does not require the self-sacrifice of a Maria or a Martin. It can be done in spare moments here and there, on the telephone, or after work; it has to do with a general attitude towards the child.

One fashionable way to over-involve yourself with your child is to commandeer him at pre-arranged moments in *your* calendar. Some childcare experts call this 'quality time' and suggest that an absent parent can make up for not being there when the child wants her, by being there in full force when she can. But as one newspaper report suggests, as a method of child-rearing, quality time leaves a lot to be desired:

> The steady erosion of life beyond work during the last two decades is clear in figures collected by Victor Fuchs, an economist. He estimates that American parents spent eleven hours less a week with their children in 1986 than was the case in 1960. The '5 p.m. dads' of the fifties and sixties, home for tea and bedtime, practically vanished; working mothers, meanwhile, have had to rely on 'quality time'. Increasingly, women are wondering whether that concept is a fallacy, and whether what everyone really needs is quantity. Half of all American parents think they spend too little time with their children.[10]

The shorter the time available, the greater the danger that it will be spent intensively. This may be because the busy parent believes she has to be just as serious about her time with the children as she is at the office. But our children may not want us to 'do' anything at all except be there.

This still leaves open to question the concept of 'quality': should we spend hours reading Topsy and Tim and providing early educative experiences, in order to call ourselves good parents? We are often told that the 'good' mother is baby- or child-centred and that we should arrange 'quality time' with our children. But such an attitude carries a great danger of interference. So keen are we to give our children 'the best', that we give more than they need. Jean Liedloff believes that

A parent whose day is centred on childcare is not only likely to be bored, and boring to others, but is also likely to be giving an unwholesome kind of care. A baby needs to be in the midst of an active person's life, in constant physical contact and stimulated by a great deal of the kind of experience in which he or she will take part later in life. The role of a baby while in arms is passive, with all his senses observant. He enjoys occasional direct attention, kisses, tickles, being thrown in the air, etc. But his main business is to witness the actions, interactions and surroundings of his caretaker adults or children.[11]

It's this notion of parenting as an active verb which keeps us all carefully on guard, gazing at our children, lest they should do something worth observing. It might be better if we kept busy so they could be watching us. In the old days, the atmosphere of benign neglect increased with the child's age – not because it was a patented method of childcare, but because benign neglect had been the lot of children all the way back to the Stone Age. Says novelist Maeve Haran,

The fifties mother may have stayed at home but she certainly didn't make the mistake of devoting herself to her children. She was too busy baking or tidying the linen cupboard. When she'd finished, she was off to coffee mornings, bridge sessions or flower arranging before you could say 'Get out from under my feet.' I remember 'latchkey kids' were who were sent off in the morning to play and not expected back until teatime, like guests in a Blackpool boarding house. What bliss.[3]

The phrase 'latchkey kid' referred to the child whose mother worked; he was given a 'latchkey' to let himself in at night to the empty house. It was not a term of approbation when it was

138

coined. It shows just how far we have come from the random childhoods of the 1950s and 1960s that we look back on such an arrangement with growing nostalgia.

Somewhere between hours of abandonment and childhood-by-appointment there must be a happy medium. To achieve a moment of genuine Quality Time, we ordinary mortals must trawl through oceans of Quantity Time when no magic moments happen at all. The idea that spontaneous quality time can be put on schedule is a contradiction in terms, as this example confirms:

> As much as we would like to deny it, women are in truth discovering that children rarely need their mothers at their mothers' convenience. Those of us who have tried – and tried and tried and tried – to make the 'quality time' theory work have, quite simply, come up empty-handed. A working mother from Virginia, whose current employer allows a seven-to-four workday so she can be home when her daughter returns from school, remembers a time circumstances weren't so favorable: 'I would be tense during the entire drive home from work, thinking "I must relate with Emma, I must relate with Emma." But when I arrived home, Emma wouldn't want to relate. Emma would want to watch television.'[12]

Having said all this, there are some situations which call for the direct attention of a parent towards an individual child. The domestic history of the Wesley family, founders of the eighteenth century Methodist movement, includes what may be the first recorded incidence of quality time. Susanna Wesley, (1669–1742) born the youngest of twenty-five children, would have been lucky to have had any private time with either of her parents. (Enormous European families were the result of babies being sent out to wet-nurse: mothers no longer enjoyed the contraceptive benefits of breastfeeding.[13])

Susanna herself gave birth to nineteen children, nine of whom died in infancy. She decided she must develop a personal relationship with each child – a revolutionary idea in the eighteenth century, when children were often treated like small adults from a very young age. Besides schooling them at home, she scheduled a private appointment with each one, every week, in order to offer encouragement and spiritual guidance. 'You know what you owe to one of the best of mothers . . .' wrote her husband, Samuel to his children, 'above all the wholesome and sweet motherly advice and counsel which she has often given you to fear God . . .'[14]

JUST BEING THERE

As most stay-at-home parents will testify, being with a child all day does not mean that he is receiving lots of direct attention. The more parents are around their children, the more they melt into the background, available in a busy-but-attentive kind of way. Many home-based parents spend their day doing housework, shopping, meeting friends, and only occasionally stop to 'play' with their child, or go along to toddler groups. They sometimes feel guilty for not doing enough. But as American mother Linda Burton describes, children are able to take all they need from an active mother who is open to interruptions, demands and cuddles *en route*. And they benefit from the relaxed presence of a parent who is not pressed by time to try and get things 'right':

> I wonder how an observing social scientist would manage to catalogue the time I spend all day working near my children. I figure he would be able to mark down the negligible-to-non-existent time I spend playing with my children with no trouble. That time is easy to quantify and isolate. But I am entirely certain that that time has nowhere near the same impact on my children than does their daily, rather pedestrian observance of how I act and what I do day in day out. How would an outside observer manage to quantify the amount of time in which I serve as a living, breathing, consistent example to my children of how to do everything from answering the doorbell to mediating major conflicts?

Children who only play in the general vicinity of their mothers are picking up lessons from her, with nary the exchange of a word. How does Mommy treat other people? What makes her curious or excited? What if Mommy wants to learn something new – where does she go to learn it? What kind of music does Mommy like – does it make her happy or sad or want to dance? . . .[15]

Quality time is a remedial measure, like holding therapy for autistic children to try to make them respond to the outside world.[16] Spontenaity is lacking. To force our children to sit still and play with us, or to be held by us, or to do any of the other delightful things that parenting magazines suggest we *should* be doing, may defeat the purpose.

Interactive play, cuddles and special moments cannot be planned for. It's great to initiate these things, but we must be prepared sometimes for a negative response. And when we stop trying so hard, the day seems suddenly full of magical moments, like this one recalled by Joanne Bruun of Maryland:

It was a beautiful September morning, a day that offered the promise of fall but retained the fullness of summer. The sky was brilliant. The air was warm and held September's special stillness, yet the trees hung lush and ripe with not a leaf lost. My baby awoke from her nap and she was warm with sleep. I carried her downstairs and as I did, Billy Joel's 'Leave a Tender Moment Alone' came on the radio. The song sang to me, the day spoke to me, and the baby warmed to me. I began to dance with her, just my little miracle and I dancing on a perfect fall day. One of the joys of being at home is being open to just such a moment.[17]

PRESENT TENSE

It is often said that children live in the present, but sometimes we forget just how complete that absorption can be. Highly competent in the physical world, a whiz at languages, the human infant is woefully ill-equipped to deal with concepts like yesterday and tomorrow. Even at the age of eight, Joe still needed me to navigate his way through the week for him. That birthday party next Saturday seemed to be 'years away!' The scrape on the knee this morning (unless visible) was a distant memory by the afternoon.

Much less could he deal with history topics as imposed by the National Curriculum on primary school children throughout the United Kingdom. 'Were *you* alive in the Roman times?' he asked me, despite the time-line his teacher has patiently strung across the classroom like a row of washing. 'Why did they used to be Romans and Victorians and now we're Humans?' There was no answer to that.

Why do children suffer from such a lack of perspective? Surely it would be helpful for them to be able to wait patiently for anticipated events, or to understand that a week ago is a relatively short time? Frustrating as it may be at times for the modern adult, the child's lack of comprehension in this area is his blessing. Living in a blissful time-bubble of the ongoing present enables the immature brain to focus on matters to hand. Children are not needlessly distracted by anxieties for the future or regrets of the past. They just keep going, presently.

It would not occur to a small child to say 'Where has the time gone?' or 'I must hurry to get this done on time.' And indeed, in human evolution, there was very little need for adults to be pressed by time-specific concerns. If only we, like parents in rural India or Africa today, were able sometimes to forget the clock, we would instantly eliminate one of the greatest stress of modern life.

I am well aware that I hurry my children unnecessarily at times. I know I am in danger of destroying their natural rhythms. Once, when Frances was only three and I asked her to hurry up and get in the car, she tried literally to do so, hyperventilating and tripping over herself to climb into her seat. It was like a parody of someone hurrying: her legs scrambling around and not getting her anywhere.

It can be disastrous for a child to be constantly pushed in this way. If it matters to me to be on time, I have simply to allow extra minutes for my child to move. If I am regularly rushing her from place to place, this is a sign that I have an over-busy schedule. Although my children like to be busy, I have learnt to introduce space around each activity and cling onto our valuable free time with the tenacity of a sea-swept limpet. Now, if an unforeseen circumstance crowds our next activity, I usually cancel whatever was coming up. Or we arrive late.

SETTING THE PACE

Time conflicts between parent and child are not an altogether new phenomenon, although they are heightened by the pace of modern living. One hundred years ago, the education pioneer Maria Montessori understood the importance of a child's inner rhythm, and also the impatience that many adults feel in the presence of one slower than themselves. 'Rhythm,' she wrote, 'is not simply an old concept that can be changed at will . . .'

It is an intrinsic characteristic of an individual almost like the shape of his body. We take pleasure in associating with others whose rhythmical movements are like our own but are pained when we are forced to adapt ourselves to other rhythms.

If, for example, we must walk with one who is partially paralyzed we feel a kind of anguish, and if we see another who has had a stroke lift a glass to his lips with a slow and trembling hand, we are pained by the sharp contrast between his halting movement and our own freedom of action. We strive to free ourselves from this inner conflict by substituting our own rhythm for his on the assumption that we are assisting him.

An adult acts somewhat similarly with respect to a child. Unconsciously he strives to keep the child from making his unnaturally slow and deliberate movements and he would remove this annoyance as he would brush away a fly.[18]

Children and old people alike may be slow and unimpressed by the speed of the modern world. But both are vulnerable, and dependent on the assistance of young adults, who are faster than themselves, and who may be intolerant of their leisurely approach. Some mothers return to work because of a fear of stagnation and boredom. They are alarmed by the slow pace of a child, and do not want to be 'reduced' to waiting around for their children to grow up. Yet they wish they were not quite so fraught in their own lives. Children can teach us a great deal about living in the moment, says environmentalist Juliet Solomon:

> We can relearn the delights of sloth from our children. Sitting in the wood, fiddling with dead leaves, looking at the light on the trees with them before they move off to investigate something else, is an antidote to stress at least as effective as those we can purchase in the marketplace, in front of the TV, in alcohol, drugs or relaxation classes . . .
>
> I used to get very annoyed when my one-year-old son insisted that I stay in his room after I had told him a story, while he went to sleep, which took about twenty minutes. But when a friend pointed out that it was a perfectly reasonable request, and that I should try to enjoy sitting still on the child's bed, because I probably had no other time during the day for that amount of peace and quiet, my twenty minutes of mild irritation turned into twenty minutes of regeneration. I was rather sad when, before he was two, he decided he didn't want me any more and sent me packing as soon as his story was finished.[19]

'If an hour seems long,' said Paul-Henri Spaak, (NATO Secretary General 1957–61), 'I remind myself that it will never return, and it immediately becomes terribly short.'

A child's tempo is an expression of himself. The speed at

which he chooses to do a thing is peculiarly his own. Evidence for this can be seen in the behaviour of the baby who is nursed on demand. He suckles whenever he feels the need, and although there may be a pattern to his feeding, he does not follow any clock. Gradually, he spaces out his feeds to greater intervals, though this may take months or even years. His way is easy, like the principle of Tao (pronounced Dao):

> Tao (the way) is the first principle of the universe. As man is part of the universe, his natural way is to go with it, flow with it, not to try and separate from it and impose his own order on things. Man is part of Tao, whether he recognizes it or not . . . Tao invariably does nothing and yet there is nothing that is not done.
>
> In other words, there is nothing to be achieved by striving. The way to 'be' is to go with the grain, to swim with the tide . . . Doing nothing brings an understanding of the way of nature. Little energy need be expended, for energy is only required for going against something, not with it.[20]

This Chinese philosophy, dating back to the sixth century BC, can be applied to many areas of parenting. Like Dr Michel Odent, whose strategy as a male midwife is to 'keep his hands in his pockets' for as long as possible during labour, a trusting mother will stand back to allow time to do its work.

One French mother whose children were born at Odent's clinic at Pithiviers in the 1970s told me that he was extremely skilled and speedy in his performance of the Caesarean section, an operation that saves the lives of many women and babies. For this reason, he could wait until the eleventh hour to see if a labour should be allowed to take its natural course. We must not confuse Taoist non-interference with neglect. A parent who goes with the flow has nevertheless to be aware of the warning signs and be ready to move in to rescue her children when she is really needed.

RITUALS THAT RESTORE

With our increased dependency on the clock, modern Western society has largely dispensed with the natural markers of time, such as seasonal changes, celebrations of nature, or the events of an ordinary day (sunrise, mealtimes and so on). When we do celebrate (Christmas and birthdays), we rarely stop: special days are usually even more busy and frenetic than the rest. Nor is there much chance for being ourselves. Every December and January, newspapers are full of the stresses of the modern family Christmas, complete with irritating relatives and divorced parents, unwanted presents and the horrors of cooking the turkey with trimmings. The combination of high expectation with harsh reality has led to a series of self-help options: workshops, for instance, and how-to-cope leaflets from family charities[21].

Rituals meant to bring us together can easily tear us apart. When community breaks down and status is based on consumer durables, Christmas – one of our last remaining heavyweight celebrations – may simply remind us how lonely we are, or how little we possess. But children rarely share our jaundiced view.

Waldorf (Rudolph Steiner) Schools throughout the world understand this: they emphasise the importance of familiar celebrations in a child's life and incorporate a wide range of seasonal festivals into their curriculum. John Davy, a British scientist and educator in the Steiner tradition, believes adult celebration has become less and less expressive: there may be some dignified singing, perhaps, but no dancing, and little evident expression of joy:

Children are closer to the older experience of festivals. On their birthdays, we wish them 'many happy returns of the day'. A birthday is something to look forward to; each time it returns, you celebrate a step in 'growing up' – towards what? Towards a grey adult world without festivals?[22]

146

Even when we do stop to celebrate in the modern world, all too often we buy our celebrations off the peg, and work ourselves into a frenzy trying to plan the occasion to perfection. Tension and a feeling of claustrophobia are the result of festivals that are organised by a few, and endured by many.

If a celebration is to be truly expressive, then it will be a product of the people who put it together. 'Festivals,' says Dutch theologian and mother Bons Voors, 'make a thread with different coloured beads over the years.'[23] Children, especially, love to have a role, and the contributions they make often become incorporated as part of the festival the following year. Bons Voors describes how her daughter was allowed to shape her own birthday party:

This year, when our daughter's sixth birthday was coming along, she took part in all the preparations. She decorated the white paper cups and plates. She helped with the making of velvet hairbands for the guests as little presents to take home. She insisted on coming to the woods to collect horse chestnuts and acorns. She loved making models of conker animals and little acornmen with beechcaps, and spiderwebs of conkers and matchsticks with thread. Thus the habit was broken that 'everything has to be quite a surprise for the birthday girl' . . .

Another element taken into consideration was the time factor. For once I had listened to the often-made remark of my daughter: 'Mum, don't be so hasty!' So we lengthened the usual time for birthday parties and did not squeeze all its activities of conkermaking, games and birthday cakes into one fat sausage. We made plenty of time for her and her friends to breathe in and out between activities . . .

So I realise again and again that a party or a festive event is not a following of strict codes, is not the cramming of activities into one afternoon, is not being scared that things will go out of control.[24]

Many of my happiest memories belong to childhood Christmases and birthdays, when the sense of family unity and purpose was at a height. The repetitions of ritual form strong images in a child's imagination, encouraging his powers of recall and allowing him to develop a sense of place and power over the passing years. Thus, anticipation becomes an important part of the ritual itself.

Each family interprets its festivals according to its own needs. Used creatively, festivals light the way, as American writer Susan Brenna explains:

> Through rituals, families create memories, continuity and a sense of being special, which in turn contribute to an individual's self esteem. Over time, as family members may develop different work, play and meal routines, tradition and rituals are especially valuable as they beat a steady rhythm behind unpredictable schedules . . .
>
> The effect of a family's taking time to recognize and celebrate traditions and rituals may be profound: a break from the speeded-up quality of daily life; a gift a family gives itself through doing service for others; or the feeling that though a family is scattered geographically, a deep, historical connection links them all.[25]

Children illuminate our lives by the introduction of small rituals of their own: 'Mummy, let's do it the way we *always* do it!' is an appeal that few mothers can resist. Children seek coherence in their lives, and rituals are an early way of glimpsing the harmony of existence. They are also a sign of bonding, of belonging. A life without rituals of any kind would be hard to imagine.

BUSY GOING NOWHERE

Maria Montessori talked about respecting the natural rhythms of the child. Some parents respond to the bright, vivacious aspects of their children; others to their quiet, contemplative sides. But many find it difficult to understand a child who does nothing at all. There will be times when our children refuse to join in, preferring to stand on the sidelines and watch. They may daydream for hours, or spend full minutes staring into space.

Often, their inactivity is taken for a sign of dis-ease. We may become irritated by their refusal to co-operate in the project in hand, and try to snap them out of it. But children sometimes need time just to be. As Juliet Solomon points out, our product-oriented society does not easily tolerate inactivity, or what appears to be inactivity:

> The myth which needs debunking is that the child needs to be stimulated. We are told that if he is not, he will be bored. But nowhere in the texts is any distinction made between those times when the child may just want to be quiet, or to watch something, and when he is what adults call 'bored'. The consumer culture, in order to sell its goods, works hard through its various agencies of publicity to make people believe that they are hardly alive unless there are tangible events or material items filling up their lives all the time . . . Something has to happen, and something tangible should result – product replaces process once again. The child who lies on his back during a walk in the woods and looks up through the trees is thought of as rather unusual – he isn't getting anywhere. And the mother whose child wants to spend hours just looking out of the window may well be told there is something wrong with the child.[26]

Most children need time to sit and stare. Sometimes a child who spends long periods in abstracted reverie is doing so as a rebellion, or as an act of self-preservation. It is his way of 'opting out' from a world that is heavily controlled by others. Play therapist Virginia Axline includes day dreaming in a list of defensive acts:

> [The child] *will* be an individual. If he cannot achieve it by a legitimate way, then he will get it by some substitute

action. Thus the child has tantrums, teases, sulks, day-dreams, fights and tries to shock others by his beha-viour.[27]

Many children switch off for a few minutes here and there. It can be a preliminary activity before joining in, time for the private screening of a fantasy, or for replaying an event or conversation. *Magical Child* author Joseph Chilton Pearce evaluates the vacant look in a child's eyes:

> All children tend to stare vacantly for long periods. Burton White [the American author and child psychol-ogist] finds that the brightest children are those who are allowed to stare without interruption. Staring may rough-in visual concepts as empty categories in the brain to be filled in later by full sensory interaction.[28]

When does a child find time to consolidate, to calm down, to take stock, if not in these moments of quiet? A four-year-old may be sent to school all day, sat at a desk, expected to wrestle with his friends during a noisy and frantic break, and then interact intelligently and politely with his mother when he gets home. If he is given space to 'come to', it is usually in front of a television, where a thousand colourful and incomprehensible images invade his mind. When does he find the time simply to 'be'?

All kinds of stalling behaviours are adopted by children to preserve the time-bubble that defines their childhood. For instance, a child who enters a new situation may choose to assess it before jumping in (in contrast to adults who act nervously but must *act*). According to British author and play researcher Alison Stallibrass,

> Another general characteristic of the children is that they know definitely what they want to do from moment to moment, even if it is to do nothing.
> . . . Some children, particularly new ones, spend much of the time watching the others. But they are not doing

nothing. Watching is an important *activity*; the child's need to watch should be respected and he should *not* be distracted from his absorption in watching others, or 'stimulated'. Some children are extremely interested in other children and their doings; some like to see others do things before they try to do them themselves; they like to ponder and consider what they will do before they do it, and I sometimes wonder if these children learn more quickly than those who rush in and therefore begin by making a lot of mistakes.[29]

Speaking as a rusher-inner, it took me a long time to accept the cautious approach of my first daughter, Frances. Continuum therapist Jean Liedloff, when she met one-year-old Frances, said: 'She's already a little wary of strangers', and instead of accepting this aspect of her, I felt bad about having 'created' a retiring child.

I should have had more faith. Frances was not at all retiring, just prudent. Even now, when nobody on earth would call her shy, Frances moves into new situations quietly, her eyes wide open, drinking in the experience before she adds anything of her own.

At three, Frances would sometimes hold on to my legs during a toddlers' music session, and decline to join in. At first, I would plead with her to sit down with the others and do her bit. My efforts, of course, were counter-productive. As soon as I stopped bothering her, and began to appreciate her way, Frances blossomed into a fully participating, active young girl.

Perhaps we should remember that the modern Western child has to face more new situations than most, certainly far more than the rural village child, who can depend on the same faces and a certain cycle of events for most of his life. His encounter with an occasional visitor will be no more than a curiosity, whereas strange moments might occur dozens of times a week for the child in an urban setting. This can leave any child quite bewildered at times.

These examples of inactivity are not meant to illustrate that it is preferable for a child to daydream, or be cautious in his approach. Such things are individual: some children learn more from trial and error than from observation.

THE RIGHT TO REMAIN SILENT

Children also move through phases of behaviour, which means we have to respect that what is appropriate for a child today may not suit him tomorrow. Alison Stallibrass describes a child as she warms to her new environment:

> A certain little girl was so silent and physically *in*active that we were a little worried. However, we left her alone; there was nothing else to be done since, when one spoke to her or even looked at her, she turned away and hung her head . . . she did nothing all morning but watch the other children. Then very gradually she began to occupy herself a little, but still she played on her own and seemed to be trying to avoid drawing attention to herself. We noticed, however, that what little she did, she did with great care and with surprising skill considering how little she had practised. She still rarely spoke to anyone, although at home, we were told, she was quite a chatter-box and also rather mischievous. One day, when she and two other children were washing their hands together, I overheard a child say to her: 'Why don't you talk? Can't you?' Then almost suddenly, it seemed, she became really lively; her gymnastic exploits and her paintings were outstandingly good, the latter brightly coloured, well balanced and well observed. By the time she left the group to go to school she had become one of the leading lights of the group – that is to say, an inventor and initiator of 'tricks' and make-believe games.[30]

It is quite clear, from her mother's description of her as a chatterbox, that this little girl was not by nature quiet or unresponsive. Yet in a more prejudicial environment, she might well have been labelled as shy, and pushed into joining in with the other children before she was ready. The child was simply holding back, preparing to remake herself in a new situation. Perhaps she was not yet ready to leave her mother and join a large group of her peers. In any case, given time, she *did* adapt, and emerged, all the more resplendent, like a butterfly suddenly breaking out of its cocoon.

Some children choose silence as their way of dealing with trauma, or just of retaining their integrity. The condition of 'elective mutism', regarded as a severe behavioural disturbance, may last for years, and is probably a self-protecting response to the pressures of the world. Journalist Heather Welford talks to educational psychologist Sylvia Baldwin:

> 'These children have a very powerful effect on those around them. They can't be tricked or manipulated into talking, bribed or threatened . . . and teachers find them exasperating and distressing to cope with.'
>
> Typically, parents, teachers and other professionals fall over themselves trying to make the child say something, anything, in school – possibly reinforcing the silence by devoting all that extra attention to the child.
>
> Yet the basic cause of the problem remains a mystery. Professor Israel Kolvin, of Newcastle upon Tyne's Nuffield Unit, who has authored a number of studies on elective mutism, says . . . 'The worst thing anyone can do is to label them too soon, and intervene in a heavy-handed way.'[31]

Adults swoop down on a non-compliant child, and compound the problem. They have an arsenal of weapons at their disposal, all of which would quell the average child. But the deliberately silent child has found strength in not speaking, and will not submit to tricks, bribes, threats or other manipulations.

The problem, we might guess, lies not with the child, who clearly has no need to speak, but with the rest of the world, who will not let him be. He senses that time is on his side. When all the professionals are baffled, and teachers have decided to accept the child as he is, he may start to talk. 'Younger children often grow out of an initial reluctance to talk at school,'[31] says Professor Kolvin. Perhaps it is just that the adults around them have shifted their focus away.

There is a tendency of professional carers to imagine that it is their input that shapes the immature child and turns him into a mature one. They forget that children grow up in their own good time. David Gribble illuminates the feelings of impatience that teachers feel with an intake of new students:

> Any teacher recognises the feeling at the beginning of the autumn term that there are no footballers left, or no musicians, or no real scholars; and every September teachers in every school in the country comment on the comparative immaturity of the pupils. There is even the feeling that a lesson learnt in school one year should automatically still be known the next, and people grumble that certain types of behaviour don't get better from one year to the next. 'But we went over all that last year,' they say, momentarily forgetting that they went over it with a different group of children. They often believe, even if only subconsciously, that it is mainly through the benefit of their instruction that the children are maturing. They forget that children grow up whatever their teachers do. When this year's class seems less mature than last year's, the teacher has an uncomfortable sense of guilt.[32]

This presents a good argument for the arrangement in Waldorf schools, whereby one teacher follows the class in its progress right through the school, so that neither students nor teacher are forced to readjust. This ought to provide a marvellous sense of continuity, although it does not always work that way. In a case where a child has a poor emotional fit with his teacher, he may suffer throughout his schooldays, instead of for one year only.

In play therapy, a counsellor is likely to encounter

non-co-operation of the silent kind, as children have a mastery of 'rude' behaviour that upsets controlling adults.

In a chapter entitled 'Accepting the child completely', Virginia Axline describes twelve-year-old Jean, a girl who comes for therapy because of her quarrelsome behaviour at home. Jean does not play or talk, like children are 'supposed' to do, but sits in silence. What should the therapist do?

> The therapist pursues her quarry. 'You don't like to play with dolls. Don't you see anything in here that you would like to play with? You may play with any of these things in here in any way that you want to.' Jean still maintains the icy silence. Then the therapist says, 'You don't want to play. You just want to sit there.' Jean nods agreement. 'Very well,' says the therapist. She, too, sits down and silence descends upon both of them. But the therapist is tense. 'Would you rather just talk?' she asks hopefully. 'No,' says Jean. The therapist taps her pencil on her barren notebook. She taps her foot. She looks a little annoyed at Jean. This silence is maddening. There's a silent battle going on between the two, of which Jean is surely aware.[33]

Even though she does not actually shout at her client or announce the frustrations she is feeling inside, the therapist is non-accepting. She is unwilling to give the child time to reveal herself. Aware of her own sense of hurry, she destroys their relationship of trust. 'Our teaching,' said experienced teacher John Holt, 'is too full of words and they come too soon.'[34]

A PLACE TO HIDE

In a candid article on the real lessons taught in schools, award-winning American teacher John Taylor Gatto identifies seven uncomfortable truths about modern schooling. The seventh of these is that the child is given no place to hide:

Children are always watched; I keep each student under constant surveillance, as do my colleagues. There are no private spaces for children, there is no private time. The time between classes lasts five minutes to inhibit promiscuous fraternization . . .

I assign a type of extended schooling called 'homework' so that the surveillance travels into private households. Otherwise, students might find free time to learn something unauthorized from a father or mother, by exploration, or by apprenticing to some wise person in the neighbourhood . . .

. . . The truth is that reading, writing and arithmetic only take about one hundred hours to transmit as long as the audience is eager and willing to learn. The trick is to wait until someone asks and then move fast while the mood is on him. Millions of people teach themselves these skills; it really isn't very hard. The continuing cry for 'basic skills' is a smoke screen behind which schools preempt the time of children for twelve years . . .[35]

With our long experience of life, you might think we could allow our children to take what time they need for themselves. Although the busy executive may be prepared to put his needs on hold until his annual holiday, a child cannot. Time to stare, time to play, time not to do anything noticeable at all, these are moments that preserve our children's emotional health, and we invade them at our peril. If we want our children to grow spontaneously, then we need to give them as much respect as they would receive in the play therapy room:

Here is at least one situation in the child's life where he is not hurried or prodded along. He can relax. If he wants to sit there and look, then he sits there and looks – for the entire hour if he decides to do so. If he begins to sift the sand through his fingers, seemingly a grain at a time, he does so to his heart's content. If he rolls the clay back and forth, back and forth, enjoying the feel of its pliable substance, then he does. If he wants to keep his mouth closed all hour, then he keeps it closed all hour. Finally, the child begins to notice that the usual pressure to hurry him along is absent. There is visible relaxation.

. . . Let [the therapist] remember that change is a gradual process and that some children move at a snail's pace.[36]

Unless we wish to be our children's jail-keepers, we should beware of hurrying them along. This should be the time of their lives.

Letting go as children grow: time

- Small children live in a protective time-bubble which prevents them feeling undue anxiety about the future or regret about the past. This frees them up to explore the apparently timeless present
- Every child needs a little time to dawdle, stop and stare to a timetable of his own making
- A child needs the chance to move and play at his own pace. However, this does not mean that parents should organise their lives entirely around him. In the balance between real-time and child-time, real-time will make its presence felt and children will learn to adapt
- Quality time with our children is rarely achieved on schedule. The really wonderful moments occur when we least expect them
- Home-made celebrations, involving all members of the family, help children to learn to anticipate the passing of time with pleasure and exercise the memory of rituals gone by
- Occasionally, children like to remain silent. This is not necessarily an anti-social act, although saying nothing may be more powerful than words. We should beware of pursuing children for a response. Sometimes they just need time out

---

6

THE TRAINING PROGRAMME –

TEACHING CHILDREN TO BE USEFUL AND BELONG

I am your mother and I will control you until the day you die.

Roseanne, Channel 4, 1992

For many of us as children it wasn't good enough just to be ourselves. We had to be *better*, even *the best*. We competed with siblings for our parents' affection, and were encouraged to compete in every sphere at school. As adults, we often find that it's the job we do, not the people we are, that most impresses the neighbours. We learn that it is unacceptable to fail, or be wrong, or be the loser, and so we battle to be one up.

With children of our own, it is difficult to avoid replaying the familiar power struggles. Like our parents, we feel we must show who's boss. A baby won't sleep at night: it's about time we nipped that little habit in the bud. A teenager rebels: we must retain the upper hand. A child's behaviour becomes less and less acceptable: the punishments escalate in the struggle for supremacy. Issues of control can range from the fundamental to the flimsy. I recall a mother having the following argument with her three-year-old daughter one sunny day.

Sally: It's raining mummy.
Mum: No it's not, darling, it's sunny.
Sally: It's *raining*.
Mum: Don't be silly, it's sunny.

Sally (increasingly upset):   It's *raining, raining, raining!*
Mum (irritated):   The sunshine is out! Can't you see?
(holding her up to the window)
Sally: No! (beside herself with fury) It's raining!

The mother, knowing her daughter to be wrong, could not allow the error to pass, or even acknowledge her daughter's point of view. The little girl, feeling unheard, started to scream and roll around the floor and was eventually sent to her room.

It strikes me that when we thwart our children in this way, far from demonstrating that we have the upper hand, we expose our own weakness. The adult who is constantly correcting the child appears less, not more in control. She is threatened by her child's mistakes and attempts at self-assertion. Instead of allowing the child to *be* a child, she drives home the point that he is wrong. Like the Queen in *Alice Through the Looking Glass*, it's 'Off with their heads!' every time there is a challenge to the leadership.

The assumption that children must be kept under control runs deep in our culture. It is expressed here by Lynette Burrows, a British parent and teacher who argues that smacking is the best way to discipline under-sevens:

Apart from simple, effective correction the other important reason why we smack our children is because we are educating their aggressive instincts. They are born with these instincts, which are a necessary part of our survival mechanism and, as psychologists in every other field stress, you should not suppress what you are hoping to educate.

So it is no good hoping that if you ignore defiance, disobedience, anger, violence and intemperate behaviour of every sort, it will simply right itself and go away. It doesn't, and only the blindest fool could ignore the fact that, as we have imposed less and less discipline on our children, their behaviour has become worse and worse.[1]

These sentiments follow a long punitive tradition dating back to medieval Christian teachings and the early history of child education. The belief that infant training requires punishment is often coupled by a passion to punish the sin out of the child as soon as possible – rather like a vaccination programme against evil. We see a similar strain of thought in this sermon of John Wesley, eighteenth century founder of the Methodist Church:

> Break their wills betimes; begin this great work before they can run alone, before they can speak plain, or perhaps speak at all. Whatever pain it cost, conquer their stubbornness: break the will, if you would not damn the child. I conjure you not to neglect, not to delay in this! Therefore, 1. Let a child, from a year old, be taught to fear the rod and to cry softly. In order to do this, 2. Let him have nothing he cries for; absolutely nothing, great or small; else you undo your own work. 3. At all events, from that age, make him do as he is bid, if you whip him ten times running to effect it. Let none persuade you it is cruelty to do this; it is cruelty not to do it. Break his will now, and his soul will live, and he will probably bless you to all eternity.[2]

Children as stubborn, to be broken in. Children with destructively aggressive instincts. Children who need 'taming' (to borrow a word from childcare writer Dr Christopher Green). This interpretation of childhood has been around at least as long as the concept of original sin, and on its back sit the parasites of control and punishment. Many parents feel they must dominate their children, on the basis that their children's natural instincts must be curbed. We achieve our domination by manipulating many aspects of their small lives.

The Empowered Manager is a business handbook addressing itself to the office worker, but its message could equally be applied to children and parents. Author Peter Block writes:

> Manipulation is so ingrained in our way of doing business that we often do not recognize it. Even if we are

aware that we are engaged in a process of manipulation, we rationalize it by saying that it is a fact of life and it is the only way to get things done.[3]

I believe the reason many of us manipulate and punish our children is because this was done to us as we grew up. We are not the only society to do this, but throughout human history, there have always been cultures in which manipulation and punishment of children is rare. In these societies, the prevailing idea of children is as social beings who are motivated to belong and adhere to the family and culture in which they find themselves. Nurtured in this belief, the children grow up, on the whole, to adopt the morals and accepted behaviour of their tribe. The tribe's ethos becomes the instinct with which the next generation will parent its children.

SPOILT ROTTEN

Whatever views we have about children, they tend to prove our point. If you believe that children are little horrors who need regular chastisement, they tend to behave according to your deepest expectations. If you believe that babies are morally neutral, but eager to learn the moral code they see about them, then you tend to interpret their actions as stepping stones in the path towards self-discovery and socialisation. When we see a baby screaming in his pram, we might imagine he needs cuddling, or feeding, or attending to in some way. Or we may believe he is being deliberately naughty, and label him as a 'little terror' who is trying to get the better of us. In either case, the infant's behaviour serves as 'proof' of our world view. Adult thinking and adult reactions interpret the baby and help shape the beginnings of our relationship with him. I believe our early prejudices can help determine the kind of baby we have: for instance a baby who cries a great deal may be 'deliberately manipulative' and 'naughty', or 'just trying to get his needs met'.

Some of us seem afraid to think the best of our children, in case we are seen as being naïve, or not in control. But assuming children want to be good makes for a more harmonious approach to parenting. Our basic assumptions determine how our children are treated, and, quite possibly, how they turn out.

If a parent hurts her child physically or emotionally, as every parent does at some time or other, she may then rationalise her actions in terms of 'the need to control'. While children crave discipline and order, they do not flourish under systematic manipulation. We interfere like petty gods in our children's lives, stamping out every form of behaviour that irritates or contradicts us. And then we claim it is the way things must be, or else chaos will ensue.

One classic argument against allowing children to have even a basic amount of freedom is that if we do so they will be 'spoilt'. I doubt there *is* such an absolutely rotten entity as a spoilt child – give the right environment, any child quickly 'unspoils' again. In any case, how he gets to be spoilt is a matter for debate. Reichian therapist Peter Jones believes that spoiling can only come about when we confuse meeting a child's deep-seated needs with catering for his every passing fancy. He offers his answer to the question 'Won't you spoil a child, giving in to her every whim like that?':

> This expresses the attitude, very common in Britain particularly, that bringing up a child is a battle of wills, and that if parents 'give in' too often to a child's wishes, she will get the 'upper hand' and rule their lives. The question implies that all the wishes and needs a child has are equally important and that there is no difference between a three-month-old baby's crying for the breast and a six-year-old's wish for a Mars Bar or ice-cream. As long as you are responding to a child's core needs, e.g. to suckle, to be held, to make loving eye-contact, to investigate the world, you cannot possibly spoil her. By 'spoiling' her I mean satisfying a child's every whim, so that she grows into a bossy tyrant . . . Becoming a bossy, manipulative brat is a tragedy for a child, burdened with the pain of unsatisfied needs, her repellent behaviour

drives away the very people whose response and love she seeks, so she suffers a double dose of frustration and pain.[4]

A SAFE PAIR OF HANDS

The child who tries always to control his parents is no happier than the parent who tries always to control her child. To be locked in an inter-generational power struggle of this sort is a sign that mutual respect is lacking. It is not uncommon to see a child who orders his parents around, while the parents hang their heads low and accept this ill-treatment.

It is easy to assume that stricter controls must be placed on the child, but many parents feel too insecure about their own authority to impose useful rules which would give their child the limits he so clearly craves. It is amazing how many parents feel 'too guilty' to stand up for their own values – and some even refuse to protect themselves against their children's physical or verbal abuse.

When asked why they endure children's disrespect, parents may respond that they are trying to compensate for aspects of their own family life. Reasons given are varied, and depend on the hang-ups of a particular culture. Perhaps the birth was not as 'natural' as a mother had hoped; perhaps breastfeeding did not work out; she did not give birth to a sibling for the child to play with; she had her children at an older age; she is a single parent . . .

We do our children the greatest disservice when we parent out of sense of our own weakness. No household, from deepest Africa to deepest suburbia, has the patent on perfection (see Chapter 10: *Practically Perfect in Every Way*). Instead of feeling guilty for our perceived shortcomings, we need to congratulate ourselves on our strengths. Only when we feel secure can we begin to offer children the security they crave, including a sense of parental direction with appropriate rules. Children need to know they are in a safe pair of hands.

For many children, the feeling of security begins at birth, in the comfortable arms of someone who neither resents his presence, nor feels that she is spoiling him to carry him so. Bio-therapist Alexander Lowen likens the babe-in-arms to the fruit on the tree. The spoilt child, he says, is one who leaves the tree too soon:

> The seed of a fruit that is prematurely detached from the tree does not root itself easily in the earth. A human being in a similar condition will strive to get back to the source of his strength, his mother. His unconscious tendency will be to reach upward to her in his desire to be picked up and held. His flight is upward, away from the ground and from independence . . . The way downward, to an independent existence, is blocked by an unconscious sense of panic. He lacks the inner conviction that his legs will hold him up.[5]

The spoilt child 'clings' to his parent. He is unable to survive on his own. As his basic needs are not being met, he feels the need to test out his parents' limits, and their capacity for love. Because he cannot voice his deep longing for acceptance, instead he may pile on superficial demands. Ice-creams, new toys, designer footwear, these are all objects the child sees around him, and he naïvely thinks that if only he has the *next* thing, his world will be complete.

'If you really love me, you'll buy it for me', is the nearest he gets to stating his core needs. The best reply he might be given is, 'Since I really love you, I won't.' When a parent is niggled by a sense of inner inadequacy – as many of us are – she may easily be bullied into buying all manner of material things to satisfy her demanding child. But the demands do not end once today's longed-for item is secured. Deep down, the child knows that expensive trainers do *not* make it all all right. There is a fundamental longing that has not been satisfied.

According to the American paediatrician Dr Ross Campbell, the problem with modern child-training practices stems from the inability of parents effectively to convey the love they feel for their children:

It is a fact . . . that most parents do love their children . . . the basic problem is that we are not aware that we *must* convey our love to our children *before anything else*: before teaching, before guidance, before example, before discipline. Unconditional love must be the basic relationship with a child, or everything else is unpredictable, especially their attitudes and behaviour.[6]

It is the nourishment given in the early days that best allows a child to grow up safe in the knowledge that he is loved and welcome in the world. If this lesson can be learnt in babyhood, then so much the better. In the words of La Leche League, the international breastfeeding support group, 'a baby's wants are a baby's needs'. Their philosophy is the opposite of John Wesley's:

With your newborn, 'giving in' to him is good parenting. Feed him according to his own timetable. Comfort him when he is upset. But, you may ask, won't such permissiveness spoil the baby and lay the foundation for problems later in life? The question is asked by many parents who are sincerely concerned about their children and want to do what is best. 'Most spoiled children . . . are those who, as babies, have been denied essential gratification in a mistaken attempt to fit them into a rigid regime.'

A mother, grandmother and League Leader, Marion Blackshear, thoughtfully considered the matter of spoiling and babies . . . Marion writes: 'When you think of a piece of fruit as spoiled, you think of it as bruised, left on the shelf to rot, handled roughly, neglected. But meeting needs, giving lots of loving care, handling gently, is not spoiling. I could carry this a step further and say that a piece of fruit is at its best when left to ripen on the tree, its source of nourishment – and a baby is at his best when held close to his source of physical and emotional nourishment – his mother.'[7]

Before we leave the fruit analogy completely, it is worth mentioning that children are *not* fruit, and that spoiling is not a once-and-for-all process after which the child is ruined. The label 'a spoilt child' can do so much damage to a young person who is merely using the tactics at his disposal to try and elicit real respect and acceptance from his parents. He wants, as desperately as them, to be freed from the unhappy cycle of demand-and-demand-again.

THE SMALLEST SHIFT

I know from my own experience that the smallest change may improve the power balance between parent and child. Frances, as she neared her third birthday, had started to whine.

Instead of saying 'Please may I have an orange juice?', she would whimper 'I'm thirsty' in an accusing way, and we would be left to guess what she fancied. She would shake her head miserably at each suggestion, and if you happened to mention what it was she had wanted all along, she replied by lolling her head on one side and looking hurt. Her new behaviour was very wearing, and we would implore Frances to make her requests assertively. We resolved to 'stop the whining', but, as pioneering educator Maria Montessori might have pointed out, this was not a useful attitude:

Even a submissive child has his own way of conquering. He gains his victories through affection, through tears, entreaties, a melancholy look, and even through his natural charm. An adult may yield to such a child until he can give no more, and then a state of bitterness is reached which leads to all kinds of deviations. The adult comes to his senses and realizes that his own way of acting has been the source of his child's defects, and he looks around for a means of correcting them.

But we know that nothing can correct a child's whims. Neither exhortation nor punishment are efficacious. It is like telling one delirious with fever that he should get well and threatening to beat him if his temperature does not

go down. No, an adult did not spoil his c
yielded to him, but when he hindered his
caused his natural development to go astray

Luckily, when we began to feel the need to ta
behaviour, we were on an unusual kind of holid   n
family festival called Campus, with groups and workshops on
all sorts of themes. I attended a taster session run by Parent
Link, thinking I might discover what to 'do' with her.

Parent Link is a course of group sessions for parents, run by
Parent Network, a support organisation with branches all over
Britain. Our leader at this session invited us to recall a positive
aspect of our 'problem' child, something we really liked about
him or her. This was refreshing to do when I felt so bogged down
in Frances' negative behaviour (and in feelings of guilt at having
caused it). It helped me to put Frances' unhappiness in perspective, and realise that she actually spent much of the day absorbed in play, or enjoying a joke. She had – and still has – a great
capacity to make us laugh. In fact, the more I thought about it,
there was more going 'right' in Frances' world than I would have
admitted earlier that day.

The group leader did not offer any specific strategy for
breaking a cycle of whingeing, but instead did a much more
valuable thing. She shared a similar experience of her own
daughter and recalled how a shift in her own emotional
understanding and acceptance had made all the difference.

I suddenly realised that what Frances was trying to do was
coax a change in attitude from me. She wanted me to accept
her completely. The whining was a naïve way of trying to
communicate a trapped need. And what was that need? Fairly
obvious, really. Just three months before, our second baby,
Alice, had been born. Frances had been an exemplary sister,
cuddling her and helping around the house. Never once did
she express anything resembling sibling rivalry. And yet she
had undergone an enormous change to her position in the
family. By whining, she was wearing the mask of a stereo-
typical baby and had us all running round her as if we were the
parents of two newborns, not one.

...ances did not know any better. Not only were we ignoring one of her core needs, but we were switching off every time she tried to voice them. As I sat with Frances that lunch-time, I tried genuinely to listen to what she was saying, instead of reacting to her tone of voice. I suddenly felt how different it was to be there for her, and not trying to control her behaviour or her means of expression. We were on the same side after all.

Without exaggeration, I can say that Frances stopped whining within a day or two and the problem never resurfaced again. After six months or so, Frances even allowed herself the occasional display of anger, which she had never really done before. Gradually I learnt the importance of the emotions behind a child's demands.

I have told this story many times in workshops, to illustrate a point, just as the Parent Link co-ordinator helped me by relating a story about her own child. While some parents know what I mean immediately, others have found it hard to understand the principle underlying the anecdote. Here is my attempt to try and make it clearer for anyone who is having a tough time 'letting go' with a 'problem' child:

- Begin by remembering the good about your child: put the 'problem' into its proper perspective. Even in his darkest moments, every child is capable of bringing joy.
- Don't rely on the angry words or behaviours of your child as your only means of communication. Tantrums and whining are a child's immature attempts to express something important – they do not realise how counter-productive their methods are.
- Don't battle over details like swear words or slamming doors. Do not insist that your child uses polite language all the time. Do not correct his speech. For the moment, let him speak from his emotions, however hurtful they may be.
- Imagine a heart-to-heart conversation with the child. Let yourself connect with him as you would with any

small, vulnerable person. Do not get over-involved in every request or accusation the child makes, but – using your judgement as an adult and a parent – accept the underlying emotion and try to sense the child's core needs.

- Empathise with your child's feelings. Offer to meet his core needs (not his unreasonable demands.) Be loving and firm. He may need you to set the rules. Be humane; give direction; be kind, forgiving, real. You can only feel your way to this level of understanding.

- If possible, perhaps when the dark clouds have passed, go back and offer physical reassurance: a short embrace, a long hug? It will depend on you and your child. Say as little as possible. He will sense when he has been accepted and the cycle of demand-and-demand again will eventually cease.

If we can follow this kind of routine feelingly, at times of crisis with our children, then small, imperceptible shifts can take place in our mutual understanding. It becomes safe for angry children to vent their feelings; safe for spoilt children to stop demanding and feel secure again.

HOUSE TRAINED

Progressive educator David Gribble believes some parents try to buy off their children in an attempt to appease them. He wonders why so many of us have a hard time saying 'no' to our children's ever-more sophisticated demands. The aim of a loving relationship, he suggests, should not be manipulation, but co-operation:

It is perfectly consistent with the idea of concentrating on a particular child to refuse to do something the child wants done. In a genuinely affectionate relationship it is absurd for either partner to dominate the other. Co-operation is the objective . . .[9]

169

Co-operation is soon sacrificed when a parent or child is over-controlling. The perennial complaint that a child won't help around the house ironically stems from the refusal of parents to hand over responsibility. In other words, the parents controls the child's usefulness.

We spoil our children when we assume unnecessary responsibility for them. We are not allowing them to grow up. Here journalist Linda Gillard takes a critical look at the reasons why our materially overloaded children have become bored, unfulfilled, 'spoiled':

> I am beginning to wonder if we have alienated our children and herded them into an attractive ghetto equipped with toys and fashionable clothes, but a ghetto nonetheless. We have separated them from the mainstream of our lives, and bribed them so we can enjoy an uninterrupted telephone call, a quiet read, a long bath – all those things that depend (we think) on our children's absence.
>
> . . . And there you have it. Toys instead of work. We struggle to keep our children 'occupied', out of the way, out of our hair. We do not incorporate them into the daily round; we give them very little responsibility; their role in the family falls somewhere between Beloved Offspring and Thorn in the Side. In our society, children lack a sense of purpose and consequently achievement. In other parts of the world, children are expected to contribute in a real sense and their role is valued by adults. They carry water, look after animals, collect firewood, cook, mind babies or run errands according to their age.
>
> . . . Children can do these things . . . If they don't behave in a responsible way, is it because we don't let them? Often we try to keep them young by doing everything for them. I remember my own mother trying to put my socks on for me when I was well advanced in years. I let her do it because it was clear that she liked doing it.[10]

The most common way of controlling our children is to over-protect them, thereby preventing them from taking on the responsibilities of advancing age. When a child reaches out to do something for himself, this is not the time to intervene. Even if a child makes mistakes with his first attempts, he should be allowed to continue trying. The American physician Dr Herbert Ratner believed that:

> The baby starts life by being dedicated to the proposition that he or she wants to grow up. More often than not the parent does everything to prevent him. Yet preventing the baby from growing up is hard work. Someone once said, 'It takes years of hard work to turn out a juvenile delinquent.'[11]

Compare this with Jean Liedloff's assessment that, at four, a Yequana child (of the Venezuelan jungle) is already contributing more to the household than he takes out of it. Alexander Technique teacher Grethe Laub believes that the beginning of fulfilment lies in the 'loving care' a child receives when young. From then on, whenever a child expresses a desire to join in, to take on new responsibilities, the opportunity should be grasped:

> Children love being useful with the household whenever they can manage and this interest should not be overlooked for later on it will be difficult to persuade them to see the point in being helpful – especially if the father hasn't reached the point where he sees it and understands the importance of being an example, then it will be almost impossible. So let the children get responsibilities from the moment they show signs of wanting to help. Let them tidy up after their play from the moment that in itself can be a play.[12]

In one British research project directed solely at the issue of tidying up, it was found that very few children co-operated at a parent's first request. Although some jumped to it when faced with 'negative parental action', the best strategy was one of 'non-coercive, positive action', such as getting down on one's hands and knees and tidying up oneself.

Out of fifty-one children in the Cambridge project, only fourteen were rated as 'securely attached' to their mothers. Secure attachment, combined with parental sensitivity, seemed to be the best recipe for eliciting a child's co-operation:

As expected, the mothers of secure children were much more positive and encouraging, saying things like, 'Shall we put them away before the lady gets back?' Mothers of insecure children issued instructions in a tone that was neutral ('Put 'em back then') or cajoling ('Are you going to help me?' – which often produced the answer 'No').

Surprisingly, few of the secure children agreed to help right away. As with the insecure ones, their first response was often to ignore mother's first request or answer sulkily and keep on playing. But though the secure child soon became positive and helped tidying up, the insecure kept on resisting.[13]

Secure children are as unlikely as any others to want to stop playing in order to tidy up. As they have not finished playing, the request is perceived as an intrusion. The 'aim' of this research was to find ways of enlisting a child's co-operation; it was not particularly interested in a child's motivation.

A child who meekly responds to all requests to tidy his room, but who never actually sees the need to tidy it up *on his own initiative*, is not being empowered. He is merely obedient. When he leaves home, he will probably tidy up only when his mother comes to visit. (Most of my male college friends saved their dirty washing for their monthly visits home.) But keeping our children tied to us does not make us better mothers, we merely deny our children the chance to gain independence. Journalist Linda Gillard says:

So much of the frustration and unhappiness of childhood is about feeling powerless. How can we empower children? Certainly not by asking them to tidy up their rooms, which is a non-starter in the Oregon trail stakes [Linda's favourite pioneer adventure story]. All children hate tidying up, which just goes to show that tidying up is the second most boring job in the world. (The most boring is pairing socks. My kids won't do that either.) I think we have to let them live a little dangerously. If we never give them responsibility how can they learn to deal with it? The following is a list of things that I do not let my nine-year-old do for reasons that are unclear to me (it may simply be that once she was two . . .): prepare her lunch box; programme the video; load the washing machine; wash her own hair; make a pot of tea; cross the road on her own; sew on buttons; lay the fire; use matches. My daughter turned nine sooner than I intended and I am having difficulty keeping up.[10]

GOING POTTY

It strikes me that in many aspects of parenting, even of quite young children, we become consumed by the parental role. This is exemplified in typical 'method' parenting, where reams are written on 'how to' train a child to meet our standards of hygiene, courtesy, sleep and so forth. The parent embarks on a programme of military precision, reinforcing her message with gold stars, minor punishments and by generally *involving* herself in every aspect of the chosen activity. This solicitous approach is a legacy of the Victorian era, in which all childhood behaviour was deemed to be worthy of control.

Take potty-training, for instance. In the seventeenth century, Louis XIII began his toilet training at eighteen months and was completely 'dry' by the age of three. It seems there was quite a relaxed attitude about training (as there was about bathing – little Louis did not get his first bath until he was nearly seven . . .) We also know that toilet training in many rural cultures consists of holding the baby out (nappies are unheard of in the hottest climates) and, later, letting the child run around with a bare bottom. Here, for instance, are the Rajput children of northern India:

During the winter, the children sometimes wear pyjama trousers. However, if the child is not yet toilet trained, he wears trousers with the crotch cut out – the very opposite of diapering.[14]

The nearest that many of the world's children come to a potty training system is being chased out of the house with a joke every time they threaten to soil the floor. Siblings are often given the job of reminding (teasing) the incontinent toddler. Parents, who have no doubt that each child will be dry when he is ready, usually play very little part in the process.

By contrast, the modern interest in potty training derives from the scientific parenting principles of the early Victorians, who believed babies could be trained out of nappies at the tender age of three months. Social historian Christina Hardyment describes how the new training was proposed in the 1840s by childcare experts like Pye Henry Chavasse:

The baby was to be held out at least a dozen times a day at three months old; if this was done, there need be no more nappies at four months, 'a great desideratum', and he would be inducted (another good distancing word) into clean habits, 'a great blessing to himself, a comfort to all around, and a great saver of dresses and furniture.' He quoted Mrs Balfour's *Hints on Household Management*: 'Teach your child to be clean. A dirty child is the mother's disgrace.' . . . Although I have found no suggestion at this time that children or babies ought to be punished for failing to perform, it is clear that if disgrace was being introduced into the matter with such intensity, there was a great deal of unspoken feeling.[15]

We may have changed our methods and our timing, but the unspoken feelings have not gone away. Potty-training can be an anxious period for a mother, and consequently for her child. There is a general lack of trust that the child will one day actually *want* to control his bladder and that he will, one day, become capable of this. But childcare experts are not entirely to blame. The advice they have given over the years has been gradually shaped by parental nervousness. Post-Victorian experts believed that the intensive training of three-month-old babies was damaging, and so, in 1946, the American childcare guru Dr Benjamin Spock recommended a relaxed approach:

> I think that the best method of toilet training is to leave bowel-training almost entirely up to your baby.[16]

If parents had been capable of doing such a thing, Spock would have had nothing more to say. But the modern parent was convinced that a dry child was a good child, and a reflection of her sensible management. She dutifully tried to abandon potty-training, but could not so easily discard the anxiety aroused by a three-year-old who wet the floor, or was still in nappies. There was a cry for renewed discipline in this area, and Dr Spock was forced to apologise to mothers for being so laid back: 'By the time the child is eighteen months old,' he wrote in the late 1960s, 'I think you should begin this training even if there is no sign of readiness.'

But this was not enough. As Christina Hardyment records, Spock's initial utterance on toilet-training was eventually replaced by a point-by-point advice section, that gave parents the opportunity to follow the recipe for 'successful' control:

> That parents continued to find it impossible to be casual about potty training . . . was reflected both by this lengthy and detailed section, and in the rash of specialist books devoted entirely to toilet training which came on the market in the late 1970s. All were confident of success, be it in a day, a week or a decade, and profusely illustrated. One thoughtfully showed mothers how to pull their toddlers' pants down.[17]

In a recent television series about children all over the world, we were treated to the scene of a Chinese mother and grandmother 'potting' a young daughter in the living room. There was much frenzied attention towards the child, who did not want to sit on the pot. As the girl started to have a bowel movement, the mother screamed hysterically, and the child, evidently frightened by the whole experience, became hysterical, too. Meanwhile grandmother flapped about unhelpfully.

This was the Chinese mother's only daughter, and, because the law limits couples to one child, she knew she was to be her last. The mother was also forced to return to work at an early stage, leaving the baby in an organised crèche. The results of alienation and cultural inexperience were clear to see, and were augmented, presumably, by the mother's own personal fears about defecation. By contrast, the film also showed the trouble-free approach to training adopted by parents supported by large, inter-generational families. Amongst the Yequana tribe of South America, for instance, there pervades an air of firm practicality on the subject of bowel control:

> . . . when house training takes place, the toddler is chased outside if he sullies the hut floor . . .
>
> If he sullies the floor before he is house-trained but old enough to understand, he is told sternly to go outside. He is told not to dirty the floor, but he is not told that he is bad or that he is always doing the wrong thing. He never feels he is bad, only, at most, that he is a loved child doing an undesirable act. The child himself wants to stop doing things distasteful to his people. He is innately social.[18]

The advent of the disposable nappy has taken the heat off potty training in the West. At the cost of around 30 million trees a year,[19] British and American parents now have a peace of mind almost equivalent to that of the nappy-free cultures in Africa and Asia. But the story has not quite managed to come full circle. Our new-found tranquillity has to be bought at the supermarket: we have not yet regained our complete trust in the child.

READY, STEADY . . .

Based on her experiences with the Yequana, continuum therapist Jean Liedloff's parenting theory[20] turns on its head most Western ideas about the impulses of children. Instead of presuming the child to be an untrained animal in need of taming, Liedloff postulates that he is motivated to conform and belong. Children want to please their parents, and, if not put off with words of mistrust, or punishment, will begin to conform to rules:

> There are those who believe reasoning and pleading for 'co-operativeness' with the child will accomplish this curbing better than threat or mental or physical insult. But the assumption that every child has an antisocial nature, in need of manipulation to become socially acceptable, is germane to both these points of view . . .
> . . . either more or less assistance than a child demands is detrimental to his progress. Outside initiatives, therefore, or unsolicited guidance, are of no positive use to him. He can make no more progress than his own motivations encompass.[16]

A spontaneous, instinctive parent who is well-tuned to her own needs, and sensitive to what is going on around her, would not embark on long, involved training programmes devised by someone who does not know her or her child. But Western parents have been taught to mistrust both the child's inclinations, and his capabilities. We are saddled with the belief that, if not trained, a child will *never* learn the basic skills. And so we interfere. In 1969, *Good Housekeeping's Baby Book* summed up the modern problem succinctly:

> Once upon a time nobody bothered about 'toilet training'. People accepted the fact that they had to mop up after their toddlers. Then came nappies and pots. Baby experts began to teach our grandmothers that if they tried hard enough they could train their small babies in

various ways, including the use of the pot. Mothers made the mistake of thinking they were teaching their babies conscious control. If a baby was not pot-trained by a year or so, his mother thought it was all her fault. She became over-anxious, he reacted, and a beautiful friendship was in danger of being spoiled![21]

In this case, spoiling does not merely refer to the unfortunate child, it is the relationship between parent and child that is soured. No matter what stratagem a parent adopts for training her child, it is her attitude that is the most important factor. This, more than anything else, will determine whether or not the child passes with relative ease onto the next stage, or whether they are both left with bitter memories.

Some parents ask whether they are interfering with a natural function when they aim to potty-train. Surely it depends on whether the child's motivation and capability are being respected. We had two false starts when I tried bringing Frances out of nappies, simply because I initiated the move, instead of waiting for her indications of readiness. Alice, at a much younger age, simply ripped off her nappy one night and never wet the bed again. I had not thought she would be ready for this, but decided to give her the benefit of the doubt. She obviously knew what she was capable of. Joe – well, I can't really remember how it went with Joe. That's how relaxed I must have become.

One big advantage of second or subsequent children, is that they are motivated to copy their slightly older brothers and sisters. Younger ones automatically set their sights on the next developmental stage. Parents will be copied too, but not in the same detail. In rural societies and large families, it is the older children who do much of the educating, 'leading out' by example.

These days, the axiom is to 'make training fun', and there is a wealth of books aimed directly at the child. Cartoon characters have brought toilet-training out of the closet. They present hilarious examples of poos done in inappropriate places, and children defying their parents' pleas.

While I am all for humour in discipline, some of these books are undermining. They start from the premise that we do not really trust the child will do the right thing. *All By Myself – The Toilet Training Book* by Dr Bill Gillham, says: 'The baby next door wears nappies. My little brother sits on the potty. But I can go to the toilet all by myself. "I don't believe it!" said Mum.' This is a book that claims to be 'Based on proven psychological principles.' Mother's mock disbelief may not sound particularly damaging, but repeated to a child over and over again it is hardly inspiring.

This particular book also comes with six 'All By Myself' reward badges. Recommended by behavioural psychologists and animal trainers, rewards are deemed to be an acceptable form of manipulation, whether at school, in the home or at the dentist. Today's children move in a world of gold stars and hovering incentives. Can this be the best way to train them into obedience?

STICKS AND CARROTS

Our lack of faith in children may help to explain the arrival of reward charts on every other fridge door and classroom wall. But contrary to popular belief, many childcare experts are cautious about the value of institutionalised praise. For instance, former teacher and educational theorist John Holt wondered:

Do children really need so much praise? When a child, after a long struggle, finally does the cube puzzle, does he need to be told that he has done well? Doesn't he know, without being told, that he has accomplished something? In fact, when we praise him, are we not perhaps homing in on the accomplishment, stealing a little of his glory, edging our way into the limelight, praising ourselves for having helped to turn out such a smart child? Is not *most* adult praise a kind of self-praise? I think of that marvellous composition that Nat wrote about the dining room in his house. I find now, to my horror, that in thinking with satisfaction about that comp, I am really congratulating myself for my part in it. What a clever boy this is! and what a clever man am I for helping to make him so![22]

Reflected glory sticks to parents as well as teachers. I have not forgotten the glow of pride I felt when Frances earned her first swimming badge or violin certificate. It's the same when any of the children play their instruments, or dance in a show – I get an almost vertiginous rush verging on embarrassment. I don't know the precise biological function of this emotion, but I know a lot of parents get it and we should not be too cynical about it. What we have to beware, is letting the feeling change our parenting. When we push children into the limelight, force them to take part in competitions or exams, make them show off in front of our friends, it is rarely in their interests. Even though we may not realise it, we are chasing the frisson of Reflected Glory. And do not be fooled – everyone around us knows that's exactly what we are up to . . .

Once when we were visiting a family whose son was taking piano lessons, his mother declared, 'Bobby would love to play his newest piece for you.' Bobby's sour expression obviously told us that he didn't want to do that at all.[23]

When children are reluctant to perform, we may bring in sticks and carrots by the cartload. 'If you ride in Saturday's gymkhana, I'll buy you those designer trainers.' 'Take your Grade Six and you'll get that silver flute.' Or this one, incredible, but true: 'For every Grade A, Mummy and Daddy will give you £1,000.' From standing up in the infant nativity to getting to university, children are taught that parents need and expect them to perform. Co-operation around the house and lessons in school are all given the same treatment.

The assumption is that the desired behaviour is not worth doing *for itself*. John Holt believes that:

We destroy the disinterested (I do not mean *uninterested*) love of learning in children, which is so strong when they are small, by encouraging and compelling them to work for petty and contemptuous rewards – gold stars, or papers marked 100 and tacked to the wall, or A's on report cards, or honor rolls, or dean's lists, or Phi Beta Kappa keys – in short, for the ignoble satisfaction of feeling that they are better than someone else. We encourage them to feel that the end and aim of all they do in school is nothing more than to get a good mark on a test, or to impress someone with what they seem to know.[24]

One weakness of behaviour modification theories is that the person is trained to respect the reward, rather than the work he has done. For example, my children from a young age have always enjoyed washing the car. If, following their eager efforts, I were to reward them with an ice lolly or some other treat, would they not be suspicious? Instead of choosing to wash the car *for its own sake*, they would swiftly decide that this activity was unrewarding. Why else should I reward them for it?

Another problem is that, used with regularity, behaviour modification soon turns upon the parent. The child, so sensitive to manipulation, twists the system to his own advantage: 'I'll wash the car for you if you give me a lolly.' Soon he is refusing to co-operate without 'payment'. Children may be even more sophisticated than this. A friend offered her daughter a mobile phone on the condition she did her homework on time. Immediately, all our twelve-year-olds were badgering us for mobile telephones. 'Please let me have one,' implored the daughter of another friend. 'Then if I'm naughty, you can always take it off me.'

It is easy for parent and child to become themselves controlled by a superfluous system. American business consultant Peter Block describes the 'bureaucratic cycle', the mechanism with which companies keep their employees enslaved. It consists of: 1) The Patriarchal Contract (strict control from above); 2) Myopic Self-Interest (personal rewards – pay, perks etc.); 3) Manipulative Tactics (where the controlling parties are strategic, cautious and indirect); and 4) Dependency . . .

Dependency. The patriarchal contract, the narrow definition of self-interest, and the manipulative strategies
feed and reinforce each other in a way that nurtures a
dependent mentality. The belief that our survival is in
someone else's hands is in part a consequence of the first
three parts of the bureaucratic cycle. Our initial willingness to be dependent also helps to create the cycle.
After twelve or so years of school systems and family that
treat us fundamentally as children, we are conditioned
for more of the same. We may not wish to be dependent,
but dangle a reward system in front of our eyes and we
are ripe for the picking.[25]

It is not uncommon to hear someone complain that they must
leave the valued and enjoyable work they do, in search of
higher status or more pay. We are soon enslaved to rewards, as
they become the most consistent monitors of our success.
Progressive teacher David Gribble is against senior-school
prize-givings for this reason:

In practice, prize-givings result in injustice. Not all the
best people are rewarded, even in a limited sense of the
word 'best'. More importantly, the kinds of behaviour
that are rewarded are not the most important kinds of
behaviour, but those that are most easily assessed, or
possibly those that are most easily marked. The implication of giving prizes for good work is that the prize is
more important than the work – you work hard *in order
to win a prize*. This removes all the merit itself, and
distracts the child from any interest the work may have in
itself . . .

The implication of the whole society rewarding an
individual is that the individual is separate from the
society, or at least that the interests of the individual
are in conflict with the interests of the group. That is
another lesson that tends to suppress altruism. And
finally, to the genuinely altruistic person, honour and
disgrace are alike indifferent; if truly the best people have

been found to win prizes, the prizes will not matter to them.[26]

Prizes are unimportant to self-motivated children. This was the experience of the earliest Montessori schools, when an untrained teacher devised a system of pendant rewards for good behaviour. Since Maria Montessori was prepared to abandon whatever the children themselves found to be worthless, the system was soon dropped:

After a little time, I discovered that the teacher had herself made other objects for the children's use. Among these were decorated gold crosses. She made these out of paper and passed them out as rewards for good behaviour . . .

Once I entered the school and saw a child sitting in an armchair all by himself in the centre of the room with nothing to do. He was wearing on his breast one of the decorations which the teacher gave out for good behaviour. She told me, however, that the little fellow was being punished. Another child had received the reward and had placed it on his own breast, but then had given it to the one being punished as if it were something useless and a hindrance to one who wanted to work.

The child in the armchair looked indifferently at the badge and then gazed calmly about the room, quite oblivious to any sense of shame. The single incident made us realise the futility of rewards and punishments, but we made further observations in greater detail. Long experience only confirmed our first intuition. The teacher even reached a state where she felt ashamed to reward or punish children who seemed equally indifferent to either treatment. What was even more surprising was their frequent refusal of a reward. This marked an awakening in the conscience of a sense of dignity that had not previously existed.

Eventually we gave up either punishing or rewarding the children.[27]

A hundred years later, and teachers are still offering un-wanted rewards to children who sense the injustice of 'stupid systems'. I was privileged to observe – from a distance – the saga of Year Six in Alice's primary school: a class of highly-motivated ten- and eleven-year-olds who staged their very own protest against a system designed to increase their personal motivation. In Year Five, good work and desired behaviour had always been rewarded by 'Peas in a Pot': a dried pea went into the glass jar and once full, all the class earned some kind of treat. This suited them all fine. But the teacher in Year Six preferred a system where children entered Merits against their individual names. At the end of the week, the winner earned a Gold Star. So many Gold Stars and you won a bar of chocolate.

Inequalities swiftly appeared. Children who sat in front of the teacher were rewarded for sitting up straight – the ones at the side of the class complained they couldn't be seen. Children were rewarded for tidying up their table first: one slow person on your table and you'd never win. Children were given Merits for good work and the class's star pupil suddenly became unpopular as she won Gold Star after Gold Star. A few children started cheating by adding extra Merits to the board, but the teacher didn't seem to notice. Within weeks, the children were despondent and angry. Appeals from parents to end the system fell on deaf ears: 'It worked very well in my last school,' the teacher replied.

It wasn't working very well for the students. One day, Alice came home full of renewed confidence. She and her friends had decided to boycott the Merit Board. Their idea was simply to refuse to claim any Merits they earned. More and more children joined in the Merit Strike, as they called it, until only the teacher and a handful of faithful supporters were still playing the game. It didn't matter, the Merit System had been devalued and the children's dignity returned. The Merit Board was still hanging there at the end of the summer term, quite why we never understood.

'EXCESSIVE PRAISE SPOILS THE CHILD' (PERSIAN SAYING)

If we are not rewarding our children for their 'good' behaviour, then we are, at least, expected to praise them. But even praise can be overdone and used as a method of control. Praise in the form of occasional and spontaneous approval is something that parents in all cultures express. It is a way of conveying cultural norms, and of making a child feel acceptable in his world. But behavioural psychologists have hijacked this feeling mode of communication and turned it into a system.

We are supposed to gush with praise whenever a young child uses the toilet correctly, or an older one brings a picture home from school. This is called 'positive reinforcement', and its aim is to make the child want to repeat the desired behaviour, but it overlooks the possibility that the child is motivated to co-operate for himself.

In fact, great dollops of praise may be about as healthy for children as high-fat mayonnaise on a bowl of salad. The child becomes hooked on approval and unable to rely on his own instincts to tell him whether or not he has behaved properly in a given situation. Here, child psychologist Dr Haim Ginott describes the pitfalls of 'global praise'. Eight-year-old Michael has just owned up to his parents for some misdeed:

Suppose Lee's husband had said to his son, 'Michael, you are a very truthful boy – the most truthful boy in the world.' What would go on in Michael's head? He'd think to himself, 'If my father only knew. If he only knew all of the times I didn't exactly tell the truth.'

Suddenly Michael begins to feel anxious. He's being awarded an honor he doesn't deserve. He's being held up to a standard he can't hope to maintain. He's cornered. Trapped. How does he get out? Maybe he can misbehave a little – just enough to prove to his father that he's not such an angel after all.

To a lay person it always comes as a surprise when he

praises a child generously and the child becomes obnoxious. To the psychologist it's no mystery. He knows that children must throw off global praise; it's too confining. As enlightened parents, we ought to be aware that when we use global praise with children, we are practically asking for trouble. I'm thinking of statements like: 'You're always so helpful. You're the most cheerful child I know. You're extremely intelligent.'[28]

If parents want to express approval or interest, Dr Ginott suggests they make their words specific and descriptive: 'Boy, Michael, I'll bet it wasn't easy to tell the truth just now – especially when Mom was yelling so loud.'[28]

Adults constantly over-praise their children in order to make them feel special, but in doing so they may prevent their young egos from learning to nourish themselves.

Self-nourishment was the evident aim of children attending Alison Stallibrass's playgroup. She also dislikes overdone praise:

> In trying to nourish a child's self-confidence, we must guard against telling him indiscriminately and absent-mindedly that he is 'doing fine'. Since he knows very well when he has or has not done what he intended to do, such behaviour on our part must cause him to doubt our sincerity. Rather, we must show him that we approve of the fact that he is doing what he wants to do, and share his joy when he is successful.[29]

A child who aims to reach the top of the climbing frame, and reaches his goal, is rewarded by the wonderful sense of achievement. The experience is complete in itself: the child fulfils his own dream, and enhances his self-confidence. To reward or praise him for his actions is to gild the lily. As the orator Robert G. Ingersoll said, 'There are in nature neither rewards nor punishments – only consequences.'

At a British conference on effective learning[30], Sir Christopher Ball, Chancellor of Derby University, related the apparently mysterious story of the child who wanted no praise. Sir Christopher's own three-year-old granddaughter, Juliet, had confounded her parents and grandparents by announcing she did not want to be praised any more. But everyone loved to praise her, believing it was good for her self-esteem. The adults around her begged to be allowed to continue praising, and eventually the child compromised to pacify them, saying they might praise her on a Sunday, but no other day of the week.

Even granddad could not understand the remarkable sense of self-preservation in Juliet's embargo. So entrenched are we in our desire to praise, we fail to see that – especially in situations where children already feel secure and loved – it may be doing more harm than good.

One of the reasons we insist on praising our children is to make them happy, and to improve our relationship with them. In our eagerness to see desired behaviour repeated, we offer unguarded praise until our children have learned to depend on it. But such solicitations are as peripheral as the decorations on a Christmas tree: they dazzle the child and conceal the plant underneath.

In fact, teachers have been warned to stop handing out indiscriminate praise, following a survey of schoolchildren in Britain, America and Russia. Almost 3,000 nine- and ten-year-olds were invited to assess their own work. Russian children underestimated their ability, with only 25 per cent rating their performances as 'good' or 'very good', compared with 65 per cent in Britain and 70 per cent in America. Yet objective tests showed the Russian children were more advanced: for instance, those who rated themselves least able in maths were scoring better than top students in America and Britain.

Educational psychologist Julian Elliot, from Sunderland University, says his report points to an over-emphasis on boosting children's self-esteem. He believes overdone praise may even be hampering children's academic progress:

> The emphasis on self-esteem is totally overdone. Of course kids should be rewarded for effort and achievement, but they should not be indiscriminately showered

with praise. Teachers are saying, 'Wow, that's wonderful,' when the kids haven't made much effort at all.[31]

The antidote to global praise is specific observation. It's as simple as noticing something the children has done, or remarking on the effort taken rather than the pass mark. 'You've worked really hard today' is so much more helpful (and honest) than 'You're the best artist I've ever seen'. And talking of art, I remember talking to a mother who was frustrated that her school-age child seemed to have a very low opinion of herself in that subject. Every time the girl brought home a picture to show her mother, she would be met with praise: 'What a lovely picture!' But the mother's genuine opinion would always be rejected by the child: 'I hate it, it's horrible, I can't draw.' The mother would insist that the picture was excellent and her daughter would, as often as not, tear it up and throw it in the bin. According to the theorists, pouring more praise in her daughter's direction ought to make the child feel better about herself. Instead, frustration was mounting, and some worthwhile paintings were being destroyed.

There is an obvious parallel between this situation and the rainy/sunny argument at the beginning of this chapter. Putting aside the rights and wrongs of the case, the parent is refusing to 'hear' the child. Before the child can move on, or can be empowered to make realistic judgements for herself, she needs acceptance from her mother.

It is hard for any parent to accept feelings of self-hatred from her child. Merely to accept these feelings would, at least in part, be a reflection on herself. So she ignores the child's pleas for recognition of separateness. If, however, she were to offer a neutral or accepting response there would be no battle. And perhaps the child would be free to start appreciating himself a little more. Neutrality is not easy to achieve, but Virginia Axline identifies it as a prerequisite of play therapy:

> It is important that the child does not develop guilt feelings as a result of his use of the play therapy contacts. En-

couragement, approval, and praise are taboo in a non-directive play therapy session. Such reactions on the part of the therapist have a tendency either to influence the type of activities or to foster feelings of guilt. The same is true of negative criticism. The atmosphere must be neutral.[32]

By the time most children reach the therapeutic situation, they have already become slaves to manipulation, through approval, bribes and the whole host of punishments at an adult's disposal. But even those who do not seek therapy are well-grounded in the art of working for good grades and adult appreciation, as Peter Block discovered when he talked to his own children:

> I would ask my own children how a class was going. Regardless of their age or subject matter, their answer was always the same: either 'The teacher likes me' or 'The teacher does not like me.' When I pressed for some reaction to course content, it seemed a matter of indifference. The teacher likes me. The teacher does not like me. End of discussion. After twelve to sixteen years of this acculturation, employees enter the organization ready to move through another approval-seeking system. The organization doesn't disappoint them. You might ask, 'What is so wrong with seeking the approval and support of those around us, including our boss?' The problem arises to the extent that others' approval becomes the driving force in our actions . . . We are not in business to gain others' approval; we are here to get work done, work that moves the business forward – even if at times our forward progress is upsetting to those around us. Approval as a dominant value is an expression of our dependency and gives rise to the feeling that our survival is in someone else's hands.[33]

If we give nothing else to our children, they at least deserve to feel that their survival is in their own hands. When we seek to control them, we make them more dependent on us. When they are fully grown, our children will have every right to blame us for all the many things we did and did not do on their behalf, and all because we were over-involved.

If we take a back seat, observing more and interfering a little less, what kind of children will we produce? Is it possible to train our children without disturbing their natural dignity? How do we begin to instil moral awareness without scaring or punishing children into submission?

It may seem that the following chapter, on discipline, comes late in an argument which advocates respect for children at every turn, but has yet to consider the need for limits, boundaries, rules and mutual respect. Now is the time for these themes. In fact, the whole of this book is really about nurturing the child's inner discipline. Only when we have done this work can we confidently begin to offer children the social rules and moral framework that will steer them through life. Discipline is an art which modern society seems wilfully to misunderstand. We mishandle it at our peril.

Letting go as children grow: training

- Before we begin training our children, they need to feel the heat of our unconditional love
- You cannot spoil a baby or young child with love, and it is not 'giving in' to meet children's basic needs. In fact, there is a greater risk of spoiling if these needs go unanswered – children's demands may become more whimsical and harder to satisfy
- Reward systems can be distracting for the self-motivated child. They presume that he would not want to do an activity for its own sake
- Children need specific, honest praise that encourages specific skills. Overdone praise just gives them a false sense of themselves and the world
- The best way to train a child is to assume he wants to behave and to give him repeated opportunities to try

---

7

THE ROOTS OF DISCIPLINE –

REAL RESPONSIBILITY AND THE POWER OF REMORSE

Laws should be like clothes. They should be made to fit the people they are meant to serve.

Clarence Darrow

How do modern parents discipline their children? They seem to split at a dramatic fork in the road: THIS WAY PUNISH-MENT AND COERCION/THAT WAY CHAOS. 'I believe in smacking,' said a friend, as she sat cradling her first-born baby in her arms. Apparently, it was my turn to respond – would I turn left or right at the fork? I decided to offer a non-committal nod. 'If you don't smack them they don't learn any discipline,' she added. Her baby was staring intently into her face, in an early attempt to decipher the meaning of life. I did not want to take either fork and I did not want an argument. 'Mmm,' I said. 'Don't you think there's more to discipline than punishment?' She looked at me pityingly, presumed I was heading towards CHAOS and changed the subject.

Threats, bribes, ultimatums, nagging, withholding treats, harsh looks, bullying, hitting, and withdrawing love are all legitimate tools for disciplining young people in our society. If you don't control the child, runs the argument, the child will soon control you. Get your retaliation in first.

Those in favour of systematic discipline have only to point out the ways in which 'permissiveness' failed the children of the sixties, and their argument is apparently complete. They might quote Vanessa Nicholson, for instance, for whom 'freedom' at a progressive school was torture:

> My parents were extremely liberal, so to them the progressive approach of Frensham Heights seemed perfectly sensible. They liked the school's philosophy of non-competitiveness and letting children develop their own personalities without too much emphasis on academia. In theory, I admire those ideas, too. But the school lacked the structure and staff to make it work.
>
> I was unlucky enough to be there in what is now known as the 'dark days' . . . Things became more and more free while I was there, rules disappeared and there was this philosophy that children should be able to do exactly what they wanted. That suited children who were self-sufficient but I felt a complete lack of direction and a desperate emptiness. I needed to know what I was supposed to be doing.[1]

When it comes to the discipline of children, modern society seems only to have two strings to its bow. Either we terrorize them into submission, or we abandon them to the vacuum of a permissive existence. In fact, children do not need systems of punishment and reward to keep them in line, but they do need discipline and structure. Children require, as Vanessa Nicholson put it, *to know what they are supposed to be doing*.

So far, our subject has been the potential of children, and how best to give them the freedom to discover it. But freedom cannot be usefully exercised without an understanding of society's rules. And children depend on us to know what the rules – the important ones – may be. In fact, good direction is essential to the idea of letting children go. In order to explore the conditions for good discipline (or 'loving guidance' as La Leche League calls it), let us first look at what happens when there are no rules at all.

REBELS WITHOUT A CAUSE

Isolated in a boarding school with no adults to emulate, no society to conform to or challenge, no direction, the children at Frensham Heights became depressed.

> Perhaps because there was nothing to rebel against, there was total apathy and depression amongst the children. If there had been a rule against smoking we could at least have felt naughty smoking a cigarette, but as it was we felt we had to go one further and smoke too much dope. We would sit and stare at the walls for hours, listening to music. If we did anything at all, it was self-destructive. People would slash their wrists just to get attention.[1]

This picture of extreme misery reminds me of the almost equal misery felt by children who are pushed too hard, who feel that, driven for years to 'succeed' in their parents' terms, life is devoid of any real meaning. In this portrait, permissiveness seems to be a licence to abandon, just as hot-housing is a licence to over-stimulate. Neither is what the child needs.

In its origins, 'permissiveness' is simply 'permission-giving', and refers to the handing-over of responsibility to a child in specific areas. Unfortunately, like so many useful ideas, it became a system, popular with post-war parents of the 1950s and 60s. But strict adherence to any system overlooks the needs of the individual child. 'No discipline' is a dangerous rule when it means depriving the child of any cultural or personal values, as some followers of philosopher Jean Jacques Rousseau discovered in the late eighteenth century. In his 1789 'Lectures on Education', Welsh teacher and historian David Williams described one 'child of nature', who,

> . . . aged thirteen, slept on the floor, spoke 'jargon he had formed out of several dialects of the family', could neither read nor write, and was 'a little emaciated figure, his countenance betraying marks of premature decay, or depraved passions; his teeth discoloured, his hearing almost gone.'[2]

This poor child, supposedly benefiting from a permissive up-bringing, had actually been abandoned by the culture into which he was born. He sounds pitifully like the two wolf girls described by Japanese violin teacher Sinichi Suzuki in his book *Nurtured by Love*. Suzuki recounts the story of Kamala and Amala, aged seven and two, who were discovered fifty years before in the Indian jungle by a priest. They had been abandoned as babies, but had survived and been raised by a she-wolf:

Head, breast and shoulders of both children were covered with thick hair. After it was cut, they looked like human beings.

In the wolf's cave the infants crawled on all fours, their eyes seeing clearly in the dark. Their noses were extremely sensitive. They ran fast on all fours, like a dog, and people could not overtake them. Their shoulders were wide, their legs powerful, with bent thighs that would not stretch out straight. They grasped things with their mouths, not with their hands. Food and water were taken in a doglike manner. Kamala was particularly advanced in the way of a wolf. She was not only fond of raw meat but showed a strong predilection for rotten meat. She was immune to changes in temperature and did not perspire. When it was hot, she would hang out her tongue and pant like a dog . . .

During the day she slept, but as soon as the sun set her activity started. At night, just as she had done when she lived among the wolves, she would howl three times at accurate intervals – at ten, one, and three o'clock . . . She did not stop howling during the nine years she was with human beings, but continued until she died, at the age of sixteen . . . Could you call this *inherited*?

A human child living among wolves and brought up by them took on their habits. To survive, man instinctively adapts himself to his surroundings. A tremendous and sublime life force works to grasp the components of our environment. I am filled with awe at the thought of this power.[3]

When their environment offers little in the way of nourishment, children start to founder. Their eager adaptability
becomes a burden, not a blessing. The many true stories of
wild children demonstrate just how strong is the impulse to
behave and to belong, even when the children find themselves
in the company of wolves or pigs, rather than humans. So
intelligent, so flexible is the human child, that he will attempt
to *become* a wolf or a pig, if necessary, in order to survive.

Children raised without rules are as keen as wild children to
know what the rules may be, in whatever continent or century
they may wash up. An upbringing devoid of direction and
appropriate guidance leaves the child bereft. <u>If his twin desires
to belong and behave are ignored, he grows up divorced from
his own culture</u>. In ancient society, making sure all members
wanted to belong and knew how to behave was the first
priority and an essential aspect of survival. It took several
millennia before anyone suggested it might be interesting to
raise children without any discipline at all. It only took a
decade or two to see how daft that idea really was.

Yet it does seem that some parents have been put off the idea
of discipline, which leaves them and their children bewildered
at every point of conflict. A frequent media complaint is that
parents are afraid to exercise authority over their children –
and as a result, they say, schoolteachers find each new intake
harder to handle. 'It is not a modern myth,' writes journalist
Steve Boggan, 'things really are worse . . .

> Teachers such as Jim West, who retired two weeks ago
> after almost thirty years, can remember a time when
> violence and discipline were not a problem . . . 'There
> has been an insidious erosion of standards of respect and
> support,' he said. 'Years ago, if you asked parents to
> come to school because their children had been in trou-
> ble, you knew that the parents would listen and the child
> would probably get a belt when he got home.
>
> 'These days, the parents invariably support the child
> against the teacher, no matter what.'[4]'

Giving the belt when they got home is precisely the kind of discipline modern parents have chosen to avoid. The hallmark of schooldays used to be a kind of organised brutality so harsh it gave discipline a bad name. But before we examine the roots of good discipline, let's consider two very different teaching styles, two very different forks in the road.

A TALE OF TWO TEACHERS

Adults who are consumed by the need to control children are usually recognised by children as bullies. The difference between a controlling and a non-controlling adult is obvious in the two following portraits of teachers, each given by their (now grown-up and famous) pupils. Cartoonist Ralph Steadman felt spiritually crushed by the headmaster of the grammar school he attended in Abergele, North Wales:

> . . . he was a real mean son of a bitch, a sadist I would say. And it destroyed me. I had been completely and utterly trusting, and then this man ruined everything, made me feel, my God, that people can be unpleasant . . . I began to live my whole life in fear of authority, and that's stayed with me ever since.
>
> We lived in fear of this man. He loved using the cane, which he applied for the smallest offences, general horseplay that kids get involved in, just anything. Many of my friends were beaten, and they said they'd never had such a beating.
>
> There was no chink in his armour whatsoever. This man meant business, and his business was to crush the spirit in children and bend them to his will through fear. I was damaged psychologically by this fear.
>
> I finally left school at 16, I couldn't take it any longer, I just had to get out . . . I got a job at Woolworth's as a trainee manager, which meant I had to sweep floors and things. I was outside the shop once, and he came by – it was as though he'd come along to catch me at it – but that would be my own paranoia probably. And he said to

me, with seemingly great delight: 'You've made a mess of your life. You left school too early, you were bottom of your class . . . and now look what you're doing, you're sweeping the streets.' And that was the last time I saw him.'

This headmaster's frequent resort to punishment was supported by his extreme views of the worthlessness of at least one of his pupils. He probably reasoned that children needed to be bullied into good behaviour, and Steadman's refusal to take the regime any longer confirmed his status as a 'drop-out'.

For the child, this is a no-win argument, and it leaves him feeling demoralised. He cannot protest without being punished, and even his attempts to escape are mocked as proof of his ineptitude. The only route to 'success' would be to surrender himself to the dominant personality. This, Steadman chose not to do. His attitude to adult aggression emerged years later in the humour and violence of his cartoons.

In sharp contrast, the Irish novelist Maeve Binchy recalls her old teacher with fond memories. Mother St Dominic was blessed with an uncontrollable giggle and a genuine love of children:

In a completely unsentimental way she loved children. She cared about them, knew their limits, stretched them but never forced them . . . Everyone she taught had this memory of someone who really seemed to understand all the horrors and rages of being a child and all the trembling fears and hopes of being about to be an adult.

It was because of her that I became a teacher, and in my classroom, when faced with intractable, terrible children I used to dream up her face and try to think how she might have handled them.

In the long hot summer of 1959 I went to the Holy Child School in St Leonards-on-Sea, telling her I wanted to teach and asking if she could give me some help. She showed me more in six weeks than any degree or diploma ever taught anyone. She had no secret, no method, no style. What she did have was a belief that children were basically decent and could probably learn anything if you told it right.[6]

It is this basic belief in children that sets Mother St Dominic apart from the average grown-up. Others, like Maeve Binchy herself, might try to copy her teaching style, but if genuine respect is lacking, the method will be empty. When Maeve Binchy stood in front of a class, she saw 'intractable, terrible children'; she feared their non-conforming behaviour. We must presume that the intractable children were not terrible to Mother St Dominic, they were just children. Good teachers earn children's respect because they are not trying to control them, or make them conform. Such adults are not frightened by the inevitable challenges that children bring to the classroom. Even the most difficult child will discover he is respected for his individuality.

But teaching our children to conform is one of the main aims of modern schooling. I have heard infant school teachers belittling new children who have not yet learnt how to stand in line, raise their hands before speaking, or ask permission to go to the toilet. These 'skills' are necessary socialisation for school-goers, but they are not of much use while the child is still at home. Pre-schoolers regulate their own lives, go to the toilet at will and choose their own activities; few institutions could tolerate such freedom. Children should be brought to school as early as possible, argued the teachers, in order to be 'socialised'; in other words, to learn the skills of being an obedient pupil.

Of course, if the aim is to institutionalise our children, then we should begin as soon as we can. Self-confident children are difficult to tame, and the longer a child is at home, the greater the chance he will be benefiting from self-education and the security of his surroundings.

A self-regulated child who has spent his first five to seven years at home can be devilishly difficult to control. He wants to eat when he is hungry, rest when he is tired, play out his enthusiasms to their limit. According to award-winning teacher John Taylor Gatto, the way to break children in is constantly to judge them. Offer them what he calls 'provisional self-esteem':

> If you've ever tried to wrestle a kid into line whose parents have convinced him they'll love him in spite of anything, you know how impossible it is to make self-confident spirits conform. As our world wouldn't survive a flood of confident people very long, I teach that your self-respect should depend on expert opinion. My kids are constantly evaluated and judged.
>
> A monthly report, impressive in its precision, is sent into students' homes to signal to within a single percentage point how dissatisfied with their children parents should be . . . Self-evaluation, the staple of every major philosophical system, is never a factor. Through report cards, grades, and tests children learn not to trust themselves or their parents but to rely on the evaluation of certified officials. People must be told what they are worth.[7]

The author's style is ironic. His actual belief is that the school system forces the child too heavily into a state of submission. He argues that there is a choice in how we bring up young people, and that traditional schooling might not be the only way to educate the young. It does not, for instance, allow for much self-education of the sort illustrated in this anecdote from the first Casa dei Bambini, or Montessori school.

> . . . a child was asked by a visitor: 'Who taught you to write?' The child answered: 'I was not taught. I learned.'[8]

Just as children are able to teach themselves many things in the intellectual sphere, so they are capable of learning self-discipline. In fact, the two go hand in hand: self-motivated learning breeds inner discipline, which in turn allows for more learning. This was observed in the earliest Montessori schools, where the environment was arranged for the use of the children, and each child was free to regulate his day to suit his own purpose or interest at the time. From the simple expedient of allowing the child to follow (and thus respect) his own inclinations, children demonstrated a natural sense of order and respect for others:

> Despite their easy freedom of manner, the children on the whole gave the impression of being extraordinarily disciplined. They worked quietly, each one intent on his own particular occupation. They quietly walked to and fro as they took or replaced the objects with which they worked. They would leave the classroom, take a look at the courtyard and then return. They carried out the teacher's bidding with surprising rapidity. She told me: 'They do so exactly when I tell them that I am beginning to feel responsible for every word I say.'[9]

This teacher's admission is revealing. In the first place, it shows that the children are listening attentively to her, a demonstration of their respect for her and her wishes. But it also reminds us how often adults do not bother to say what they mean to children, or to be responsible for their words. We sometimes say ridiculous things like 'Don't pick your nose or it'll drop off'; we make idle threats: 'If you don't do as I say, you won't *have* a birthday party'; and we nag because we don't actually expect to be heard the first time.

In this Montessori classroom, where the children were taken seriously and allowed to arrange their own lives, the teacher found herself treated with equal respect. The children naturally looked to their teacher for direction, and because they could trust her not to abuse her power over them, were obedient to her wishes. There emerged a new sort of discipline, not a wielding of threats or punishments, but discipline born out of mutual respect and personal responsibility.

CULTURE CONVEYED WITH HUMILITY

Children adapt to the conditions of life as they find them. If, like the biblical seed, they land on stony ground, they cannot be expected to flourish. In this context, we cannot separate discipline from love. A child requires two main things from his parents: a) to offer him unconditional acceptance, to love him for what he is, rather than what he does, and b) to show him the ways of the world. By demonstration and involvement, parents *bring* children *up* to the level of understanding and fulfilment that they have attained.

A child who is not given the benefit of direction, and not allowed to participate in the real world, will have little to aspire to. Institutionalised permissiveness deprives a child of the necessary components for survival. This was realised by the educational thinker Reuven Feuerstein, who worked with Jewish migrants arriving in Israel during the 1950s and 60s.

Professor Feuerstein asked himself why it was that some immigrants, such as the Yemenis, adapted easily to their new Israeli home, while others, the Moroccan *Mellah* for instance, were considered so backward they would never integrate. He did not believe it was merely a matter of genetics. The *Mellah* had a strong history of Talmudic scholarship. Yet on arrival in Israel, some fourteen-year-olds could not even name the Hebrew days of the week.

Feuerstein discovered that, back in Morocco, the *Mellah* had been subject to European colonisation, that had resulted in their becoming alienated from their own culture. Fathers were traditionally away working during the week, and mothers were left to care for livestock and to carry out domestic duties. The task of transmitting culture had always been left to grandparents. When families uprooted to live in the new urban centres, there was rarely enough space for grandparents to come too. No one had time to teach the children the ancient Jewish traditions. The Moroccan Jewish children were being deprived of the transmission of their culture. Feuerstein discovered quite a different story among the Yemeni Jews, who were airlifted *en masse* to Israel:

The Yemenites were among the most technologically primitive groups to emigrate to Israel. But they had, according to Feuerstein, a cultural system of community-wide relationships where the children were respected participants and had special roles in the customs of the community.

The children had the same rights and duties as the adults as regard the prayers: they gathered together around the *Torah* [Jewish scripture] praying together and were accorded real status. This had a tremendous impact on the children, all of whom were literate between the ages of three and four years.

Moreover, how they read was an interesting metaphor for the way that culture influences learning. Because there was a great scarcity of books in the villages, everyone had to sit round to read the same book. As a result the children learned to read from every angle – upside down, straight on, left to right, right to left. There were no illiterates among the Yemeni Jews and their incorporation into Israel was remarkably free of problems.

Feuerstein's hypothesis is that individuals from different but nevertheless rich and still coherent cultures, having learned one culture, usually have the means to learn another. Those children who have been deprived of their own culture do not.[10]

Out of these observations, Feuerstein developed his 'Mediated Learning Experience', a practical teaching method that imitates the real-life transmission of culture. Facts are not intended to be learned without context; they must have a function in a child's life if they are to mean anything to him. Ideally, they will connect with other facts that the child has already absorbed. They should certainly be relevant to his own life. Good-enough parents offer such an education to their children all the time, without realising it. One of the roles of parenting is to hand down meaning: to present the rules that bind people together. This is the context for life:

Our parents and relatives, acting as the agents of culture, impose meaning on the otherwise neutral stimuli that continually bombard us, and, in this way, ensure the transmission of values from one generation to another. When parents say, for example, that objects or events are 'good', 'bad', 'sad', 'happy', 'important', 'unimportant', 'worthy of respect', 'unworthy of respect', 'right', wrong', they are assigning cultural meanings to our daily environment . . .

Our senses alone cannot do this. It must be through the human endowment of meaning onto a non-human physical environment that a child's cultural universe is established, and different cultures are continued.[10]

Judgemental adjectives such as 'good' and 'bad' are known in counselling jargon as labels. They are generally considered unhelpful when they are applied directly to children, in phrases like 'You're a good girl', or 'a bad boy'. Parent Network classes in Britain, and the Kids' Project in America give parents a new vocabulary with which to convey their emotions to their children, *without* labelling.

Professor Feuerstein is not suggesting that we all go back to labelling our children, thereby offering them the 'provisional self-esteem' described by John Taylor Gatto. But he is saying that we do a disservice to our children when we fail to hand down our own cultural values, in other words, offer a structure for discipline. It is possible to give value to aspects of our culture without judging the people in it.

Some parents refuse to label objects or events as good or bad, in order not to influence their children. Feuerstein believes that children need our personal values in order to grasp the meaning of the world. At a later stage they may reject our interpretations if they wish. The challenge for parents is to convey meaning without closing the book. 'This is what *I* believe . . .' is not as dogmatic as 'This is the one truth . . .' Culture conveyed with humility is the most wonderful framework for life. We can convey meaning and feed a child's inner world, while still allowing room for growth and dissent.

The excessively 'liberal' parent, who does not allow her child to see her true emotions, know her opinions, share in her faith, or understand her own limits, is depriving her child of discipline. 'Children need to be given meanings because they act as bearings in an otherwise impenetrable world,'[10] says Feuerstein's interviewer. A child is dependent on his environment for his direction in life.

In the view of Alexander Technique teacher Rob MacDonald, giving a child too much freedom can be tantamount to rejection:

> In a lot of schools, the pendulum has swung the other way and they have serious problems using this idea of freedom and freedom of expression as their sole basis . . . The question of direction is not properly touched upon when you just consider freedom. What do we mean when we say 'let them be free'? Children are given freedom because their parents aren't interested. That is freedom with rejection. That makes them very anxious.[11]

It is now generally accepted that systematic permissiveness is an incomplete environment for the child. In a chapter titled 'Freedom, Not Licence', teacher David Gribble explains how a progressive school might establish a set of rules:

> There can in fact be no total freedom in any society, because the mere presence of other people imposes restrictions. Even if you live alone you are not free from the need to eat and sleep, and you are not free to flap your arms and fly. What the true progressive school tries to do is, first, to create a society with as much freedom as is compatible with the *children's* objectives, and, secondly, to make sure that the *children* appreciate the reasons for the nature of the society and are free to improve or alter it if they can reach agreement.[12]

Permissiveness has been largely discredited because of the way it has been misapplied in the past. But the better elements of permissiveness still exist in many homes and schools today where there is an atmosphere of respect. Permissiveness towards a child's emotional life does not have to be translated as 'no rules at all'. Even in the deliberately tolerant context of play therapy, Virginia Axline believes a therapist needs to be clear about her own boundaries, both in and out of the classroom. For instance, she explores 'The value of limitations':

> Any attack upon the therapist should be stopped immediately. There can be no value in permitting the child to attack the therapist physically. There can be harm in such a practice – and not only to the therapist. The therapeutic relationship, to be a success, must be built around a genuine respect that both the child and therapist have for one another. A child needs a certain amount of control. He is not entirely self-sufficient. The control that is the outgrowth of mutual respect seems to be far more conducive of good mental attitudes than any other method of control.[13]

If we care for ourselves at all, we will not allow ourselves to be punished or victimised by our children's behaviour. We will heed our own feelings just as we heed theirs. We will give meaning to their destructive actions, so that they can come to an understanding of what is and what is not permitted in our culture.

WANTING TO BELONG

In a traditional, rural culture, the rules for life will be upheld by the majority. The rules for the next tribe, living perhaps only ten miles away, may be completely different, but they, too, will be largely respected. The price for stepping outside certain boundaries is usually expulsion from the tribe, which is a living death for someone who loves his people. Expelling a child from a school in which he felt alienated anyway will not have the same effect.

Expulsion was, in fact, a blessing in disguise for thirteen-year-old Kiley, an adopted child who was dismissed from school for disruptive behaviour. He was neither violent nor delinquent, but 'attention-seeking', according to his parents. At his first school, Kiley was one of a large group with diverse needs. Then he was moved to a special school for children 'with a wide range of learning and behavioural problems.'

Small classes, a democratic approach and discipline rooted in good pupil-staff relationships, were just what Kiley needed:

> Kiley's first year at the school has transformed him. He loves the space – the school is in the Oxfordshire countryside, with a lake in the grounds. He is the chairman of the fishing club, looks after ducks and grows vegetables. And with an average class size of six, the staff can give him the attention he demands. The school's democratic, child-centred regime has taken away his constant need to challenge adult authority. The head, Maurice Cooling, says that his staff can push back the levels of tolerance in a way that a comprehensive cannot
>
> But it is no Liberty Hall. Discipline relies heavily on relationships with staff, backed up by a system of nine 'levels' of privileges related to behaviour. Kiley approves: he has already reached level six, which means twice-weekly trips to nearby Banbury . . .
>
> Mr Cooling: 'Swancliffe Park doesn't work for every child with problems. There's no magic formula. It's a question of finding the right school for the child.'[14]

This headmaster understands the roots of good discipline. He knows that if children are to *want* to obey the laws of their community, they must feel bonded to that community, and be given responsibility within it. He cares not just about children's compliance, but about their motivation. Swancliffe Park's discipline is based on good relationships and empowerment. Its system of privileges is really no more than a manifestation of the pupil's growing ability to cope in the outside world.

Traditional tribes and modern schools exclude those who refuse to live by the rules. But it would be a sorry story if parents expelled their offspring on a similar basis. What sanctions can parents employ when children test the rules to the limit? (Since testing rules to the limit is exactly what children are programmed to do.)

Before sanctions, before punishments, before applying loving guidance, parents tend to get angry. And it's their anger that children seek. Because only when they know what makes their parents mad do they learn about what matters. Small children need to cross the boundaries of behaviour in the same way that babies need to taste shoe laces and soap and any other object that lies in their path. Children need to experience what it means to have done a bad thing, so that they can choose to do a good one. And when their parents are angry, they sense they are standing at the frontline of a really powerful emotion. The question is: will they survive?

TEMPER, TEMPER

I remember clearly the first time I felt angry with Frances. She was not yet two years old, and we were making pastry together in the kitchen. She started throwing the flour and pastry crumbs on to the floor. I was furious, though I couldn't really say why. I think I shouted loudly at her to stop, and she looked at me, stunned. I was stunned, too, hugged her and said I was sorry. It felt quite frightening. I had never dreamt that something so small could make me feel that way.

Everybody's anger will be triggered at different times, by parenting experiences that relate to forgotten experiences of our own. We have the choice of 'acting out' our anger, suppressing it, or conveying it constructively to our children.

A child watches closely for his parents' reaction to his challenging behaviour, not so much for her words, which can be misleading, but her real feeling. Is mother undermined by my behaviour, and if so, why? A child seeks out discipline, in order to assimilate it in his inner world. The parent who will not be genuine is infuriating to the child. He knows exactly what will wind her up, and so he uses every ploy to elicit an honest reaction from her. Perhaps this was the case with children's picture book character, Harriet Harris:

> While her mother was gardening, Harriet pulled up flowers instead of weeds, just like that.
> Her mother didn't like to shout, so she seethed instead.
> 'Harriet my darling child . . .
> Harriet, you'll drive me wild.
> Harriet, sweetheart, please don't dream.
> Harriet Harris, you'll make me scream!
> Harriet, honey, what are we to do?
> Harriet Harris, I'm talking to YOU!'[15]

While Harriet commits a series of dreadful misdeeds: falling over, dribbling jam and painting unintentionally on the carpet, her mother's temperature soars. She starts off smiling (through her teeth, presumably) and progresses through moaning, groaning and hissing to the final showdown:

> When they arrived home again, Harriet banged the front door hard and all the glass broke, just like that. And her mother SHOUTED.
> 'Harriet Harris –
> That's IT!
> I've HAD it!'
> And she shouted and shouted and shouted, whilst Harriet stood there, just like that.
> But later that night they were the best of friends, And that is where the story ends.[15]

I recognise something of Harriet's mother in myself when I started out. I tried to be an all-loving, tolerant parent, but eventually something had to give. Now I am more aware of my own needs and limits, and find it easier to express them and make sure they are respected. Most of these are conveyed to the children without the need to become angry at all.

I still get mad at times, but I have also learnt to recognise the kinds of events that make me feel this way, and to head them off at the pass. I am learning to convey my anger without labelling my children, or hurting them, and to let them know when 'danger' has passed.

I believe children can survive occasional outbursts, so long as we do not actually destroy something in the child as we rage. We owe it to our children to let them know our limits, and not merely in a clinical way. As Feuerstein would say, there is no point setting out rules unless we also convey to the child their emotional significance. Even small babies depend on a mother's genuine emotions, including displeasure, to guide them towards full growth. It is OK for a mother to be angry, so long as she can convey to her baby that her love for him has not gone away. British mother and author Bronwyn Hocking began to realise this as she researched the possible effects on her baby son of her own post-natal depression:

> . . . I had recently read about the work done by a doctor who videotaped the responses of new-born infants to the different expressions that appeared on their mothers' faces. The results were striking. The babies showed the most distress not when shown an angry face, as might be expected, but when shown an apathetic face with an absence of expression such as would be worn by somebody who was depressed.[16]

Being genuine with our children is, I believe, one of the greatest gifts we can give them, and for this reason I disagree with the following summary of the parental role from *The Children on the Hill*. It seems to me to place an unreal pressure on the parent, and to deny the child any sense of direction:

> The mother must also be aware of the importance of avoiding any kind of conflict, or charged relationship with objects, animate and inanimate, or people. Any such disturbance will be transmitted to the child and will delay

the process. It is for this reason that Maria has tried to keep violence, frustration and pent-up emotions out of her life as far as possible. Children detect upset in the surrounding atmosphere very readily, even if it isn't openly expressed by their parents. Recently Maria was staying with her family as guests in a friend's house. Just before the time came for them to leave, she asked the children not to go to the fridge, for fear there would be accidents. Nevertheless, their desire to experiment was too strong, and a cup full of ice cubes was produced as a play-object. Maria, under the pressures of the social situation, whipped them away.

'You've *destroyed* them,' Paul cried. 'Why have you *destroyed* them?'

For Maria this seemingly trivial incident represented a failure . . .[17]

The advice on handling negative emotions is to hide them or avoid them. I would argue that such a strategy would be likely to increase family stress, rather than dissipate it. Maria's choice of an isolated cottage in mid-Wales for the family home certainly made it easier for her to avoid social conflicts. But in so doing, she also avoided society.

THE FULL RANGE OF EMOTIONS

Unless we wish to wrap our children up in cotton wool, they need to learn to face conflict and deal with it. We might work on making our days with our children as pleasant as possible, but that does not mean we have to avoid our more unpleasant emotions.

Family therapist Dr Robin Skynner wrote that many parents attempt to present a perfect image of themselves to the child, thereby depriving the child of a real adult model. The pattern repeats itself through the generations:

Instead of accepting to be, in Winnicott's phrase, 'good-enough parents', they try too hard, conceal their own needs and limitations, and present to their children the same impossibly perfect model they received from their own mother and father. The children are then in a double-bind. They sense their parents' neediness and see their inconsistency, but cannot recognise it openly without hurting their parents by making them feel even more inadequate than they do already . . .[18]

In another article, Dr Skynner assured us that stormy emotions at home are not necessarily a 'bad thing'. A study of exceptionally healthy families carried out by Dr Jerry Lewis and his colleagues at Timberlawn Research Foundation, Dallas, revealed that communication in disturbed families was confusing, with underlying meanings, often containing incompatible messages. Mid-range (average) families communicated in a clearer, but more restricted way, everything tended to be pedantic and controlled. But language and communication in healthy families was uncalculated and free, involving the full range of emotions:

This honesty seems to be possible because of a general feeling of confidence and trust, and assurance that everyone will be listened to respectfully, and accepted and loved for themselves even when there is disagreement or temporary disapproval over some action. The book reporting Timberlawn's findings, *No Single Thread*, describes this nicely: 'Part of the sensation of joy the observer feels in observing the interaction of healthy families is the obvious lack of calculation, the openness of honest feeling and thought on the part of different family members – especially the children. There is freedom without chaos – a feeling of the three-ringed circus, yet with everything under control.'

. . . The most healthy seem to achieve control not so much by restriction and repression of strong feeling, as the mid-range tend to do, as by their unusual capacity to balance and manage a wide spectrum of emotions instead of keeping the lid on them. This is no doubt one explanation for the playfulness, humour and creativity that observers so frequently describe.[19]

CONSISTENCY: AN OVERRATED VIRTUE?

Many parents are reluctant to allow their children to witness their conflicting emotions. There is a belief, for instance, in 'consistency' with children as a basis for good discipline, and research backs up the thesis.[20] As was demonstrated in Chapter 1, a baby needs to be able to rely on his carers to meet his needs faithfully. His security depends on it. But parents often interpret consistency as the need to be strict and unyielding.

Consistency with children, they would admit, often means putting on a false face. It means sticking to your guns when you have changed your mind. It means being unswerving in your stated point of view, and therefore less receptive to the child's argument. It means pretending you know what's best, when inside you are full of doubt. Consistency, I believe, is a greatly overrated virtue.

Perhaps 'genuine' would be a more valuable attribute for parents to cultivate. Children need parents to be *true to themselves*, which may mean being flexible, understanding, open to change and even inconsistent at times. Dr David Fontana, a psychologist at Cardiff University, says:

> Kids have to know where they stand. We don't really know what the other variables are. Either of the extremes [being too authoritarian or too relaxed] are equally bad. People who argue for one or the other are blind to the evidence. In Victorian times the incidence of human misery and law-breaking was just as bad as it is now. There is no virtue in harking back to the idea that if we suddenly get strict with children we will solve all our problems.[21]

Stating that a child needs consistency does not take into account all the inconsistencies of the real world. It presumes that a child cannot cope with doubt or complexity, which is

212

simply untrue. Paradoxes, exceptions to the rule and subtle shades of meaning are all aspects of life that attract and fascinate children. They want to know why it is, when such-and-such a rule applies on Monday, it does not on a Sunday. They delight in the variety of life, and are happy to abide by its complex demands, provided they are secure in themselves and in their relationships with their parents.

Grandparents understand this law perfectly. They do not attempt to make their house rules consistent with the house rules children are used to. They have the confidence to be different, as author, journalist and grandmother Angela Lambert describes:

> With my own children, I followed the dictates of Dr Spock. My daughter is entirely yielding, tender and indulgent with hers. When those small grandchildren first came to stay, I told them firmly that my rules were different from Mummy's. They would have a nice supper, a nice bath, a nice long story and a nice kiss, and not a sound did I want to hear once they had been settled in bed. Astonishingly, it worked. They recognise that funny old Granny has different rules and you might as well obey them.[22]

Grannies not only make their own rules, they make them sound warm and inviting. Children are well able to adapt to this kind of inconsistency in their lives – in fact, they are expert at deducing the kinds of behaviours any number of adults expect of them. Sarah Ferguson, mother to the Princesses Beatrice and Eugenie, imaginatively appealed to this infant skill when devising a programme of discipline for her royal daughters. Rather than expecting them to behave like little princesses all the time, she laid down a graded code of conduct at the table:

> A is for tea with granny (at Buckingham Palace); B is for a meal in public, and C is relaxed – just dinner at home with mama when we can have fun. Oh, there's a D, too. That's a tray in front of the television.[23]

DANGERS OF DOGMA

At a meeting of our mothers' support group in Manchester some years ago, we once tackled the subject of childhood happiness. We brought along photographs of ourselves as children, and discussed how we felt about our childhood selves. About half of us rated our upbringing as contented and happy, the other half as unhappy on the whole. But when we compared life events, highlights, moments of sadness and so on, there was no discernable difference between the two groups. Those who rated their memories as positive had plenty of unhappy moments to recount, while those who deemed their childhood to have been miserable could recall happy times.

Eventually we stumbled on a significant difference between the two groups. Those whose parents had been strict, who valued consistency, and who were unlikely ever to change their minds or 'give in', spawned the negative memories. Those whose parents offered flexibility and humour in their dealings with their children, who would admit to being wrong sometimes, and could be seen to change their minds, left their children with positive feelings. Such parents had allowed their genuine selves to shine through, for good or bad. I counted my parents amongst this group, and considered my early childhood to have been happy.

Author Carol Clewlow's story illustrates the dangers of dogma. She was brought up as a member of Plymouth Brethren, a faith, she says, 'in which chinks are not allowed.' When, at seventeen, she admitted to her parents that she did not know whether or not she believed in their faith, it was as if their world began to crumble. She explains why:

> You can't really replace the Plymouth Brethren, you can't replace a faith that doesn't allow for any doubt, because as soon as you allow doubt, it will crumble. The compromise faiths just crumble up against that great edifice of certainty, which is what fundamentalists know all over

214

the world. But, of course, doubts are a vital part of faith . . .

The fault is the absolute certainty. When I look back now I see that was the problem, it wasn't anything to do with lipstick or dancing, it was to do with having an inquiring mind, and it was education that brought the whole thing to an end . . .

I have a recurring dream. I dream of a house, and I dream I am inside it and it is all broken up, the floor-boards are smashed and cracked, the beams are falling down, the plaster is coming off the walls, and there are holes everywhere. And that is the house in which I was born and brought up, and it is blindingly obvious what that represents.[24]

Carol's parents presented her with a single version of truth. When she challenged this, the whole edifice of certainty was destroyed. Her parents even offered to change church, but for Carol this was not the point. The Brethren were the context for all the years of her growing up, and she did not *want* to throw all that away. She did not want to change her parents, but to be allowed to make up her own mind. Had they only allowed Carol her doubt, her parents would have been able to cement their relationship with her.

At Bath University, psychologist Dr Helen Haste has spent decades researching aspects of moral behaviour. She suggests that when parents lay down unbreakable rules, they may limit the child's capacity for moral reasoning:

We can bring them up to be a conformist, a Rotarian, obedient and good. This might not produce people who can stand up and say 'Hey, this is wrong'; it might not even enable them to say 'Stop beating up that kid'. But they probably won't steal your car. Or we can adopt a different approach and teach teenagers to ask questions. Then they are going to be rather a nuisance and question everything, which can be very uncomfortable. But you will, in the end, have people who are capable of changing the system, either in the playground or, later, in society.[25]

It would be lovely to think that we could inculcate good morals in our children by spoon-feeding them our own. But experience teaches children to question the rules they learnt at home. At some time, our deepest-held beliefs will be up for scrutiny, compared with those of their friends' parents and bandied around for ridicule or rejection. If we are sure of ourselves, we will not need or expect our children to share our values unquestioningly. Humour and an attitude of acceptance will see us through.

THE SUBTLE ART OF CAVING IN

In the 1990s, the US comedy series *Roseanne* tackled issues of parental consistency and control. Here, parents Dan and Roseanne consider the implications of changing their minds to allow daughter Darlene to meet boyfriend David:

> Dan (ironic): We don't have to look at it as a double standard, let's look at it as different kids need different rules.
> Roseanne (also ironic): Yes, that's good!
> Dan: And we didn't cave in on this David thing, we adapted to a difficult situation.
> Roseanne: Well done my man. Hey, I got one. Darlene isn't totally out of control, she's spunky!
> Dan: Quite.[26]

There is an art to changing your mind, and women have historically held the copyright on this particular skill. The patriarchal model is to present a consistent front. Margaret Thatcher, who, as prime minister, earned herself the title of 'The Iron Lady', managed to corner both images at once. Her famous utterance, 'U-turn if you want, the Lady's not for turning'[27] conveyed her consistency and strength, while the coyness of 'Maggie may . . .' helped to retain her feminine mystique.

Changing your mind with strength means being consistent with your feelings, which is the kind of consistency that a child can truly rely on. If our feelings are fairly steady and triggered off in predictable ways, then a child soon learns to know his parents' emotional landscape.

We should, perhaps, worry less about being consistent with our children, than being humane, as child psychologist Dr Haim Ginott told one mother who felt she'd 'caved in':

> In my eyes, Nell, you didn't have a failure. You felt that the need for sharing a beautiful moment with your son was more important than the need to be consistent. You trusted your inner voice, and when we heed that voice instead of sticking to the rigid rule, we usually don't go too far wrong. There is seldom a time we cannot demonstrate our humanity by saying, 'I've had second thoughts . . .' 'I've reconsidered . . .' or 'Tonight we'll make an exception to the rule.'[28]

Family therapist Dr Robin Skynner talked about the 'playfulness, humour and creativity' that characterised exceptionally healthy families. The idea of *disciplining* our children with humour is alien to our culture. If we believe in consistency and unwavering authority, then humour might undermine us. But if, instead, we view discipline as a part of the tapestry of cultural transmission, as the educational psychologist Reuven Feuerstein believed, then humour is one of the best ways of getting our message across. Older children know this, when they tease younger ones who are being 'naughty'. Even adults may be disciplined with humour, as in this case, where the Efé Pygmies make a joke out of a marital fight:

> What usually happens when a husband and wife fight, says Hallet [Jean-Pierre, the Belgian anthropologist], is that they are encouraged. If a man is about to hit his wife, the others will give him a stick and say, 'Hit her with this. You are a strong man. You can kill her!' By this time, the husband already feels a little ashamed. The others group

around and call out, 'OK! Go! Go for it!' And then he realizes how foolish he looks. They end up making a joke out of it, a sort of soap opera. Then everybody claps, and they are happy.[29]

Humour is strong and flexible. Tragedy is brittle. If we turn all our children's misdeeds into tragedy, they soon learn the unhappiness of existence. If all their mistakes are exposed and judged, as before the High Court, they swiftly feel themselves to be victims of an unyielding system. Soon they feel not only that what they did was bad, but that they are intrinsically bad, too.

But if a child can make mistakes in safety, learn through the warmth of a cuddle, or through laughter, his trust and feeling of parental acceptance is not destroyed. The lesson will, however, still be learned. Humour defuses a situation; seriousness intensifies it.

A ROUGH GUIDE TO RULE-MAKING

Discipline is not something you do at the end of the day, or when Daddy Gets Home. It's in your every interaction with your child; it's in your bones. Discipline is the main dish of parenting, because – whether we like it or not – our unconsciously expressed attitudes are educating the child hour by hour. Children learn from the way we talk to our friends, from the way we cringe when someone else's child steps out of line, from our body rhythms and what we cook for tea (and whether or not they are expected to eat it all up.)

- The first rule of discipline to our children is to discipline ourselves. We are the signposts to our children's future, and they are always looking to us to see where to go. It makes sense to take responsibility for our own actions, because it is our behaviour, not our words, that children most readily copy.
- After setting a good example, the next thing is to notice and remark upon desired behaviour in the child. There's always

something. Excessive praise is unhelpful here – in fact, it doesn't have to be praise at all. Something simple like 'Wow, just look at all those shoes arranged in a line!' or 'What a lovely smile you gave to your teacher!' Children love to be noticed for the small things. It also saves them having to beg for constant attention.

- Conversely, it makes for a calmer life to notice as little bad behaviour as possible, (allowing for the fact that siblings may notice it for you and try to 'correct' it on your behalf.) When the child does need correction, a quiet word is more powerful than a public dressing down. Children are more likely to co-operate if they are not constantly embarrassed by an exhibition of their errors. A few whispered words, pointing out that 'We speak quietly in restaurants', give the child a chance to appear to decide to behave for themselves. Children need lots of practice at appearing to do the right thing, and it doesn't matter if they weren't always the ones to think of it.

- Try to limit the number of commands you give and make these as polite as they would be to an adult. E.g.: 'Please would you fetch me the orange juice?' Always keep commands positive, so the child can focus on what he is expected to do, not what he is being forbidden. And even better, present the rules as society's norms, e.g. 'People walk on the pavement,' not 'Don't walk in the road.'

- If you do feel you want to impose sanctions, then let them be a real consequence of your child's actions. For instance, if a toddler's behaviour is disrupting the session of gym tots then a natural outcome would be to apologise to the teacher and leave. (If it matters to the child to join the class, then he must join in appropriately. If not, then perhaps he shouldn't be there anyway.) All-purpose sanctions – smacking, being sent into isolation, the withholding of distant treats – can be self-defeating, because they give the child a chance to stew in his own little cauldron of hurt and resentment. He's considering the consequence of *your* actions, not his own!

- Behaving is belonging. Don't give small children the chance to practice misbehaving, i.e. behaving contrary to social rules. If you are saying 'No' to something the older baby is about to do, simultaneously remove him from the scene of impending danger or destruction. Distract him swiftly with a suitable alternative. This way, you both avoid a cycle of nagging and disobedience.

- It can be fun to reward children for good behaviour – but spontaneously, not systematically. A small treat, a note, or even a 'thank you', just occasionally, helps to make a child feel appreciated. It's another perk of belonging and behaving.

- Finally (and this is a very rough guide, as it's far more important to be creative about rule-making than it is to follow any recipe) we can appeal to our children's own moral sense.

By following the child, observing his tendency to want to do good, and to make good when he has done wrong, we can allow him to discipline himself. The psychiatrist Dr Ross Campbell says that

> . . . if a child is already sorrowful for his inappropriate act, his conscience is alive and well. That's what you want! He has learned from his mistake. A good healthy conscience is the best deterrent to repeating misbehaviour.
> . . . When a child already feels genuinely contrite and remorseful for his act, his conscience is dealing severely with him. He is punishing himself.[30]

ATONEMENT

Atonement is an old-fashioned word and it's not the first thing we think of when we talk about child discipline. But allowing children to mend their own mistakes is a marvellous way of empowering them to do the right thing. Even quite senior children may be visibly relieved to find something practical to do to make amends for misbehaviour or a mistake.

The answer to the question of discipline is not to dispense with all rules, which would be to deny one's own needs, and the demands of the culture, but to *allow the child to make good*. Some parents reading this will shake their heads and say, 'If I waited for my child to mend his behaviour, I'd wait for ever.' At first, they may be right. But as with learning to climb, or to talk, learning to discipline oneself requires time and exercise. Children may be immature in the ways of the world, they may certainly break the rules and make mistakes, but what they need is practice, not punishment. Teacher David Gribble believes that:

> . . . just as in order to develop a healthy body you need to take physical exercise, so in order to develop healthy moral perceptions you have to take moral decisions. If you are told what to do all the time at school, you will not be able to direct yourself when you leave. You will have been trained vigorously as a follower of rules, and you will only survive as a healthy (i.e. normally rational) individual if you rebel . . .[31]

One way to encourage the child's conscience is to ask him for his own ideas on sorting out a difficult situation. One American study[32] found that children who were encouraged to develop their own judgement used the same tactic when playing with their friends. 'How shall we make sure we each get a turn?' they might ask, just as their parents would ask them. Children whose parents routinely shouted and threatened tended to shout at and threaten their peers. Even in nursery school, the study found that the most popular children were the ones who approached situations with constructive questions rather than blame.

I have found that the most satisfying way of dealing with my children's mistakes or unacceptable behaviour, is to allow *them* to sort it out. When something is spilled, I hand them the cloth. If as toddlers, one of them should hurt another child, I would invite them to decide what they want to do about it. Invariably, they wanted to hug, and kiss and say sorry.

When something goes wrong I find the quickest way to make matters worse is to launch in with my own fury, or insist that they repair the damage *my* way. This takes the moral initiative out of their hands.

I shall never forget a poignant incident at a supermarket some years ago, when a little boy deliberately (I think) rammed into my leg with a trolley. He caught me sharply on the shin, and because of the pain, I reacted with a loud 'Ow!' He saw my angry face, and although I said nothing, he knew he had upset me. His mother missed the whole incident.

As I was putting my shopping into the car minutes later, the little lad (he was only about seven) came up all by himself and said, 'I am sorry for hurting your leg.' I was very touched. It is rare for children even to be given the chance to say sorry for themselves, and we do not often see them do it. I accepted his apology, and told him I thought it was lovely of him to come back to me. We parted with a smile and a wave. If the child's natural mechanisms are not disturbed, he really does learn his discipline from within.

In Chapter 1, the child psychologist, D.W. Winnicott was quoted saying that mothers are human, that humans make mistakes, but that we are all the time mending our mistakes. There is an interesting example in *The Continuum Concept* of a parent making a mistake with his child. Because his moral senses are alert, and his self-discipline strong, this father knows instantly that he has done wrong, according to his own, inner set of rules:

> I saw a young father lose patience one day with his year-old son. He shouted and made some violent motion as I watched and may even have struck him. The baby screamed with deafening, unmistakable horror. The father stood chastened by the dreadful sound he had caused; it was clear that he had committed an offence against nature. I saw the family often, as I lived next door to them, but I never saw the man lose respect for his son's dignity again.[33]

Like Harriet Harris, who 'later that night' was best of friends with her mother, the Yequana baby, following this incident, could still expect a deep level of acceptance from his father. He could rely on his father's sense of self-discipline to mend whatever mistakes might be made. And it is the mending that we remember.

Having worked in business, I know this to be one of the basic tenets of customer care: customer loyalty is earned through the mending of mistakes. You may, for instance, have been taking your car to the same service station for years, with no particular feelings of loyalty to the firm. Say, one day, a mistake is made on the repair work, and you march in with your complaint. Instead of the fight you were expecting, you are greeted with a genuine smile, concern and an assistant who takes your complaint seriously. She takes the problem out of your hands, arranges for it to be sorted out immediately, and offers you a small token of reparation for your trouble. *Now* you are delighted. You are also likely to feel committed to the company, and to recommend it to all your friends.

The mistakes we make always bring with them opportunity. This is as true for our children as it is for us. When they step out of line, they are naturally motivated to step back in line again. Unless, of course, we hover over them with our punishments and rewards, and confuse them completely.

Discipline worries many parents. Some feel guilty for being too harsh, others for not being harsh enough. But play worker Alison Stallibrass takes the dilemma out of our hands:

> Parents will not worry about whether or not they are exercising just the right amount of indulgence and firmness if they are aware that the most important thing of all is to give their child every opportunity to *feel effective*.[34]

If we can hand over to our children, as with every other area of their lives, responsibility for themselves, they will grow to be true and strong. They may not become the kinds of people who live only by rules, or who use rules to control others, but they will always be able to draw on their self-discipline to tell them what is right.

Letting go as children grow: discipline

- Good discipline emerges from a child's sense of belonging and responsibility. He also seeks clues from the behaviour he sees in adults and older children around him
- Discipline should not be confused with punishment. Punishment is an overused disciplinary tool
- We owe it to our children to convey the rules of our culture, although we may expect them, as they grow, to question those rules
- Even small children have a strong moral sense and are able to express remorse, sympathy and spontaneous acts of kindness apparently beyond their years. These acts increase when they are noticed and encouraged
- Children need boundaries: they do not need unflinching consistency
- Model good behaviour, notice good behaviour, occasionally and spontaneously reward good behaviour – and most of the bad behaviour will take care of itself
- Keep sanctions real. Children need to learn that bad behaviour can have its own consequences
- Children's mistakes and misdemeanours are an opportunity for them to make amends

8

SHOW SOME EMOTION –
IS IT SAFE TO TALK?

My parents were deeply loving, that's the hardest thing. I think most parents make the biggest mistakes out of love.

Novelist Carol Clewlow

Love? What good is love? The most overrated commodity there is. It's only when you can channel it into your behaviour that it has any relevance.

Mother and author Bronwyn Hocking

Most of us believe we know our children well. We are there when they smile their first smiles, take their first steps, scrape their knees, struggle with homework, fall in love and out again. They depend on us for so much, for so long, that we might feel they belong to us. We may find it hard to understand when they want to go their own way, and make choices we would not have made. We can forget that their experiences and feelings about life are not the same as ours.

Because our children are relatively inexperienced, we may presume that little is going on beneath the surface. But a child's inner life is rich and complex, and as play therapist Virginia Axline suggests, there are many emotions that children keep to themselves:

The child lives in a world of his own and very few adults really understand him. There is such a rush and pressure in modern times that it is difficult for a child to establish the intimate, delicate relationship with the adult that is necessary to enable him to lay bare his innermost secret life.[1]

In fact, the very young child does not know that his feelings are all his own. It takes a long while for him to realise that his mother or other primary carer does not actually *share* his experiences and feelings. Aged two and nine months, Frances was sitting in the back of the car, when she asked me, 'If I put my tongue here in my mouth, it's all soft. Can you feel it?' At a slightly earlier age, she also believed I could control all her experiences: after watching a train speed by, she asked me to 'Make it do it again, mummy.'

From birth, children encounter new experiences for which they have no words. This need not deter them from trying to express their feelings. Frances invented words, and having used them once, would discard them. In the bath, washing her hair under the water, she once exclaimed, 'My ears are flickling!'; and another time: 'When my hair is clean it cricks.' Alice (at two) preferred to borrow words from other contexts. While watching a programme about snakes on television, she declared, 'I doesn't like a snake, Mummy. Too spicy.' Joe, at three, took this a stage further, with 'I've got a tummy ache on my shoulder.'

A child's inner world is vibrant and alive. He is all the time making new connections based on his own life experiences. Nobody else before him has been through exactly the range and order of emotions that he is experiencing. Nobody else can tell him how he feels.

TELL ME HOW IT FEELS . . .

We do not really need to ask children to communicate their emotions to us. Body therapist Thérèse Bertherat argues that, as a child's body expresses his state of well-being, we should learn to read his body language, instead of expecting him to describe his feelings with words:

> Impatiently, we wait for our children to be able to express themselves verbally; we congratulate them for speaking like adults and being able at last to protect us from the raw truth that they had been continually trying to express through their body. We're reassured when, like us, they can use verbal language as a screen to hide their true desires, to modify their natural tendencies, to master their sensations. 'Talk to me. Tell me what's on your mind. If you don't talk to me, how do you expect me to know what's wrong,' say parents to children emitting distress signals that they don't see.[2]

In fact, the average parent, while asking what is wrong, is desperately hoping that nothing is wrong at all, and is ready to pounce on the negative emotion and deny it. We phrase our questions to our children to ensure that they will deliver the required response: 'Are you happy, darling?' 'Yes Mummy.' Parent workshop leaders Adele Faber and Elaine Mazlish, here in conversation, describe the way in which adults give coded messages to signal what their children's emotional responses should be:

Faber: I find even the question 'Did you have fun?' to be irritating. The expectation is, that to make me happy, you have to have fun. Why does your child have to have fun? All you actually have to say is, 'So, you went berry picking.' And let your child tell you the rest: 'Yeah, it was boring,' 'Yeah, I got bitten by a mosquito,' 'Yeah, it was fun, Mom.'

Mazlish: Very often, the more we move into our children's domain, the more they will pull back, and the less they will tell us – particularly with adolescents and preadolescents. Being invasive in our children's lives is another form of

	disrespect. Sometimes just our facial expressions say, 'Please say you had fun, because that will make me happy.' Children read their parents' faces and try to please: 'Yeah, it was OK.' 'Yeah, I had a good time.'
Faber:	And then you've lost the opportunity for your child to tell you how Jimmy got three acorns and he or she only got two, or about the leaf that your child floated down the river.[3]

Real emotions are not always acceptable in adult culture. When we greet an acquaintance, we may offer the shorthand, 'How are you?', but our brisk tone and manner signal that we do not really want to know. The stock response: 'Very well thank you', glosses over the subject nicely: we have dispensed with the need to become involved.

Psychotherapist Solveig Sandström Taylor believes we can share our real feelings with our children, to show them it is safe to share theirs: 'If you always say, "Yes, I'm fine", children will say the same,' says Solveig, whose work is aimed at empowering children to protect themselves against sexual abuse. 'You can say, "I had a really good day", or "a shitty day", and that's honest for children. They can take that.' She gives us an example:

I was collecting my daughter and her friend from school. The friend had been given a minus house point at school, and she was crying when I picked her up. I accepted that was the way she was feeling. She was in a good mood by the time she got home. The next day, when I collected her from her house, I said 'How are you?' and she replied 'OK.' Her father was angry. He told her, 'Don't be rude, say "Very well, thank you"', then turned to me and apologised: 'My wife has just shouted at her.' The father had forgotten what his daughter was going through. She wasn't allowed to feel what she was feeling at the time.

POTTERING PARENTS

Parents often complain that their children don't tell them anything, and yet they may not be providing an atmosphere in which the children feel free to reveal intimate information. Because 'good' parents are supposed to be interested in their children's activities, we may bombard our children with invasive questions that make them recoil.

When Frances started nursery school, I was desperate to know how she was getting on, and would give her the third degree: 'What's your teacher like?' 'Who did you sit next to?' 'What did you do?' 'Did you like it?' I soon realised that the answers to questions like these were unrevealing. If a child can be bothered to deal with invasions of this sort at all, it is usually with monosyllables and 'facts', not the meaty stuff, the emotions that have been building up all day.

Instead, when she began full-time school, I set aside an opportunity for Frances to come (or choose not to come) for a cuddle. I would say very little, perhaps only 'You went to school today': something descriptive, non-probing. In this quiet time, Frances would tell me a few of the feelings she wanted to express; like somebody not wanting to be her friend any more, and how she had felt about and dealt with it.

Sometimes she would come for the cuddle and say very little. Perhaps she had nothing to say. We cannot *make* our children talk to us. As long as we try to coax their feelings out of them, they are likely to feel pressurised. We have to respect their right to deal with their time away from us by themselves, and give them room to decide to bring their problems to us if they choose.

Sometimes even a cuddle is too much. Linda Burton, founder of the American support group Mothers at Home, recalls, as a child, sidling up to her mother, while busy in the kitchen, for problem-sharing sessions. This was non-focused, non-quality time, where she felt safe to share her emotions:

> . . . it is often much easier to share our most intimate feelings and heartaches if it *seems* like we are not actually

doing it. If what we are doing is dicing the onions or peeling the potatoes – if we are somewhat diverted from the strength of our feelings for a moment – it seems somehow easier to express them. After all, if we become too embarrassed or overwrought, we can simply return to making the salad with a vengeance. So the kitchen is often an especially 'safe' place to talk. No one is calling us on the carpet, as it were, to Open-Up-Your-Heart-And-Be-Quick-About-It.

Certainly, the creation of this low-key, cozy atmosphere is therapeutic for adults. But for children, I think it is crucial.[4]

Cuddling the smaller child, or dicing onions while older children prowl around the kitchen: these are simple techniques for making ourselves available to children should they wish to talk. It's the pottering parent who gets to hear about her child's successes and fears and who has the chance *not* to over-react, but to keep on listening with half an ear and all her heart. This peaceful oasis is the antidote to quality time. It's just time.

It also is the permissive atmosphere that is the aim of play therapy. No one is coaxing the child to speak, or directing the content of his words. Solveig Sandström Taylor says her job is to 'allow people to express their emotions in a safe environment. Children are great at this. They are the healthiest people in the family. They are very undisturbed . . . Children see things clearly, and they have a very strong healing power. We encourage them to listen to their bodies, getting them to trust themselves so they can learn to say "No".'

REAL CHILDREN WELCOME

It is a vital component of play therapy that, whatever feelings are expressed, they will not be judged by the listener:

The therapist is concerned with the *feelings* the child expresses. A child seldom goes into the playroom and straightaway plays out his deep feelings. First there is a period of exploration, of testing, of getting acquainted. The child must have a feeling of confidence in the therapist if he is to share his feelings. He must feel so secure in this situation that he can bring forth his 'bad' feelings as well as his 'good' feelings and not be fearful that this adult will disapprove of him.[5]

Few of us can approach another person and be certain to be heard without disapproval. Few of us grew up in an atmosphere in which all our feelings were accepted at-face value, where no judgements were offered. In fact, for many of us, our parents were the ones most *likely* to give us their judgement, not only of our actions, but also of our emotions. Even positive judgements are off-putting to the child. He guesses that his feelings will be amplified and given the parental seal of approval.

Instead of allowing their child's emotions to be, parents often declare war on his expressions of feeling, in essence telling him he cannot trust his own senses. A child declares he feels cold: 'No you don't,' says his father, 'it's a hot day.' A child has a tantrum: 'He's not himself today,' says his mother. To suggest someone is 'not himself' whenever his mood is negative, is an astonishing denial. Is a child only 'himself' when he is in full health and displaying positive emotions? When we flatly deny certain aspects of our children's emotional lives, we might as well issue a warning: 'Real children not welcome here.'

We want our children to be happy, and we may expect them to wear their happiness on their sleeve. A happy child is supposedly proof of a 'good' parent. But we cannot force children into happiness, any more than we can prevent them suffering. As a result some parents merely pretend suffering is not there, and give themselves the mighty task of trying to 'make' their children happier.

Research shows, however, that it is not what we experience in life that determines our 'happiness quotient', but the way we deal with it. Children can survive bad experiences, if they are allowed to express their emotions about each experience in an appropriate way. They will not survive satisfactorily without expressing their emotions.

Piers Partridge, a psychotherapist and former public school boy, works with groups of adults who were emotionally damaged by being sent away to boarding school. He describes the grief experienced by young children who are forced to separate from their families, and then given no outlet for their pain:

> Partridge thinks children suffer enormously from the early enforced separation from their parents, but usually receive no help in dealing with it. 'It is a major bereavement. It's a bit as if your family and pet dog were wiped out in a traffic accident. But this is not even touched on by the schools.'
>
> All the children can do is to swallow their feelings. 'They learn to suppress fear, because fear is not acceptable. They learn to suppress love, because loving other boys is not acceptable, sadness is not acceptable . . . so you are left with being happy . . . The typical boarding-school boy or girl is "happy". But if you can't express feelings, you can only have limited relationships with other people,' says Mr Partridge, who is campaigning against children under the age of eleven being sent away to school.[6]

British actor Jeremy Brett recalls his unhappiness at Eton, where he was regularly beaten, and so often approached sexually by other boys, that he began to question his own sexuality. But he could not share his fears with his parents, who had sacrificed a good deal to send him there. He was trapped, and in a uniform that made it difficult to breathe:

> I remember the desolation when Mummy's car left and I was marooned. I found that so frightening. And having my own room made me instantly lonely. I cried the first night because I was alone . . .
>
> I remember the first morning trying to open my

starched collar with a nail file so I could breathe. I was crippled by a kind of beauty, which was hell for me, and I got a lot of wrong responses . . .

But you never told your parents you were unhappy, because you knew, especially me, the youngest of four, that it was costing them practically everything they had to keep you there.

I was beaten a great deal. You had to wait until after the beating when they asked: 'Do you have anything to say?' You would say: 'No.' 'You may leave,' they then said. And you must then say: 'Thank you.'

The first time, I got up, and out of panic, I immediately said thank you. 'Oh,' they said, 'he likes it, bend over,' and I got another five.[7]

The beating scene is a cruel parody of conventional manners. Under the guise of discipline, a boy is forced to exchange niceties with his attackers. This was surely not what Brett's parents had sent him to Eton for.

Pressure on children to avoid the full range of emotions is so usual, we may fail to notice its insidious influence. When our neighbours were involved in a car crash some years ago, the local newspaper reported the incident under the headline: 'Family's crash courage'.[8] The mother, who was badly injured, was quoted saying how horrendous the accident had been and how angry she felt.

But the children (who also suffered injuries and the temporary loss of their parents who were treated for months in hospital) were pictured smiling in the arms of the ambulance staff who had rescued them. 'They were all as good as gold,' said the paramedic. 'There were no tears.' Would the children have been 'bad' if they had cried, made a fuss, or expressed any emotion other than smiling acceptance? What kind of a world are we creating, where courage means not crying and only 'good' children will do?

There are many ways of denying and ignoring our children's emotions. We may simply pretend that their pain is not real: 'You can't be upset about a silly thing like that.' We may blame them for the feelings they are experiencing: 'It's your fault you are in such a bad mood.' We may try to make their feelings more palatable: 'You don't hate her really, darling.' We may even substitute our own feelings for theirs: 'Now *I'm* not frightened, and neither are you.'

One tactic of parents is to turn the emotional tables on our children. We interpret *their* actions in terms of *our* needs. I remember a teenage childhood friend announcing to her single-parent father that she wanted to take a year off to be an *au pair* in Germany. He was distraught. 'How can you do this to me?' he asked. There was no recognition of her needs, it was all about him. She never did take her year abroad.

Solveig Sandström Taylor suggests we count up to ten before launching in with our own emotions: 'Stop and ask yourself,' she says, ' "Who is being the child here?" ' Bio-energetic therapist Alexander Lowen believes we do great damage when we prevent our children from being children, from expressing their emotions in full:

> The ego grows through the perception and integration of body sensation on the one hand, and the expression of feeling on the other. If a child is inhibited in the expression of feeling or made to feel ashamed of his body sensations, his ego will not mature. If he is prevented from taking the measure of himself, from exploring his strength and discovering his weaknesses, his ego will have a precarious foothold in reality and his identity will be nebulous. If, moreover, he is indoctrinated with 'shoulds' and 'shouldn'ts' and brought up to fulfil a parental image, his ego will become devious and his identity confused.[9]

The following exercise might help you to discover whether or not you inhibit the emotions of children in your charge. Ask yourself, how safe is it for my child to:

1) express his fears?
2) make mistakes?

3) break something?
4) answer me back?
5) admit he has done something I won't approve of?
6) tell a lie?
7) be different from me?

How accepting are you of your child's emotional states? How often do you wait for your child to reveal those states, rather than stepping in with your own feelings? Parents are often surprised at the various shades of denial they use with their children.

THEIR SIDE OF THE STORY

We may not actually believe we are harming our children, and yet we may have created an atmosphere in which they are afraid of expressing their true feelings to us. This not only damages their emotional growth, but diminishes their powers of self-protection. Here, a newspaper report touches on the unsavoury fact that many crimes against children go unreported because children are afraid to speak up, even to their own parents:

> Thousands of crimes perpetrated against children never find their way into official statistics, according to research commissioned by the Home Office. It has found that children fall victim to a range of unreported crimes, including assault, extortion by bullies and theft, but they may be too frightened to tell their parents or ashamed to tell a parent or teacher . . .
>
> The case last month of a six-year-old boy who spent ten hours alone with his mother's body after witnessing her murder is seen as an extreme example. He dialled 999, but police in Taunton, Somerset, did not act on the call . . .[10]

We know that children sometimes deal in fantasy, and are apt to confuse what is with what might have been. But unless we listen to their side of the story, however it is told, we have little chance of hearing their emotional truths. It is perhaps a cherishable difference between you and your child that *he* has not yet learnt to keep his 'unacceptable' thoughts, emotions and needs to himself. He shares his fantasies, his dreams and his fears.

I am particularly grateful to my parents for protecting my inner world. I remember when I was quite young stating to my mother that after this life I would be born again as another person. Though she did not hold this belief herself, she accepted my idea and informed me that there were entire philosophies and religions based on that very premise. I did not instantly become a Buddhist or a Hindu, but I felt validated.

British psychotherapist Susie Orbach believes parents disregard children's ideas and emotions because they habitually disregard their own. She suggests that parents and teachers need to become 'emotionally literate', in order that children with fears and deep-set needs will receive the acceptance they crave:

> . . . we become wary of vulnerability seeing in it a sign of weakness. We define adulthood by the way we manage our vulnerabilities and needs. Most often this means over-riding them. We develop psychologies which deny personal vulnerability while over-developing our capacity to split off problematic or troublesome feelings. But responsible parenting requires precisely the opposite skills. It means becoming emotionally literate . . .
>
> Disallowed feelings don't just conveniently slip away. On the contrary, having one's feelings ridiculed leads to bad feelings, confused feelings which hang around, albeit in distorted form, motivating many of our acts in ways that belie our capacity to be rational.[11]

When children see their ideas and feelings squashed by adults, their feelings of self-worth diminish. Paradoxically, this may force them into a state of chronic bravado and bluff. Orbach gives an example of a boy who, having been ridiculed for his fear of water, acts in 'counter phobic' ways in order not to be ridiculed again:

> Ashamed and humiliated, he works hard to banish fearful feelings in himself . . . goading his mates in the playground and himself to overcome the scariest of activities. By the time he is an adult, he has a complete contempt for anyone or anything fearful. He is unable to confront fear, experience fear and live through fear. When his child expresses fear, psychic alarm bells propel him to decry it and the cycle turns.[11]

Agony aunt Angela Willans experienced a parent's denial when, at the age of three, she and her twin sister were put into the care of an abusive nanny. Angela recalls the extreme cruelty of the nanny as less devastating than their mother's refusal to believe that anything was amiss. To the physical and psychological torment of the surrogate parent was added the emotional abandonment of the real mother:

> . . . this Olive was totally responsible for us and had enormous power over us.
>
> There was a lot of physical abuse, slaps and cuffs and things, and she had a terribly severe way of washing you; she'd poke things in your ears and up your nose, and her favourite thing was holding me by my hair while beating me with a hanger. She should never have had anything to do with kids . . .
>
> After that it was 'into the cupboard' – and this was the cupboard under the stairs . . . we had to stay in there for God knows how long, and one imagined she'd camped outside, because if you made a whimper of a noise, it was, 'You be quiet, be quiet!' And then, eventually, when it was bed time, she put us to bed, and we just lay there trembling, because the bloody bitch, she'd come in every twenty minutes or half hour, '. . . [The police] haven't come yet but they're coming . . .' and this went on all through the night . . .

Olive's cruelty, I suppose, didn't hurt nearly so much as the fact that one had a slightly uncaring mother, and when I first tried to tell her what Olive was like she just didn't want to know. I mean, she had her own life to lead and she depended on Olive to look after us so she could enjoy herself, and so it was inconvenient to know: '. . . Angie, oh no dear, no, no, no, no, that's not happening.' She would never acknowledge it.

I really didn't get through all that until I had psycho-analysis.[12]

FORGIVE AND MOVE ON

We may imagine that, by denying our children's pain, we can make it go away. In fact, the opposite is true: only when we accept their hurt do we help to ease it. We forget that until unpleasant emotions have been expressed, good feelings cannot come in. Here, Alexander Technique teacher and author Glen Park talks about the quality of acceptance:

When a person does not have an habitually harsh judge-mental attitude, the quality of his response is one of acceptance. It is possible to feel critical of something but still accept it ('I do not like this, but I can accept it'), whereas it is not possible to attach a harsh angry quality to an attitude of acceptance. When we move to a position of acceptance our view of the world changes dramati-cally. Everything can be seen as part of the whole, operating in a way that is totally appropriate to that part. Acceptance puts us in present time, in touch with what is, and not what ought to be. In order to accept we have to be able to let go of the past, and of our expecta-tions of the present and the future . . . In order to accept we have to be able to forgive. Forgiving is a way of letting go emotionally.[13]

Many people spend their lives suppressing emotions they were not able to deal with at the time, and which keep re-emerging.

It is hard work, and potentially frightening, to have to go back over old ground, to deal with our personal history. But it is even harder to hang on to our bitterness, which eats away at our lives and prevents us fully enjoying the moment. How wonderful if, instead of forcing their children to store up *their* pain, parents could provide an environment in which it was acceptable to express real feelings. Parentcraft author Adele Faber describes such an environment:

> Your child cries, 'My finger hurts', and you say 'Oh, honey, it doesn't hurt; it's just a little scratch.' He or she cries more. But if you understand how to describe rather than evaluate, you say instead, 'Let me see. I see a little cut. Gee, even a little cut can be painful.' And your child says, 'Yeah, well, it's not so bad', and runs out to play.
>   Our fear is, that by acknowledging pain we reinforce it. The thing we need to learn over and over again is that *the moment we acknowledge pain, the pain becomes somewhat diminished*. So the best comfort we can give is to acknowledge pain, to allow sorrow, allow grief, welcome suffering. As we say in our book, 'Your tears are as welcome as your laughter.' I don't only want the happy part of you. I want all of you. I'll take the whole package.[3]

Acknowledging our children's pain does not have to be a tortuous process. It is not necessary to embellish the occasion with tedious reiterations of the child's feelings, or even to end it with a group hug. The quality of acceptance is, at its best, a simple 'yes'. Just as a magic kiss heals the grazed knee of a wounded three-year-old, so acceptance is usually enough for emotional pain. It's surprising what can be achieved, merely by refusing to deny or interpret children's feelings; by being there.

If a baby is unhappy, he will cry. A small child will cry freely if necessary, but he may swiftly learn that screaming is un-acceptable, even when he is frightened. Older children, boys especially, will suppress crying, too. Soon we are left with only words to express our emotions, and even our words are likely to be denied. One by one, our feelings are hidden away, locked in our bodies, where others can pretend not to see them.

Words are feeble in comparison with the unsuppressed body language of, for instance, the Efé Pygmies of the Ituri rainforest in central Africa:

> Pygmies express their emotions freely. Turnbull [Colin, English anthropologist] refers to the bright-eyed, open look of the playful Pygmies and is surprised by the extent of their emotional freedom: they may even fall to the ground and roll around while expressing intense sorrow or laughter. According to Hallet [Jean-Pierre, the Belgian anthropologist], if Pygmies feel like crying, they cry. If they want to scream, they scream. They yell. It is also acceptable for a man to cry openly. The Pygmies do not suppress their emotions; instead, they say, 'Tell the truth. Do not hide it – let it out.'[14]

When Westerners talk about Truth, they are usually referring to either religious wisdom or factual evidence. The Pygmy looks inside himself for his truth; he recognises that his emotions make him what he is, they define him. To deny your emotion is to deny yourself. This same realisation came to Herby, an eight-year-old boy, while attending play therapy:

> 'All of a sudden, I'm free. Inside me, I'm free.' (He flings his arms around.) 'I'm Herb and Frankenstein and Tojo and a devil.' (He laughs and pounds his chest.) 'I'm a great giant and a hero. I'm wonderful and I'm terrible. I'm a dope and I'm so smart . . . I'm good and I'm bad and still I'm Herby. I tell you I'm wonderful. I can be anything I want to be!' Apparently Herby felt that during the therapy hour he could express fully all of the attitudes and feelings that were an expression of his personality. He felt the acceptance and permissiveness to be himself. He seemed to recognize the power of self-direction within himself.[15]

This is an extremely powerful illustration of empowerment. By simply accepting the person before her, the therapist allows the child to rediscover his potential. She certainly does not deny the child's feelings, or blame him for them, or attempt to stamp them out. And that is not all. There are other, subtler manoeuvres that are *not* taking place in the therapy room.

REASON AND REASSURANCE

One of these is reassurance. It is very common, when a child presents us with his fear or his pain, to reassure him that it will go away, that 'everything will be all right.' But, as *Magical Child* author Joseph Chilton Pearce says, even reassurance is out of place if we wish to empower the child:

> If the four-year-old cries out in the night that there are bears under his bed, the parents accept that statement. His tears indicate not only a genuine perception to that effect but also, most importantly, specific needs that lie beyond the issue of an illusion. The mother does not go in, flip on the light, and berate the child for being silly and imagining nonsense. She does not insult his system and accuse him of being a fraud. Nor does she just cuddle the child and tell him everything is all right. Things are obviously not right. She does not show him that there are no bears under the bed. Instead, she recognises the youngster's terror as loss of personal power, loss of control, some inarticulate fear projected onto an object of imagination, and fear that has an object is tangible and can be attacked . . .
>
> The mother plunges to the heart of the matter; the bear *is* the focus. Immediately, she does that for which the parent is designed; she functions as the matrix. She lends the child her power. She gives her child the strength to enter fully into the reality he has created, and she joins him in that world. Together they get rid of that bear. Perhaps she holds the child and charges the bear and chases it completely away. Perhaps she corners the bear

and cows it into submission. Or perhaps, holding the child, they make friends with the bear, win from him some boon, and make of him a guardian for future nights.

She has not turned on the light to prove her child a liar, to show that his perceptual apparatus is faulty. She has not tried to override the child world with the idea system of the adult. She has met the child where he is, in his need, taken her cues from him, and responded according to the needs of the situation. Rather than trying to dispel the reality creation, the mother has joined in transforming it. Personal power has overcome powerlessness and the fear of the unknown.[16]

In storybooks, children's feelings are often represented by fantastic animals or magical occurrences that children believe in, but that adults deny. As a result of their denial, parents miss out on the wonderful experiences that only the child characters (and the child reader) can share. Youth is preserved by those who believe: in J.M. Barrie's *Peter Pan*, Wendy's growing up means she will no longer be able to fly.

Another way to deny young children's feelings is to reason with them. Before the age of about seven, children are not equipped to accept reasoned argument in the face of emotional crisis. But in a society that admires facts and logic, it is not surprising to see parents offering their children large doses of both, when all they really want is emotional food. Co-authors Valerie Walkerdine and Helen Lucey, whilst researching a book on mothers and their ten-year-old daughters, discovered that turning every encounter into a lesson was a way of denying children's needs, or, as they put it,

. . . comfortable environments could hide an oppression too, 'the way in which the middle-class mothers had to make every minute of the day into a pedagogy.'[17]

The over-rational, pedantic parent may isolate a child with his emotions. To insist that the bear under the bed is not real (and could not possibly be there, since it wouldn't fit underneath, and is anyway a species native to the North Pole), may be factually correct, but it is not what the child needs to hear.

Our job as parents is not to protect our children *from* their emotions, but to protect their right to *express* them. Sometimes, children need help to articulate what they feel, and parents can be the best people to help them do this. Child psychologists John and Elizabeth Newson discovered that parents are often very good at reading their children's underlying emotions:

> Because our society places a certain value on courage and the stiff upper lip, fears and worries, even when they are engendered in the school situation, are often concealed from teachers and other adults, however potentially sympathetic, and saved up for mother. She is the person who is most likely to realise that the child has anxieties, and she usually recognises as her responsibility the task of comforting him and building up his confidence. Her acceptance of this responsibility will make her sensitive to small signs which may not be explicit at all: 'I think he does worry, and yet he's the type of kiddy that sort of shrugs it off,' says a window cleaner's wife – 'he's a child that *makes out* he's bold, and yet he's not as bold as what he thinks he is.'[18]

DO NOT DISTURB

The danger is that, rather than helping the child to articulate his emotions, a parent will probe too deeply. She amplifies her child's feelings, in order to augment her own role. This will be done in a spirit of love, but in fact it represents over-mothering, or 'smother love', of which any adult caring for children may be guilty.

An over-mothering parent may attempt to prize out every nuance of feeling from the child, because she lives vicariously through her child's emotions. She needs detail, because she feeds off the intimacies of her child's life. She has become over-involved in her parental role, and does not understand the laws of what the Japanese violin master Sinichi Suzuki called 'natural growth':

> A seed is planted in the earth. We don't see when the germination begins. That is the doing of Mother Nature; it is the fundamental working principle. We have to wait patiently. We cannot dig up the seed to see whether it is really growing; to do so would be to destroy everything.[19]

The over-involved parent disturbs her seedlings. Her children are encouraged to grow in a way that satisfies *her* ideal, not in their own direction. The child who grows up to be himself inevitably grows away from his parents, and this can be difficult for them to bear. It deprives them of their nurturing role, leaving them with only themselves to tend to. Letting go is especially hard for single parents, as Wendy Oberman, author of *Mothers and Other Loves*, describes in this interview:

> Divorcee Wendy Oberman is terrified she might fall into the trap. Since her marriage break-up three years ago, Wendy, 46, has centred her life on her only child, nine-year-old Ben, and now sees the danger signs in herself.
> 'When he first went abroad on holiday with my ex-husband I wept every night,' she says. 'I knew he would be enjoying himself but it was agony for me to be separated from my baby.
> 'I get upset over ridiculous things. When he made his first Valentine card at school, all his friends sent their card to their mums, but Ben sent his to a little classmate and I felt terribly sad. When he went off to a camp I couldn't stop myself phoning up on the first night.
> 'I once had a boyfriend whose mother waited up every night to feed him sandwiches, even though he was in his twenties. She wouldn't allow any other woman to get close and I don't want to have that effect on Ben.

'The mother who doesn't let go of her son is guilty of emotional abuse. She is choking his emotional development . . . When you don't have a good partnership with a man there is a great danger of turning your child into the perfect lover.'[20]

Psychiatrist Dr Ross Campbell writes about the 'too much love' controversy: the difference between mollycoddling a child and offering him unconditional love.[21] He says parents must ask themselves, 'Is the love I am giving my child appropriate?'

According to Dr Campbell, children need 'a superabundance of appropriate love', but no inappropriate love at all. He identifies four categories of inappropriate love: possessiveness; seductiveness (which may be more common than we may realise); vicariousness (living one's life through the child); and role-reversal (where the child is placed in charge of the parent's emotional needs, and becomes a confidant to emotions he cannot really cope with or comprehend).

Psychotherapist and counsellor Carole Rudd described to me the principle of 'consonance', which is what the over-involved parent seeks. Consonance is the state of harmony or merging that a baby feels with his mother, and it is entirely appropriate for babies. As the child grows older, he moves out of the state of consonance into a state of increasing separateness. The primary task of parents is gradually to allow this process to happen. It is not our job to keep up with children at every stage, to feel what they are feeling, or to force them to be more like us. It is to let go.

If a child fully bonds with his mother at the appropriate time, he may continue to seek consonance with others, to 'be like' them, or to attempt to make them like him. But the truly strong and independent adult does not seek to merge. She is content in herself and is happy to meet others at their boundaries. The over-mothering parent suffers from ill-bonded beginnings. Rather than face up to her own needs, she seeks to satisfy them by merging with her children.

Continuum therapist Jean Liedloff examines what may happen if a parent reverses roles with her child, acting out her own needs, and demanding love. When parents are so involved in their own emotions, there is simply no room for the child to be heard:

> The mother, regarded as possessive or over-attentive, is in fact not *giving* love in her concentrated efforts to win her child's undivided interest; she is demanding it. She often plays the role of 'little girl', and tries to beguile her child with infantile cues into paying attention to her or feeling sorry for her. Unable to prevail against her pull on him, the child's pull upon *her* goes unnoticed . . .[22]

We are all, to some degree or another, still children inside. So when our children raise issues that we have long buried, when they appear, in their youthful vitality, to be stronger than we are, we may turn to them for comfort, and insist that they take care of us. This is damaging for the child, who is not equipped to handle his parents' longing. It confers on him a maturity that he does not possess, and robs him of his childhood.

It is all too easy to mould our children to fit the emotional roles we require of them, says Solveig Sandström Taylor: 'Children will push themselves very hard to see their parents happy. They are dependent on their parents in every way, that's why they are so vulnerable.'

MY FEARS, YOUR FEARS

A recent British study of 114,000 schoolchildren attempted to find out what children really did in the mornings. Who woke them up? Did they eat breakfast? Watch television? The study contained some fascinating asides and direct quotes from the children, including the following remark:

> One boy explained that his mother laid out £1.50 a day for his bus fares and food. By his own swift arithmetic, he reckoned she spent £500 last year getting him to school.

School was an expensive item. It worried his mother. Did that worry the children? Their hands shot up, yes, they worried about their parents' worries.[23]

Although many of us believe we shield our children from adult fears, the likelihood is that children take on board their parents' concerns, as well as their own anxieties about exams, friends, puberty and personal appearance. Being aware of others' emotions is, in itself, no bad thing, but it helps if we understand that children soak up their parents' moods subliminally and are therefore highly suggestible to emotion.

When we examine our motives, we may discover the subtle ways in which we use our children. Giving ourselves the job of maintaining our children's happiness, for instance, is one way of ensuring that we feel needed. But it also enhances our feelings of guilt, and makes parenting an arduous task. As parentcraft author Elaine Mazlish said, when she realised that her children were responsible for their own happiness:

> It is a tremendous relief not to have to take so much responsibility all the time. I used to feel that if my children were happy, then I must have done something right. If they were unhappy, then I must have done something wrong. If they caught a cold, it was because I didn't dress them properly. It was wonderful to finally be able to reduce some of my guilt by putting the responsibility, not blame, back on the children and by treating them as if they were responsible.[3]

We cannot make our children happy, and nor do we need to allow them to make us miserable along with them. It does not help the sad child if, when he shares his emotions, his parents become depressed, too. In fact, it makes things worse, because instead of attending to the child's feelings, parents become overwhelmed by their own. What the child seeks is sympathy, not mood-sharing, as Faber and Mazlish describe:

Just because Andy was dejected about having no one to play with for the afternoon didn't mean that I had to share his misery. Just because Jill was almost twitching with fear over a unit test didn't mean I had to twitch along with her. Dr Ginott had often pointed out that it was in the interest of a parent's mental health not to be infected by his child's moods. He'd say, 'A doctor would be of little use to his patient if he were to catch his every illness.'

My parents could never have understood this. They would have been ashamed to smile when we were unhappy. To them it would have been a sign that they didn't care. A *real* parent suffers along with his children.[24]

Moods tend to be infectious, and it is often difficult to allow one family member to get on with his or her suffering, while the others retain their own feelings. In many families, it is expected that children take on the mood of the parents. But a parent who expects her child to share her moods is seeking consonance, and is out of order.

VIVE LA DIFFERENCE

Very often, all a child wants to say is, 'I am different from you', to be acknowledged as a person with his own feelings, his own mind, the right to make his own mistakes. Teacher John Holt saw through the disruptive tactics of a child in his class, to an individual who wanted to be accepted. 'Jane' was, in fact, his favourite in that particular class, and here he gives his reasons:

The more I see of our troublemaking Jane, and the more I think about her, the clearer it becomes that she has a great need to feel truly loved, but feels that being loved when she is nice, good, obedient, etc., does not count. *Loved* is a tricky word here; perhaps I should say admired, appreciated, or even honoured and respected. She is like Cyrano; she thinks nothing could be more contemptible than to try to get approval and affection from others by saying, doing, and being what they want.

Isn't there much to admire in this? Perhaps someday she will feel that she can oblige and help the people she likes without having to worry about whether she can get anything out of it for herself. Right now, she finds it hard to show her natural affection, as other children might, just by being affectionate. On the contrary, she feels she must continually test, by misbehaving, the affection of others for her . . .

She is at my lunch table these days, and is delightful company; she's even making vague gestures in the direction of better table manners. I wish I could persuade her that she need not every day give our affection for her the acid test, but I guess only time will do that. At lunch the other day she said to me, 'I *hate* teachers!' and then gave me a 1/100-second smile and a hard sock on the arm. How much easier her life would be if we did not continually oblige her to choose between our adult approval and her own self-respect.[25]

A child constantly seeks the reassurance of a safe environment. He has a great deal of love to give, and does not judge the adults around him for their moods, but he soon finds himself judged. All children want is to be accepted, their mistakes to be forgiven, and their emotional truth to be heard. If the-world-as-he-tells-it does not seem to satisfy the adult audience, then a child may resort to lying instead. His lies may be a product of his ingenuity, but they can also be motivated by fear, as bio-energetic therapist Alexander Lowen describes:

All children lie at some time or other in their lives. They do it to explore the role of deceit and to sense the power it carries. Children will lie to test their ability to deceive their parents. It gives them a feeling of control if they get away with it. But they will also lie if they are afraid of the consequences truth may bring. In both cases they have gained something and lost something. The gain was in the sense of power and control or in the avoidance of punishment. But the loss is in the pleasure of being straightforward.[26]

It feels good to tell the truth of our own feelings and emotions. Children who are used to being heard are likely to respect their own feelings, and to be self-empowered. When faced with a dangerous situation, they are more likely to protect themselves, to say 'no' to strangers, for instance. You can teach a whole class of children the word 'no', but it requires a lot of courage and self-awareness to sense a truly suspicious situation and stand up for yourself in it.

A young child's feelings constantly seek expression, and we should recognise this as a healthy sign. The child may irritate us with his complaints and demands, but perhaps we should be honoured that he has chosen to bring them to us. Here, a teacher is flattered to be trusted with the unsavoury truth by one of her young pupils:

> One day a little first-grader said to his teacher, 'I just love to hit people and bite them and scratch them and hurt them. I *like* to make kids cry!' Another teacher chanced to overhear this remark. She said later to the boy's teacher, 'Now I've heard everything. Why, if that child stood there and told me that he liked to hit people and bite them and make them cry, I'd have told him what I thought of him!'
>
> 'But Pete was complimenting our relationship,' said Pete's teacher. 'He was telling me the most unflattering things that he could about himself. Soon he will be able to go on to a more positive way of thinking.'
>
> 'You mean it's a compliment to have a child tell you exactly what he thinks?' said the skeptic, with more than just a trace of derision edging her voice.
>
> The next day she stopped Pete's teacher. 'Say, I tried that technique of yours,' she said.
>
> 'What happened?' Pete's teacher inquired.
>
> 'You know that ornery, sulky Jacob in my room? Well,

as he came in my room this morning, I reached down and grabbed him by the shoulder, and I said, "Look here, Jacob, tell me just what you think of me." And Jacob stared at me blank as ever. "I mean it," I said, "I won't do a thing to you no matter what you say." And Jacob growled and said, "I think you're *crazy* if you think I'd tell you what I think of *you*!"' And Jacob's teacher laughed heartily. 'Not so bad for a first try, is it?'[27]

We may grab our children by the shoulders, but we cannot force them to share their feelings with us. It is easy to destroy the atmosphere of trust by acting as judge, by simply arguing with them, or shouting them down. Roald Dahl, the best-selling children's author, refused to play the role of superior grown-up in his books. When asked to write a safety manual for the British Railways board, he included this disclaimer:

I have a VERY DIFFICULT job here.

I am totally convinced that most grown-ups have completely forgotten what it was like to be a child between say the age of five and ten. They all **think** they can remember. Parents think they can remember and so do teachers. Some of course actually can, but very few . . . I can remember exactly what it was like. I am certain I can . . .

. . . The child is surrounded by beastly GIANTS, and the trouble with these beastly giants is that they seem to spend most of their lives telling the child WHAT TO DO and WHAT NOT TO DO . . .

What is the result of all this? I'll tell you precisely what it is. Deep down inside the child's mind (subconsciously) the giants become THE ENEMY. Your teachers become THE ENEMY. Even your loving parents become THE ENEMY. Not outwardly, but inwardly, subconsciously.

This explains very clearly why **Matilda** is far and away the most popular children's book I have written and was bought by over half a million children in Britain alone in the first six months. In it there are a pair of perfectly revolting parents and a foul tyrant of a teacher. The young reader is invited to hate them all and he does. He says to himself, 'Thank goodness we have here a writer who understands our secret feelings.' Children may not realise it themselves, but that is the real reason why **Matilda** is so popular among them.[28]

Roald Dahl invites children to hate. Most authors, parents and other adults with power over children invite them to be happy, to love, to see beauty everywhere and to deny any negative feelings that may creep in. But Dahl knew that a bit of good old hate wouldn't do any harm. He helped children to express their bad feelings, and make them feel a lot better. And he sold millions of books in the process.

We may not all have the narrative skills of Roald Dahl, but we do not need them. If we do not know what to say to our children, we could simply say less. Ginott Haim, the child psychologist, used to advise parents, 'Whenever possible, replace a paragraph with a sentence, a sentence with a word, a word with a gesture.'[29] When a child wants comfort, simply holding him may be enough. The less we say, the less harm we do, and the more we are inclined to listen, as Adele Faber describes:

Once, at a workshop, I heard some of the parents asking their children if they had had fun in the playgroup. When one child said, 'No, it was boring', the parent didn't know what to say and just replied, 'Oh.' That was genius. 'Oh' simply acknowledges the child's experience. He or she is allowed to be bored, allowed to be unhappy, and it doesn't have to destroy the parent.[3]

We don't have to be ready with quick replies for our children. We don't have to be able to give the right answer, or know how best to deal with their problems, or offer them our solutions. They have enough nous to sort out their own problems, and they do not want to know the acceptability (or otherwise) of their feelings. A child ideally needs his parents to be true to themselves, and to give him the space and permission to find out what *he* truly feels. Children want much less of their parents than most parents are willing to give.

Letting go as children grow: emotions

- Children's feelings are primarily expressed through their bodies: babies use the entire body to cry; older children will slump. It helps to learn to read the signs
- Asking a child to put all his feelings into words may be asking too much
- One way to encourage children to talk is make yourself available and then appear to be slightly busy. Let them draw you in
- Children do not need us to anticipate, interpret or deny their emotions. Reason and reassurance are rarely helpful when dealing with feelings
- Children have a high body awareness and often sense others' emotions and fears. They may also have a surprisingly wide range of anxieties of their own
- If children can express their fears and negative emotions as they go along, before long, other emotions will follow

---

9

BREAKING AWAY –
WHY TEENAGERS NEED US STILL

. . . her instinct to leave is stronger than the bond with her parents.

a lesser black-backed gull leaves the nest, *Survivors*, BBC1, 1990

You can't control an independent heart . . .
If you love somebody, set them free.

'If You Love Somebody Set Them Free' from 'Dream of the Blue Turtles',
1985, Sting

Of all the transitions in our lives, adolescence is perhaps the
most obvious. The shift from childhood to adulthood may be a
time of rebellion, of turmoil, of intense passion, or of anti-
climax. As a child adjusts his position in the world, adapting to
his new-found status and responsibility, parents have the
choice of resisting or accepting the pull. And since adolescents
stand uncertainly on the threshold of adulthood for many
years in our culture, the pulling and resisting can take a long
time.

Until I had one of my own, the nearest I ever came to
parenting a teenager was on our annual holiday. Cousin Laura
came away with us to help look after Frances and Alice when
they were small. It gave me an inkling of what was in store for
us, and I decided we weren't ready for it yet. When your oldest
child is five, fifteen seems a long way ahead. My husband Paul

and I did not have the run-in or the experience that would have helped us to deal with issues of freedom and control, negotiation and participation. I talked to other parents of teenagers at our campsite, and was impressed with their laid-back attitude and sense of humour. I was panicking because I hadn't seen our teenager all day. The other parents reassured me: 'Don't worry, they come back when they run out of money.'

The funny thing is, that when we did come to deal with the highs and lows of our adolescent and pre-adolescent children, the intervening years had in many ways prepared us for the experience. Without being instant experts, it felt as though we had been rehearsing for this phase all along. And with the high volume of research and media discussion on the Inner Life of the Western Teenager, parents can hardly be caught by surprise. The reality of living with teenagers is not always as terrible as our imaginations would have us believe.

When asked to describe the behaviour of their teenage children in a survey, parents gave a long and varied list of adjectives: marvellous, unpredictable, changeable, volatile, well-mannered, considerate, intense, changing all the time, assertive, vulnerable, sensitive and insensitive, intelligent, irrational.[1] 'Teenage years' is a comfortable term to classify the stormy period between immaturity and maturity, but it does not tell us much about the variety of experience one might expect. Two fifty-year-olds would not expect to be lumped together because of their age, and yet we are happy to talk about a group of 'teenagers' as if they fitted the same mould. The word tends to make adolescents sound like a gang, sharing the same interests and going through the same problems, but this is obviously not the case.

ONLY CONNECT

Magical Child author Joseph Chilton Pearce identifies adolescence as the fifth matrix shift: childhood is nearly done. But even though the child is preparing to stand alone, to leave home and, perhaps, to find a partner of his own, the emotional connection with the parent is always there:

By adolescence, the biological plan is that we become our own matrix, consisting of mind-brain and body . . . That is, the mind-brain should eventually become its own matrix, its own source of power, possibility, and safe place to stand . . .

So long as we live (or she lives), the physical mother remains the primary matrix even though we separate from her and move into larger matrices.[2]

This is one of the paradoxes of letting go. It is never about total separation. Now that we are reaching the end of the journey, we might assume that our aim should be a complete disengagement from the child, so he can take a grasp on adulthood. But in a healthy society, children never walk away entirely and parents do not sever all connections.

In this context, 'letting go' has more to do with respect than turning away. Children, if they are brought up to bond with their parents, their families and the wider community, will want to return – and they especially need us as they go through the turmoil of transition to adulthood. As social psychologist Terri Apter puts it:

There is a common confusion between the concepts of individuality and separation. Without being aware of it, many parents think their children can only develop their individual identity through psychological distance or separation from their parents. But in fact, people gain an identity as much through their sense of belonging to a person or family or religion or locality or nation as they do from refining their points of difference . . . Human development is relational.[3]

For the Western adolescent, moving towards independence is unlikely to be a smooth affair. It is possible that he has not moved with confident ease through the various developmental stages so far, and that instead of feeling fulfilled, well-bonded and empowered, he arrives at puberty in a state of frustration and bewilderment. What happens during adolescence cannot be divorced from all that has gone before. A twelve-year-old who is still treated like a six-year-old by his parents is likely to have difficulties adjusting to the demands of the teenage years.

There are few rituals to ease him through the changes he is going through. Confirmation or bar mitzvah may confer on a child the honour and responsibilities of religious maturity, but they are rarely matched by social responsibility. There is no symbolic cut-off point, after which a child becomes a 'woman' or a 'man', with the privileges, power and status that entails. Modern society does not even offer a reliable definition of what it means to *be* a man or a woman. As Dr John Coleman, director of the Trust for the Study of Adolescence describes, the teenager bears the brunt of this confusion:

> . . . imagine the pressures upon any teenager. In the first place their own bodies are changing, and growing, leading to radical alterations in size, shape, strength, and self image. With these changes come pressures inside the individual towards adult, mature behaviour. At the same time friends also act to encourage young people to grow up fast, as does society at large through advertising, television and so on.
>
> On the other hand parents often try to hold back any rapid moves towards independence, feeling anxious about whether their son or daughter is mature enough to cope with the temptations of the real world. In addition the teenager too will have doubts about how fast he or she wants to grow up. At times the freedom of being an adult will seem very attractive, but there will be moments when standing on your own feet will feel very scary indeed.
>
> These conflicting pressures from within the young person and from the outside world almost always lead to a sense of confusion. The teenager is not sure, cannot be sure, exactly what he or she wants, and this uncertainty will of course be reflected in behaviour. Furthermore we must remember that society itself cannot decide how to treat adolescents. What sense can you make of the

fact that in the U.K. sixteen-year-olds can join the army and get married, yet they cannot vote, give blood, drive a car or own a credit card? . . . Is it any wonder that they feel confused? If adults can't make up their minds how to treat young people, how can young people themselves work out how to behave?[4]

At around the age of twelve, fantasy play (if it has been allowed to continue for this long) will usually cease. Fantasy is the playground of the emotions, a safe place in which a child can explore new situations, experiment with 'what ifs' and rehearse for the next stage of his development. As the child enters adolescence, he starts to become capable of pure abstract thought. His new ideas often challenge the status quo, as it is fitting they should. Now he does not role-play his way through inarticulated fears, but enacts them through his everyday behaviour. He may become withdrawn and uncooperative, he may undergo drastic mood swings, or he may choose friends who allow him to experiment with different lifestyles. All of these forms of behaviour are an attempt to come to terms with the transition to adult life.

It is too late now to play 'mummies and daddies', the adolescent is old enough to *be* a mummy or daddy, and in many rural cultures would already have begun this role.

Traditional societies hand over responsibility to children very gradually from a young age. Toddlers are allowed to prepare vegetables; children as young as six or seven carry their baby siblings around on their backs; youngsters of ten or eleven will have already honed the necessary skills for survival and hunting, including the use of sharp tools. By the time they go through their puberty rituals, such children are merely celebrating the end of years of active involvement and effectiveness in the wider community.

By contrast, Western culture prefers to offer a cerebral education, to separate children into peer groups and to encourage them to enjoy their childhood for as long as possible. Their years of usefulness have scarcely begun before they run up against a raft of rights and responsibilities (work part-time at fourteen; get hitched at sixteen; drive a car at seventeen, to take the British model . . .) There is a tendency in our society to remove children from the raw edge of experience. Children are sometimes banned from hospital wards, especially where birth and dying are involved. It is often assumed that children cannot cope with death or severe illness, and parents may try to protect them from such first-hand experience. We as adults even contrive to protect *ourselves* from the messier aspects of living. The Western teenager may be aware that he has not yet finished being a child, that he is not ready to assume the full weight of responsibility and commitment. And for this catastrophe, he may blame his parents.

PARENT SHOCK

Parents are sometimes stunned by the accusations and rebellions that come from their teenage child. If life seems hard for the young person, it is equally hard for them. Life may have been humming along quite smoothly until now. Parents may have settled nicely into a 'way of being' with their children, when suddenly they find themselves challenged. Their parenting strategies gradually become inadequate as their child refuses to be a child any more.

Everything, from the level of intimacy to their level of control, can be up for grabs. Their lifestyle comes under scrutiny. Their attitudes and opinions are greeted with cynicism and derision. Parents who feel they have nurtured and cared for their child to the best of their ability, and are happy to continue to do so, suddenly become a source of embarrassment to their offspring. American writer Elizabeth Berg describes the new role prescribed to her by her pre-pubescent child, in all its glorious negativity:

> One minute they swear they want to live with you for ever; the next, they tell you to take a hike because their friends are coming over – after you've provided a non-embarrassing snack, of course.

All of this might be easier to take if you could remember that all parents are, or will be, in the same boat. But the distressing message that you get from your child is that *everybody else's* parents are better than *you*. For example, apparently I am the only mother around who hasn't wised up to the obvious virtues of eye shadow. My husband and I are apparently much meaner, more unfair, and less hip than anyone else in the world.

There is no predicting when this decline in stature will begin, but when it does, you may find that you have trouble keeping track of the constantly changing rules and regulations for parental behaviour. Here, then, is a list of (a few) dos and (a lot of) don'ts to help other parents whose status has deteriorated in a similarly distressing fashion.

1. Do not come to your child's classroom to visit when you are invited to do so. Although you may believe that the school is sincere in its offer, the overture is a sham, simply a device for exposing parents who are nerds.

2. Do not put anything healthy in your child's lunch box, including whole wheat bread.

3. Do not attempt to chat with your child's friends.

4. Do not ignore your child's friends.

5. Do not inquire as to who is on the other end of a telephone line, since this is 'gross' . . . [5]

And so on. The list of 'don'ts' includes such clauses as: '15. If you are the father, do not lose any hair'; '20. Do not make those wheezy noises with your nose when you breathe'; and '23. Do not suggest, ever – in any way, shape or form – that you are, uh, intimate with your spouse.' I was reminded of these commandments recently in the swimming pool changing rooms, when a woman confided that her teenage son had instructed her not to grunt while playing tennis: 'It sounds as though you're bonking,' he told her.

Just as a parent is coming round to the idea of giving her child more freedom, more responsibility and the chance to make up his own mind, in waltzes the child with his own set of demands. In his immature way, he is trying to claim control and to help his parents to see that there are viewpoints other than their own.

One irony is that, while some children are going through rapid personality shifts, they may accuse their bewildered *parents* of changing. Parent workshop leaders Bill and Win Sweet recall hearing this accusation from their adolescent children:

> There was a time after Jill and Jim went back to school, following our home-based schooling experience, that they seemed to be wearing masks. Words kept coming out of their mouths that we couldn't recognize. Especially frustrating were the assertions that *we'd* changed: 'You feel . . . about me,' 'You expect me to do . . .,' 'You're going to explode because I got a B in English,' and on and on. Jill and Jim knew us well and knew we had never reacted as they described. So, who were these people standing in front of us? They couldn't be Jill and Jim even though they looked familiar.[6]

I came up against the power of the pre-adolescent child in an interesting way with my second daughter, Alice. Alice was lucky to belong to a lovely, flexible group of friends throughout her primary school years and their friendship remained intact, despite the inevitable separations which came with the transfer to senior schools.

Aged only twelve, the girls, some armed with mobile telephones, ensured that their Young Girls' Network stayed in frequent contact. They arranged social events, planned impromptu parties and generally organised their lives with an efficiency which left their parents breathless. We mothers, running a step or three behind our daughters, sometimes resorted to phoning each other in private to find out what was going on.

In these conversations we tried to form a vaguely united front, while retaining our individual rights as parents to make our own house rules. It was through the support of friends that I learnt how to parent this particular adolescent child.

To some extent, I think we were coerced into concessions the girls would never have won by themselves. 'So-and-so is getting her ears pierced as soon as she is thirteen,' Alice would tell me, with a pause for contrast at her own plight at being still ear-lobus intactus. Or: 'Such-and-such a person is allowed to watch fifteens.' [15-rated movies].

If we ever had any guns, they were suddenly swathed in grease and it was becoming almost impossible to stick to them. Peer pressure, they call it, but it's more than this. It's an advanced form of communication which proves that the human species is still evolving and that all the technology is on the children's side.

As they attempted to slip under the trip wire of adult consent, the girls used all the persuasion skills at their disposal. They were aware that their mothers relied heavily on each others' judgement. They reminded us, often and separately, that we were the 'only one' who ever laid down any rules or caused a fuss even though we knew otherwise. If life had been up to them, it would have turned into one long sleepover, featuring liberal amounts of hot chocolate, painted nails and piercings. And this was before any of them really discovered boys. This was only the beginning.

COMPENSATORY PARENTING

When you resort to ringing other parents in private to find out what the consensus ought to be, you have already admitted your own vulnerability. But lucky the parent who has other parents to ring. The difficulties of managing the modern teenager are dissipated when they are shared with a laugh and a little adult solidarity. Checking in on what's normal can help parents gain a sense of perspective and a feeling of strength. And strength is needed if we are to withstand the storms of adolescence without getting swept out to sea.

Studies of how teenagers change the family dynamic suggest that parents – as well as children – need a strong sense of self-esteem in order to cope. Today's parents seem all too willing to accept whatever blame is flying around: from their children, from unsupportive partners, or from the media. In a paper called 'The Balancing Act of Parenting', social workers Peter Currie and Elin Evans uncover the cycle of frustration experienced by parents of adolescents with 'unacceptable behaviour'. What is evident is the parents' willingness to take full responsibility for their grown children's behaviour, as they have done since those children were small:

> Most of the parents attending our groups tend to question themselves and try to find excuses for their children's behaviour . . . They look for events in the past for which they feel responsible, in order to explain the child's unacceptable behaviour or the breakdown of their relationship. Typically these past occurrences range from very minor to major life-events, from having spent a single night in hospital to adoption and parental divorce. Although we acknowledge that these life-events may well be significant, we state that neither the parents nor ourselves can now do anything to reverse them. Our argument at this stage is that we need above all to reinforce the parents' need to look at their situation in the present and work towards improving their relationships in the future. In an attempt to help explore the necessity for looking forward, we go on to highlight a cycle of events common to virtually all these cases with which we deal.
>
> The cycle usually begins with the parents' guilt feelings. Because they feel guilty, or in some way responsible for their child's behaviour they tend to compensate for, or overparent the child in an attempt to correct the behaviour.
>
> The parents have difficulties in separating their own rights from their assumed parental rights and are consumed by the parental role, which directly places them in conflict with their child's growth towards independence and the child's wish to assume greater responsibility for itself.[7]

In a sense, parents are right to take responsibility for their children, because, given a completely different set of circumstances, things would have turned out differently. But we cannot change the past, we can only come to terms with it. Blame is futile. We need to let go of the guilt that we carry around, and to which our teenagers may alert us.

Researchers have noticed that parents respond to perceived inadequacies (to their guilt feelings) by trying to *do more parenting*. They clamp down more firmly on their children, or they overprotect them, to compensate for 'a bad birth', or 'not having been breastfed', or 'the divorce'. This is categorically not what the adolescent wants. Whatever the perceived failures of the past, children need to be freed from their parents' guilt in the present. Parents also need to be freed from the intolerable burden of 'babying' their nearly adult children:

> We put it to parents that they are currently assuming far too much responsibility. This is denying them the right to consider their own individual needs. As the balance is redressed and they hand over more of the responsibilities to the child and to others they can at last fulfill some of their ambitions and dreams themselves, such as going away for a weekend on their own, spending an evening out and Sunday morning in bed.[7]

TESTING, TESTING

At adolescence more than at any other time, the child is likely to be testing the parent. This is largely an unconscious process. Deprived of a reliable social model for adulthood, or a ritualised transition period, the child challenges his parents instead to lay down the limits and to let him know how strong and reliable the framework of his family really is. If a parent adopts a doormat-like approach, giving in to every demand, then she deprives her child of her own strength and leadership. It is important that family limits are known and understood.

But if a parent reacts by trying to regain the upper hand, she may be in for a bloody battle. Laying down by-laws on every form of behaviour known to man is likely to alienate the teenager and make him rebel. Dr Coleman advises parents,

Don't waste your time and effort fighting battles over minor issues. Keep your energy for the major issues – things that you know will make a difference. Parents have a right, for example, to make rules about behaviour which can threaten health or safety, and young people will usually appreciate that such rules are for their own benefit, and reflect their parents' care and concern. Teenagers will not feel like that about rules which seem petty, and which appear to them to be for the benefit of the adults rather than the young people.[8]

Asked what they thought teenagers needed from their parents, parents replied with the following qualities: understanding, patience, boundaries, tolerance, affection, reassurance and discipline, time, love and security.[1] In other words, acceptance and direction. 'You do not lead by hitting people over the head – that's assault, not leadership,' said US president Dwight D. Eisenhower.

WHEN THE WIND BLOWS

What a teenager needs one minute may be quite different from what is required the next. Cuddles and intimate moments may be just as important as privacy, and if a young person feels he can have his own space when he wants it, he is more likely to indicate his need for tenderness. Adolescence is like a wind; it can be a warm, wet south-westerly that is vigorous but does no damage; or a cold north wind that is destructive and rips up everything in its path.

Parents are under great pressure when the wind starts up. Even if they do not feel in control, they may want to appear so. It takes a great deal of inner confidence and self-awareness to stand by as your child undergoes a radical transformation. As teacher David Gribble says,

The reason we do not always behave kindly and well is that we are not sufficiently sure of being loved, admired and approved of if we do. Far too often we are afraid of being thought soft, unfair, foolish or unconventional.[9]

Many parents are motivated by what other people will think. We want our children to have good manners, good friends, a neat appearance, a loving and reliable nature . . . and we want them to do it all in front of our friends. But no method of control yet devised can make our children live and act exactly as we want them to. Instead, we might be thankful for the ways in which they are different from us; this is a mark of their independence, and a sign that they are busy creating themselves.

We might, as parents, imagine that the child's pull is always away from us. We assume this from our teenagers' challenging behaviour, from their glue-like attachment to their peers, and even from their clothes, which seem designed to create intergenerational ripples of dismay. But as Terri Apter points out, the road to maturity is more of a zigzag than a straight line. Like the baby who goes through many regressions, the adolescent (despite outward appearances) may be frightened and insecure. What feels to us like a stormy wind must be a Mistral to him, tearing up all his childhood assumptions. Or could it be like the tornado that whipped through a certain farm in Kansas?

> Perhaps *The Wizard of Oz* is such a popular story because it taps into this common dilemma of the threshold years: the longing for independence and adventure, and the constant search for a way home again.[10]

The Wizard of Oz, it so happens, is a film used by movie therapists in Britain and America to help young people work out their angers and fears.[11] The Lion, the Scarecrow and the Tin Man embody Dorothy's anxieties as she approaches adulthood: where will she find the necessary courage, intelligence and warm-heartedness? By the end of her journey, of course, Dorothy realises she possessed these qualities all along. It is no coincidence that the Yellow Brick Road zigzags all over the place, or that Dorothy has to rely on her friends to guide her on her way. Reliance on family and friends is a crucial aspect of the transition towards autonomy. It helps to keep the child grounded during the storm.

When a child goes through a turbulent adolescence, there may be grief on both sides for the child that has left. The adolescent himself may regret the force and unpredictability of his feelings, and wish, in part, at least, that life could be as simple as it used to seem to be. For their part, parents may wish that they could have their little boy or girl back again, the one who wanted cuddles, who looked up to them in awe, who was happy to come on the family holiday, and who said 'When I grow up, I'll marry you, Mummy.'

But this child has to leave home. He may not actually walk out of the door, but he must stand back from the all-enclosing family pattern in order to discover his own values.

THE MOTHER'S BLESSING

In medieval romance, which is the origin of the fairy-tale, growing up was symbolised by the hero's going out to seek his fortune. (He was always a hero, but the analogy applies equally to the modern girl.) Typically, the hero would come from a disastrously poor single-parent family, and it was essentially the mother-figure he was breaking away from. In one version, the poor old woman offers her departing son a choice of two gifts: a curse and the last scrap of bread, or her blessing and no bread at all.

Only the fool chooses the bread, and soon comes crawling home again. The good son chooses the blessing, which equips him to go out in the world. Our hero then spends years (or a year and a day) in the wilderness (adolescence), undergoing various tests of his inner strength. The reward for his valour, impetuous courage and, in particular, his patience, is the hand in marriage of a noble, virginal woman. In one symbolic swoop, he moves into manhood and secures a prosperous future for himself and his ageing mother.

The widow's blessing is her letting-go. She does not resist

the loss of her child, for she knows she *must* lose him if he is to become a man. In the fairy-tale, the mother offers her son the choice between a harmonious and a bitter farewell. In real life, it is usually the parent who decides. Children may put their parents through a hell of a time during adolescence, but *it is the way parents react* that will determine how easily the wounds heal. Parents retain the power to love a child unconditionally, or to reject him (because they feel rejected themselves by their children's behaviour). Historically, this involved throwing a child out because of an unsuitable marriage partner, or an unwanted pregnancy. Today, it is more likely to be a falling-out over political differences, or a drifting apart into conflicting lifestyles. Or it may be a general feeling on both sides that neither party likes the other very much.

So how can we 'bless' our children, while they seem to be blaming us, blaming themselves, or blaming the world in general? Social psychologist Terri Apter suggests a list of measures: accept some regressive behaviour; provide a steady stream of information about the family; listen and respond calmly and key in to positive areas in the child's life. Journalist and author Kate Figes confirms that the short-sharp-shock approach to letting children go is no longer appropriate in an already short-sharp world:

> Liberal sentiments in family life tend to work; authoritarian ones tend to provoke insurrection, animosity and great unhappiness. Tough and repressive regimes at home force teenagers to flout authority more as a means of defiance and in ways which will most aggravate their parents.[12]

Figes reminds us of the everyday agony in Anne Frank's diary. Cooped up as she was with parents and friends hiding from the Nazis, Anne became understandably engrossed in the emotions of her own adolescence. She wrote:

> They criticise everything, and I mean everything about me: my behaviour, my personality, my manners; every

inch of me, from head to toe and back again, is the subject of gossip and debate. I'd like to feel that Father really loves me, not because I'm his child, but because I'm me, Anne.[13]

There is an astonishing wisdom in these words. Anne wants to be loved (unconditionally accepted) for being herself, *not merely because she is her parents' daughter*. When we 'let go' with adolescents, it is not a question of giving up on the child, but of demonstrating that unconditional love which is the only blessing they need.

A SENSITIVE TIME

If a teenager is personally abusive to his parents, it is not surprising that they take it personally. But the adolescent bitter words may sound harsher than they are meant to. Dr John Coleman advises parents not to become too involved in their teenager's anger:

Remember . . . that, even if the anger or hostility is directed at you personally, it is rarely intended to wound or harm you. Just as a toddler, throwing a temper tantrum, might try to kick or hit you, so a teenager expresses feelings which are hurtful or rejecting, but which in reality are more to do with his or her own inner turmoil. If you can remain slightly detached, if you can stand back a little and not let yourself become too personally involved in these angry feelings, you will find it all much easier to deal with.[14]

Although 'tantrum' is a perjorative way to describe the emotions of the child who is expressing his anger, Dr Coleman correctly identifies the inner turmoil of the child. The sensitive teenager often hits out in frustration – it's just that parents sometimes find themselves in the firing line. A lot has been written on how to 'deal with' tantrums, little of which suggests that parents take their children's anger seriously, or that they should look for the root cause of the child's lashing-out. Italian educator Maria Montessori had a lot to say about tantrums, and her words could as well be applied to the teenager as to the three-year-old:

> The tantrums of the sensitive periods are external manifestations of an unsatisfied need, expressions of alarm over a danger, or of something being out of place. They disappear just as soon as there is a possibility of satisfying the need or of eliminating the danger. One can at times observe in the child a sudden calm following a state of agitation that seemed almost pathological.[15]

Montessori's 'sensitive periods' are a specific reference to a child's learning patterns in the early years. But the word 'sensitive' applies to adolescence in general. The teenager may be sensitive in his approach to the world, having discovered a passion for animals, ecology or community works. He may be sensitive in his emotional life, ready to light up with anger or elation at the mildest remark. Even his skin may become sensitive, as hormonal changes wreak their havoc. We should perhaps not forget that he is also sensitive to his new role in life, that of self-discovery.

PERSONAL POWER

The adolescent is at a highly acquisitive stage, where he is open to the experiences of imminent adult responsibility. During this phase, he absorbs a lot of new information and has to find ways to process his findings. Deprived of the opportunity to exercise his new personal powers, the adolescent may become frustrated and angry.

Everyday occurrences, such as eating at the family table or going out, provide opportunities for the parent to hand over responsibility to the child. The adolescent will often use the most ordinary occasions to make his mark, to challenge parents and their ways of relating to him. What he really wants to know is that his parents trust him to make his own judgements, and to be involved in family decisions. Research into decision-making has demonstrated that this is a vital stage for adolescents:

> One barrier to competent decision-making is the belief that decision-making is of no personal concern or relevance, or that it is entirely in the domain of adults . . . 24 per cent of thirteen-year-olds, 22 per cent of fourteen-year-olds, and 9 per cent of fifteen-year-olds believed that decision-making does not affect young people, or were uncertain in their beliefs. A small number of fifteen-year-olds believed that important decisions should be made solely by adults.
>
> . . . Low confidence to make decisions may stem from the limited opportunities given to adolescents to participate in decisions that affect them. For example, many adolescents believe that the school system excludes them from decision-making and they are powerless to influence decisions . . .
>
> It is argued that if adolescents feel constrained in their choice of goals, they become low in 'activation' and 'concentration' . . . Some adolescents develop a negative or even cynical attitude about the possibilities of influencing important decisions, and therefore become detached and apathetic.[10]

Having a voice in family matters is important to the teenager, even though he may not appreciate its value in building his self-esteem. The adolescent who is used to being dominated by his parents may not be ready to make decisions about his own life. For such a child, it would not help to insist that he suddenly take responsibility for himself. The work of handing over power should begin slowly.

In the 1970s, child psychologists John and Elizabeth Newson made a ground-breaking study of seven-year-olds at home in Nottingham, England, amply demonstrating the different ways in which families deal with issues of responsibility. The first child has already learnt a great deal of self-discipline at seven, while the second child waits for his parents to discipline him:

> Lace hand's wife:
> 'Last Sunday I wasn't feeling very well and I asked her to wash up for me, you know, and she turned round and she said "I'm not doing them", she says, "it isn't my job". Well, it's the first time she's ever said that to me. Well. I was really, you know, hurt, and I just looked at her; and she just sat there and looked at my face, and she said "Ooh, I'm sorry", and she did it.'
> Machine operator's wife:
> 'I think what it is, you know, he's had so many little smacks to *get* him to do things that now he doesn't even hear you if you just *tell* him to do things; I mean he's much worse for that than what he was, he used to take *some* notice of you – but now – you can tell him till you're blue in the face, he just seems to have to have that little smack to go with it, you know.'[17]

Communication between the machine operator's wife and her child is becoming increasingly less subtle, as she tries to take control. She succeeds only in being ignored. As she says, her son does not even hear her any more. Parents who cannot let their children be, often find themselves sucked further and further into a spiral of punishment and control. By the time they reach the teen years, many children are thoroughly alienated from their parents. Far from being invited to make important family decisions, they are not even trusted to get themselves dressed in the morning.

SECRET FEARS

The teenager's sensitivity, often felt so deeply, may not always surface in outward displays of emotion. Some adolescents keep their feelings bottled up – and then parents are left wondering exactly how or whether they should prise the lid open.

The first rule for concerned or suspicious parents is to avoid prying. Personal diaries and locked cupboards may contain some of the clues you are seeking, but unless you suspect serious crimes or face an obvious emergency, they are best left shut. Once trust has been destroyed, it becomes almost impossible for the sensitive teenager to confide in you again.

Childcare author Kate Figes reports that over-protected children are those most likely to become secretive. They are less likely to seek parental guidance for fear of being misunderstood.[18] So, since the aim is to stay in touch with our children's problems, we must paradoxically seek a little distance and demonstrate some respect in order to encourage them to be open about things.

Children with deep-seated problems often leave a trail of evidence for parents to respond to. If a child becomes completely withdrawn, he evidently needs help. But a certain amount of anxiety is as normal for teenagers in modern society as it is for their parents. Levels of tension vary enormously from culture to culture, family to family – and children swiftly learn to fret like adults do. One survey found that 79 per cent of teenagers worried about the perennial subject of exams[19] – far more than those who worried about domestic problems, divorce, or bullying. But children can fret for ages over the smallest of things, simply because they have no frame of reference.

Boys, in particular, are prone to keep their concerns to themselves. While girls may share intimacy with friends, chat freely with their mothers, read teen magazines and write in diaries, boys have fewer outlets. Journalist Nick Fisher, who helped to answer the trickle of boys' letters addressed to a teenage magazine, noticed how lonely and fearful the boys seemed to be:

A teenager boy's greatest fear is from his peers. To be known among your mates for having a tiny dick, an ugly girlfriend or, the absolute worst of all, being gay, is tantamount to social leprosy. And teenage boys can be immensely cruel to each other. Often, they delight in others' unhappiness and misfortune.

273

To show weakness and ask for help is like putting your neck on the block. So many boys finish their letters with lines like: 'I'm writing to you because I've no-one else to turn to,' 'I can't talk about this to my friends/parents/ teacher' or 'I could *never* go to a doctor about this.' They live their lives and contain their fears in a gut-wrenching world of isolation.[20]

It is important that we do not belittle children's own sensitivities, however trivial or transient they may seem to us. In the words of journalist Ruth Picardie,

> Teenagers have always worried about things. The world's mythic teenagers – Holden Caulfield in J D Salinger's *Catcher in the Rye*, James Dean in *Rebel Without a Cause*, the suicidal heroine of Sylvia Plath's *The Bell Jar* – are the biggest worriers of all. Being agonised is the whole point of being a teenager.[21]

We may not be able to take the agony away, but we can make sure our children know that we are available and willing to try.

ANYONE FOR SECONDS?

Parents may prepare themselves to be open about the big issues of adolescence, only to find that these are not the battlegrounds at all. Activities that a child has enjoyed all his life may suddenly become the major issues. It can infuriate parents to discover that every activity has a political sub-text, like the teenager who accuses his mother of being authoritarian and bourgeois because she asks him to join the family at dinner. To the adolescent, every activity can take on a symbolic importance.

Eating is one area that is fraught with difficulties. It is widely acknowledged that anorexia nervosa, an obsession with weight and a refusal to eat that mostly affects teenage girls, is a young person's attempt to regain control of her life. This, at least, is one area where she cannot be forced to comply like a child. Recent evidence from the United States suggests that boys and girls as young as ten suffer from the disease. Children would sometimes rather die, than eat to please those in power.

Not-eating represents, albeit negatively, what little power a person has left. It is, for instance, the method sometimes chosen by prisoners to bring their protests to public attention. Not-eating carries a profound message, as pacifists such as Gandhi were aware. Assertive toddlers know that there is nothing more likely to get mother worked up into a frenzy than refusing to eat.

For the mother, rejection of food may feel like a rejection of herself, whether her child is three or thirteen. American psychotherapist Kim Chernin, author of *The Hungry Self*, explains that food battles are intimately connected with the child's struggle for identity:

> . . . all the issues of development through which the child passes between infancy and adolescence are negotiated in a first, essential form through the relationship to food and feeding. Our efforts to gain a vital sense of trust, autonomy, initiative and industry – these struggles that take us into adolescence – are all issues that are experienced, perhaps even in their most crucial form, by the way we are taught to conduct ourselves with the food we eat . . .

> 'You'll sit there until you finish your meal,' we say to the child who refuses to eat, without in the least realizing how potently we engage in this way a heated debate about identity. 'Don't make a mess, I'll do it for you,' we say when the child reaches out to mix a chocolate milk. Food is so charged, so significant, so informed with primal meaning and first impressions of life, mothering, and the world that we might well expect the communications that take place through food to carry even more weight than those that arise when a child totters about knocking into furniture or pushes a truck across a floor.

And so we come, stage by stage in this way, to

adolescence, when the youth must struggle to form an image of what she is and may become. Is it a wonder, then, that she continues to express this struggle through her relationship to food?[22]

Kim Chernin describes young women who eat by themselves, vomit in secret and refuse to share food with other people in the family. Although anorexia nervosa and bulimia can affect adults, the onset of eating disorders is most usual in the teenage years, when issues of control, responsibility, autonomy and inner direction come to a focus.

The real life story of 'J', a sixteen-year-old orphan whose emotional integrity was shattered after the death of her grandfather, illustrates how the teenage struggle is expressed through food. Her refusal to eat was the only way J could think of to retain her integrity. The authorities could not respect J's decision. Journalist Carol Sarler reports:

Having manifestly failed to provide J with any kind of happiness – foster parents, we are told, 'could not cope' because she was traumatised after her grandfather's death (well, well!) – and having spotted that J was developing a tendency to lose weight, they consigned her to an adolescent psychiatric unit. And there, when the weight loss began to look more serious, it was duly decided that 'treatment' was in order. At the age of fifteen, the girl was subjected to the horror of having a tube forced through her nose and into her stomach . . . while her arms were encased in plaster to prevent her from removing it. This lasted three whole weeks.

Now they have come up with a smashing new idea: J should be moved, against her will, to a specialist unit for eating disorders and there, also against her will . . . be subjected to more 'treatment', as her doctors see fit. J fought this with the only card she had left: her status, now, as a sixteen-year-old . . . she and her solicitor argued that she had the right either to refuse to move or to accept the treatment. But last week three Appeal Court judges overruled that right and her wishes. They were profoundly wrong to have done so.

That J should have developed anorexia nervosa is not particularly suprising. Nobody yet has arrived at a full understanding of the disease, but it is widely accepted that an element in its structure is a strong desire for control. When a patient feels he or – much more commonly – she has control over nothing else in life, it can still be exerted over the flesh. Poor J could not control the shocking toll that death was taking upon her family – but, by heck, she could get her weight down to under six stone . . .

J had made a decision and, no matter how much we may wish that she had decided otherwise, she is old enough – and apparently sane enough – to have it respected . . . we certainly cannot tolerate a position where we say, through our legal system, 'You have the absolute right to your own decisions. Except sometimes.'[23]

It seems tragic that young people are still having to assert their basic need for autonomy at sixteen, an age when empowerment should be all but complete. Carol Sarler believes the issue of anorexia nervosa obscures that of childhood and the law. But it seems to me that these two issues are essentially one. The child is struggling to gain control of her own life, and society (*in loco parentis*) is unwilling to let go.

EASY DOES IT

One way or another, our children assert their differences, and they need to have them accepted. When we encourage our children to be dependent on us for any longer than is necessary, we curse them like the old woman in the fairy-tale. If we keep on interfering in their lives, it becomes difficult for them to break away, and to reach a fulfilled and independent maturity. Each teenager may be different, but each one is capable of letting us know how much power he feels he would like to handle.

While acknowledging a teenager's need for freedom, a parent will not necessarily agree, for instance, that their son is ready for an all-night party, or that their daughter should travel alone after dark. Parents' experience is valuable, and their opinions on safety and propriety should be respected. But often, when consulted for his opinion, the child will impose stricter restrictions on himself than a parent fears. Self-regulation, if taken in small doses, does not generally lead to decadence and stupidity. Parent Network founders Ivan Sokolov and Deborah Hutton describe the gradual process of the taking and giving of responsibility:

> An important aspect of our understanding and skill as parents concerns just how much responsibility we can usefully encourage our children to take as they slowly develop, learn to walk, talk, feed and dress themselves. As they grow, each at their own rate, children move from a state of total dependence, when we are one hundred per cent responsible for them, to a state of total (theoretical) independence, whereby they are one hundred per cent responsible for themselves. Although our children can always be seen as equal to us in terms of *value* as human beings, their degree of independence must inevitably depend on their level of physical and emotional development – with us relinquishing control and them taking it on as we, and they, feel ready.[24]

Puberty hits us all at a pre-set time in the biological calendar; we can't put the physical stuff on hold. But increased body hair is not in itself a sign of maturity. Some children experience a delayed adolescence, perhaps because it was not 'safe' for them to rebel in their teenage years.

At the time when I might have been starting to dye my hair orange and stay out till all hours, my parents were in the process of divorce. This would not have been a good time for displays of teenage angst, for painting my bedroom black, or for earnest late-night discussions on the meaning of life. However, like every other adolescent I needed my privacy. I especially needed to escape from the emotional turmoil that my *parents* were going through.

I cultivated (consciously and subconsciously) an air of responsibility, so that I would be left alone. I held my breath on my own emotions, worked hard at school, and went out in the evening, that was my time off. This saw me through a difficult period, although it meant that my adolescence had to be delayed. I did not put my parents through the short, sharp shock of teenagehood; my rebellion and self-discovery came a little later on.

There is no single cultural format for adolescence in the industrialised world. Its manner and even its timing depend on the individual. But the same is true for the modern teenager as for the medieval hero: liberation and self-discovery are most likely to occur when parents are willing to let go.

The ways in which parents hand over responsibility to the child are outlined in Parent Link groups. Parents are invited to describe their own role with regard to their children, and then to consider this list:

When your child is:	your role will mostly be:
a baby	protector/nurturer
a toddler	protector/nurturer/guide
in mid-childhood	protector/teacher/friend
an adolescent	guide/teacher/friend/consultant
an adult	friend/consultant

Parental roles do not divide easily into compartments, but this list usefully illustrates the trend towards separation. Experience can be likened to a wedge that drives itself between the parent and the child. Their relationship is forced to change. Continuum therapist Jean Liedloff describes what she feels to be the roles specific to mother and father in this context. She is talking about an older baby's perceptions of his parents:

His mother's remains steadfastly what all people's roles have been until now: that of a giver and caretaker who expects nothing in return but the satisfaction of having given. His mother cares for him simply because he is there; his existence is reason enough to guarantee her love. Her unconditional acceptance remains constant as his father emerges as an important figure interested in developing social behaviour and his advance towards independence.[25]

The roles are blurred in our society, where fathers may be around to help with much of the 'mothering', and mothers may be involved in developing social behaviour. The important sentiment here is that the parent 'expects nothing in return but the satisfaction of having given.'

If we allow the child to take gradual responsibility for himself, adolescence need not be a massive shock, but one more stage in a process that began at birth. When a child discovers values of his own, this is not necessarily a rejection of yours. The day your child leaves home may feel like the end of your life because it is, in a sense, the beginning of his.

IT'S NEVER TOO LATE TO LET GO

Many children enjoy watching television soap operas. Here, day after day are enacted the small dramas of people's lives. The observer can see in minute detail how ordinary people deal with their problems and emotions, which gives older children invaluable clues about the way life works. Based purely on the evidence of soap operas and series, the Americans seem far advanced in matters of 'not disturbing' the child. Parent-figures in the British and Australian soap operas tend to be manipulative, neurotic and controlling. The interfering tactics of the Australian *Neighbours* parents in particular make me wince. But US soap writers, thanks perhaps to years spent agonising on the therapist's couch, know all the theory by heart. Here is the parenting philosophy of one of America's *Golden Girls*:

In the animal kingdom, the whole idea is to teach off-spring to fend for themselves. Humans are the only ones who think it is their duty to care for children their entire lives.[26]

And from Leland, the fatherly figure at Mackenzie Brackman, the famous law firm in *L.A. Law*, we get an unexpectedly deep insight into the role of the parent:

The ultimate job of the parent is to know when to stop parenting – to know when to let go.[27]

The quotation from American novelist Lisa Alther at the beginning of this book, that 'parenting is a series of . . . small daily deaths', describes letting go from the parent's point of view. In nature, the old dies back to make way for the new. The ultimate job of parents is to stop parenting. The child, reciprocally, develops and blossoms in a series of births.

In *Fear of Life*, bio-energetic therapist Alexander Lowen writes about the quality of birth. It is just this sort of transition that the adolescent goes through in order to become a woman or a man:

We know, of course, that the bursting forth of life is preceded by a long period of preparation. A baby bursts into the world at birth, but it was slowly being prepared for this event. A flower seems to open over-night, but it, too, had a long development. The bursting is always the breaking into light of a process that previously went on in the dark, and it is this aspect that seems magical. There is a sense of liberation, as if a force previously bound breaks free. There is also a sense of creation, as if a new being or new state of being is suddenly there.[28]

The process of adolescence is not merely a blot on the developmental landscape. It is a preparation for adulthood. A lot of changes for the adolescent are taking place in private, in his head and in his heart, and he does not necessarily want to share the details with his parents. One of his greatest needs is to be left alone. At this time in his life, the 'Do Not Disturb' notice on his door should be respected more than ever before. Adolescents need to be given more space and time; to be allowed to do more things for themselves; to experiment and to fail. They need to sort out where they stand in the world, and who they are within it.

The more a parent can stand back, offering her blessing when a curse might be expected, the easier the changes might be. It helps to have the attitude of Jean Liedloff's continuum-style mother from the start. But it is never too late to let go.

THE ART OF SIMMERING

We can learn many new skills in order to communicate with our adolescents, but deep down all that is required is respect. Let us return to Linda Burton's memory of talking to her mother in the kitchen (see Chapter 8). As the daughter sidles up to her subject, note the sensitivity and restraint exercised by Mom. She senses that all she has to do is keep on simmering:

I would come home from school and see Mom in the kitchen simmering chilli. I would open the refrigerator, close it, and say, 'Why don't we ever have anything good to eat?'

Then I would go downstairs, take off my sweater, throw it on the floor, come upstairs, open the refrigerator door again, and say, 'What's for dinner?' Mom would tell me. 'Ugh,' I would say, 'We just had that.'

Then I would call my best friend and be told that she was at a yearbook meeting. I would walk around the living room, pick up a magazine, throw it on the sofa, go into the kitchen again, and open the refrigerator. I would tell my mother that I did not *want* a nice, fresh apple. Then I would heave an enormous sigh, look in the cupboards, leave them open, listen to Mom ask if there was anything wrong, and tell her, 'No.' I would go downstairs, bang on the piano, have an argument with a sibling, come upstairs and look in the refrigerator, shut it again, and agree to chop the green peppers for Mom.

Then – observing her still simmering the chilli on the stove – I would sit down on a stool and say, 'You know that stupid Tommy Morgan? I hate that stupid Tommy Morgan!'

Then Mom, not looking up from the chilli (most moms knew you'd stop talking if they looked up from the chilli) would say, 'Oh, really? Why do you feel that way?' And somewhere between chopping the green peppers and running the dishwasher, I would tell her.[29]

Simmering (*noun*) – being around in a non-obtrusive, but available kind of way when children need to talk. The older the child, the more subtle this art becomes, as adolescents in particular become wary of the glare of attention whenever they have something interesting to say.

'Josie started her periods'; 'I got 20 per cent in maths'; 'Peter asked me out today'. 'I just know you're going to kill me' (a surprisingly frequent accusation levelled at pacifist parents.) These are the kinds of comments likely to elicit our over-excited responses, which is why it helps enormously if we have some activity to distract the hands – and apparently the brain – while teenagers talk.

Diffused listening is a skill which comes belatedly to many of us and never to others, but it allows adolescents the chance to air some of the riskier topics which are giving them grief. And while we listen, and 'simmer' (or sew, or read the paper, or walk the dog) we might remind ourselves of the descriptive list of the qualities of letting-go, as compiled for Families Anonymous, a support group for the family and friends of drug users. This list could be useful for parents of children of any age, but especially for the parents of adolescents, because adolescents are ready to shoulder many of the responsibilities of adulthood. A lot of the parental qualities listed here are to be found in the simple act of listening to a child over a simmering chilli:

> To 'let go' does not mean to stop caring, it means I can't do it for someone else.
> To 'let go' is not to enable, but to allow learning from natural consequences.
> To 'let go' is not to fix, but to be supportive.
> To 'let go' is not to judge, but to allow another to be a human being.
> To 'let go' is not to be in the middle, arranging all the outcomes, but to allow others to affect their destinies.
> To 'let go' is not to be protective, it's to permit another to face reality.
> To 'let go' is not to deny, but to accept.
> To 'let go' is not to nag, scold or argue, but instead to search out my own shortcomings and correct them.

It is not easy to let go of our protective, all-embracing, judging, arranging selves, in order that our children can break free. Even when we do stand back to give our adolescents their freedom, our reward is that they leave us. The parent is then left with her grief.

As American author Nancy Friday said, 'There is only one thing in this world that approaches the pain of letting go of our mothers . . . It is separating from – letting go of – our daughters.'[30] The transition is all the harder in our culture because of the physical distance our children place between us and themselves.

CUTTING THE APRON STRINGS

As to whether the child returns one day to take care of his ageing mother, it may depend on how far he feels able to be himself in her company, or how far she accepts the new person he has become. When he telephones, does she complain that he never keeps in touch? When they meet, does she tell him how he ought to behave? If a parent is unable to let go emotionally at this late stage, she may find her child keeps as great a physical distance from her as he can. What adult wants to live near, or with, the only person in the world who still treats him as a child?

This was the question television presenter Anne Robinson began to ask as she watched her daughter, Emma, enter adulthood. While battling with drink and journalistic ambition, Anne lost custody of her small daughter. Years later, she wrote candidly about their relationship in *Memoirs of an Unfit Mother*. Yet even when Emma was in her mid-twenties, Anne would find herself behaving badly during their precious visits together. As long as Anne played the overprotective mother, Emma fell into the role of imperfect child:

> Why, as soon as she turns up, do I begin to sound like an old seventy-eight record of my mother? What is it that makes me ask umpteen times if she has clean knickers or needs to borrow some black tights? She is nearly twenty-five, for gawd's sake . . . Why does she clear off for months, independence written all over her determined face, yet question me accusingly when she finds a few of my things hanging in her wardrobe or that someone has moved around her doll's-house furniture? . . . I bought us each a copy of Virago's *Mothers by Daughters*. Inscribe it, she pleaded. 'A mother's love is unconditional; sometimes,' I wrote.[31]

The child who is cursed with an interfering parent takes his freedom at a cost, that of intimacy between the two of them. Or, should parents have succeeded in making their child feel inadequate without them, he may stay behind, fearing to strike out on his own. There are increasing numbers of adult children who do not move out into independence, although their parents dearly wish they would. The child feels comfortable where he is, so it is up to the parent to untie the apron strings.

Jean Liedloff says '. . . one can never free oneself from a non-continuum mother. Need for her cannot but continue.

One can only struggle on the hook . . .'[32] I agree that a lot of work needs to be done by the child who is forced to empower himself despite his parents. But I do not believe that children need be forever hooked. If an adult lives a life of regret, blame or bitterness towards his parents, he does so out of choice. It is possible to glimpse unconditional love in one's own lifetime, as the author Bernice Rubens did, despite a mother who could not let go:

> My mother died recently at the age of ninety-four, and I loved her very much, but she never *never* let me go. In the end, though, I realised it was a kind of loving and I didn't resent it. She came to terms with all of us before she died, and we came to terms with her. You are lucky if your mother lives long enough to give you the chance to do it.[33]

The sooner we can begin to allow our children their integrity, the sooner they will come to feel the love we have for them. In good time, the child follows his instinct to leave, which is stronger than the bond with his parents. When he goes, all he needs is a blessing in his pocket.

Letting go as children grow: adolescence

- 'Letting go' with teenagers does not mean giving up on them: adolescents go through many regressions on the path to adulthood
- All children take a long time to reach maturity: in Western society, this process may happen much later than we expect
- Adolescents grow best when they feel firmly rooted in the family and community
- The earlier children can begin to feel useful among adults, the more at home they will be with the rights and responsibilities of adolescence
- Boys, in particular, may find it hard to share their fears and anxieties. We need to be especially aware of their emotional needs in a society which expects men to repress their feelings
- If we insist on treating young adults like errant young children, we should not be surprised if they behave like errant young children

10

A TIME AND PLACE FOR US –
A CHARTER FOR SANE PARENTS

When I'm inspired, everything is fine, but when I try to get things right it's a disaster.

Keith Johnstone, *Impro*, director and theatrical improviser

The ideas in this book will only work if we apply them to ourselves as well as to the children in our care. Parenting as an act of self-sacrifice is as damaging for the child as it is for the parent. It is not a case of us *or* them, but us *and* them, working things out both together and separately. We owe it to others, as well as ourselves, to listen to our own needs, to accept and respect our own feelings, to give ourselves time, space and some privacy. We may not be children any more, but there is room for growth none the less, and this can only take place if we are good to ourselves.

Guilt is the emotion most likely to destroy our good feelings. Bio-energetic therapist Alexander Lowen believes it is essential that guilt is erased from child-rearing:

Guilt destroys the integrity of relationships and distorts the behavior of a person. A normal relationship is maintained by the pleasure and satisfaction it provides. When guilt enters the relationship, pleasure and satisfaction disappear . . . The devastating effects of guilt are usually seen in relationships between parents and children or husband and wife. The parent who acts out of guilt towards a child resents the child, who in turn resents the parent and feels guilty about it . . .

Parents want to love their children, but a guilty parent seduces the child instead of loving it. The aim of seduction is to gain closeness, but its result is alienation. It is motivated by love but distorted by guilt. Eliminate the guilt, and whatever love is felt will come through honestly and directly, uncontaminated by negative feelings. Whenever negative feelings arise, they should also be expressed honestly and directly. One can cope with such negative feelings, since they are open and aboveboard.[1]

We have looked at ways in which adults might give their children more room to grow. This means giving yourself some room too, an exercise that will be hard for anyone who is habitually over-involved in her child's life.

CRACKS IN THE PAVEMENT

Take, for example, a parent who divorced when her children were young. She tried to 'make it up' to the children by becoming the perfect mother. She worked hard to bring in enough money to live on, chauffeured her children everywhere, and refrained from bringing boyfriends home, in order not to upset them. Now the children are teenagers, and their mother wonders why they are not particularly happy, or helpful, or understanding of *her* needs. She still blames herself for the divorce, and yet at the same time resents her children's attitude. Whenever she asks them to co-operate with tasks around the house, she ends up with a battle. Then she feels bad about rowing with them: 'After all,' she reasons, 'it's not their fault they haven't got a father.' She backs down, and devotes herself once more to maintaining the lifestyle to which her children have become accustomed. Her guilt keeps her enslaved, but she does not know how to break free.

Lowen believes that the healthy ego does not feel guilt. Instead of acting upon judgements of right and wrong, the healthy person is guided internally by her emotions and externally by the situation before her. Such a person accepts that there may be conflict between feeling and circumstance, and that sometimes she will be disappointed by her decisions.

However, such a parent is almost always supported by a caring, involved community. She does not – would not – attempt to parent alone. An acquaintance of mine returns to her original homeland of Brazil whenever she gives birth, in order to enjoy the welcome and unequivocal support of friends and neighbours for the first two years. She says she would not consider staying in Britain, where criticism, comparison and blame are the miserable outlook for many new mothers. She does not want to be left to struggle all day with a baby while simultaneously questioning her own ability to nurture.

In Brazil, there are many hands eager and willing to help with the baby. This mother gets time off one or two evenings every week. She is not nagged about her childrearing choices, but supported, because she (and those around her) presume that the first rule of parenthood is to cater for the infant's needs. In the simple act of doing her best, this mother receives boundless practical help and frequent applause.

Guilt grows like a weed in the cracks of an unattended pavement. Parents may provide the solid paving stones on which children walk, but community fills in the gaps, leaving no room for guilt to grow. This is the way children have been raised throughout human history. Such a system – though cynics might call it old-fashioned and idealistic – still exists in traditional cultures all over the world. Only in the post-industrial, decaying half-life of nuclear society do we consider it reasonable for one or two parents alone to pave the way for their children.

Guilt disturbs many of us. It may be the internalised voice of our parents, though they may no longer be around to reinforce their message of non-acceptance. It may be the internalised voice of the ante-natal teacher or doctor. It may be the friend who likes to chip in with unwanted words of advice. It may be the voices of certain school-teachers or of unwitting childcare authors who seem always to know better . . . After a while, these voices start to sing a daily chorus of non-acceptance in our heads, until we find we are unable to evict them. We may not even realise they are there, except for the feelings of self-hatred and self-blame that follow us around. American healer and author Louise Hay lists some of the ways in which guilt eats into our lives:

> Our partner is tired and grouchy. We wonder what *we* have done wrong to cause it.
> He takes us out once or twice and never calls again. We think something must be wrong with *us*.
> Our marriage ends and we are sure *we* are a failure.
> We are afraid to ask for a raise . . .[2]

Sometimes the inner voice lectures us on the issues of our own childhood, such as the dangers of crossing the road, the importance of finishing our meals, or the 'fact' that we'll never be a first-class footballer. But our inner voice does not stop there. It will quite happily tackle issues such as sex, body-weight or adult relationships. And from here, it's a short step to believing we are not good enough parents. Despite the many hours of loving attention we give our children, some of us dwell only on the bad moments, or moments in the child's history which we know we can never retrieve. We have internalised our culture's negativity, and made it our own.

In her book *Feel the Fear and Do It Anyway*, psychologist Susan Jeffers describes the chatterbox inside our heads:

> This is the little voice inside, the voice that drives you crazy – and often succeeds! I'll bet some of you don't even know it's there (I was shocked when I became aware of it), but I promise you it holds the key to all your fears. It's the voice that heralds doom, lack and losing. We're so used to its presence we often don't notice it is talking to us. If you are not aware of your Chatterbox, it sounds something like this:
> If I call him maybe he'll think I'm too pushy, but

maybe if I don't call him, he'll think I'm not interested. But if I call him and his message machine is on I'll wonder where he is and it will ruin my whole evening because I'll know he's out with another woman, but if I don't call I'll wonder anyway. Maybe I shouldn't go out tonight. He might call and then he'll think I'm out with someone else and he'll think I don't care. But if I call he'll really know I'm interested . . .[3]

Many of the letters and phone calls I receive from mothers hinge on issues of guilt. Parents who have put their children's needs *before* their own needs in every way are terrified that they might not have done 'enough'. In some ways they are doing too much.

WHO'S THE PARENT AROUND HERE?

Being a parent means acting the grown-up, embracing children's fears and making executive decisions. You may not always know what is right and you may often have to admit you are wrong, but nevertheless, you happen to be the one in charge. An important aspect of parenting is feeling strong enough to make the changes, big and small, which are needed to keep family life running smoothly for all. The task in decision-making is to consult our own feelings, in addition to the external circumstance (our children's needs and any other relevant factors) and then make up our mind. The healthy ego will be happy to do this, in the full knowledge that the decision may or may not work out. New decisions can be made later on, once we see where *this* decision leads us. Guilt confuses this process. We become so concerned about our part in making choices, and how we will feel about the range of possible outcomes, that we may be unable to proceed. We judge our decision before we make it, with a list of what ifs that makes us feel worse. We feel bad about the feelings we have, and as a result find ourselves feeling guilty about wanting to act on them.

If we can possibly identify and accept our emotions, we

begin to see more clearly. We realise that our feelings are separate from circumstances, and are valid in their own right. Sometimes merely knowing that our emotions are OK is enough for us to carry on with things as they are. Sometimes we make a decision for change. As we let ourselves off the hook, we begin to see that doing our best is 'good enough'. We cease to make moral judgements about our emotions, i.e. the guilt that comes when people disapprove of our feelings, and the righteousness that comes when others agree with us. We may still be aware of others' judgements, but they matter much less than being true to ourselves.

Parents tend to forget that they owe it to their children to take care of their own needs, too. They forget their own power. It is possible for us to initiate change when we feel it to be necessary, just as a child would. I am not suggesting that we ignore our children's needs, but that there are many ways of satisfying them without putting ourselves through misery. We deprive our children when we deprive ourselves. In the words of one child expert, 'Children grow well when their parents are growing well.'[4]

As a reminder of what it means to be guilt-free, let us return to the empowerment list from Families Anonymous:

> To 'let go' is to admit powerlessness, which means the outcome is not in my hands.
> To 'let go' is not to try and change or blame another, it's to make the most of myself.
> To 'let go' is not to regret the past, but to grow and live for the future.
> To 'let go' is to fear less and love more.

Admitting powerlessness is not easy. We might assume that good parenting is strong parenting, but this does not mean we have to be infallible, omnipresent, omnipotent and clairvoyant too. If only we could do a little less to achieve more. By far the easiest way to 'let go' is to share the parenting: not necessarily all day, every day (as in some village communities), but by the simple act of surrounding ourselves with tolerant friends and willing neighbours. By re-inventing the community which was once our heritage, we begin to relax and stop trying to be everything to our children at all times.

COMMUNITY VALUES

Before the Victorians, child-rearing was generally a communal activity. It was never designed to be a one-person task, or to be conducted in an atmosphere of social hostility. The strangers who criticise our children's behaviour in the streets would have considered themselves at least partly responsible for their welfare. Perhaps that is *why* they criticise: they sense the removal of their social responsibility. Or perhaps they feel they *are* exercising their social responsibility, and do not realise how critical they sound.

There's no doubt that the disintegration of local communities has had an effect on the way that children are raised in urban culture. It's had an effect on almost every aspect of human relations. At the dawn of the twenty-first century, less than a third of Londoners claimed to know most of their neighbours.[5] Only 59 per cent of Londoners said their neighbours looked out for each other – and we may expect these figures to decline as crime, social fear and suspicion increase.

When we hear that every month in London up to 1,000 people die unnoticed and alone[6], we should not be surprised that babies are often also born into an environment that is friendless and unsupported. Surprisingly, older generation mothers (the grandmothers we hoped to be able to lean on) are not necessarily sympathetic to the modern mother's plight. A wide-ranging questionnaire of British mothers young and old uncovered a mutual mistrust which makes matters worse. Biographer Claire Harman reviews the work of motherhood researcher Vivien Devlin:

> The resentment and aggression of the older generation towards the younger is striking: modern mothers are wasteful, spoilt, neglectful, lack endurance and sit down too much during pregnancy. They don't have to tolerate

bad marriages or unwanted pregnancies and expect not to have their careers disrupted by having a family.

The younger women, the so-called have-it-all generation, harp on in turn about the stresses and guilt of modern mothers, the lack of community support and the feeling that their children, for all the money and attention spent on them, are on the whole 'very discontented.' Unfortunately, no single example promises a fail-safe formula for happiness.[7]

As community support disappears, guilt increases. The hard-won improvements in benefits, standard of living, contraception, ease of divorce and career continuity have not eased the stress and blame which modern mothers feel heaped upon them. Nor are their children demonstrably happier. So unfriendly is modern society towards the young family, that parents would, apparently, rather go to the dentist or complete their tax returns than take their children to the supermarket![8] As parents from other parts of the world might tell us, community is the key.

But many mothers make life harder for themselves. They stoically refuse help with children or housework. Leaning on others is no longer viewed as a necessary aspect of domestic life, but as a sign of weakness and ineptitude. Other women are likely to judge us for it: 'I know she's got four kids, but I don't see why she can't get round to her ironing.' Women are good at putting on a brave face, especially for other women. American social scientist Susan Maushart is furious that women's coping mechanisms are stronger than their ability to admit defeat:

The mask of motherhood mutes our rage into murmurs and softens our sorrows into resignation; and it gives the semblance of serenity . . .

The mask is a useful coping mechanism, too. There have been times when I have almost consciously gone into denial about how truly awful things are (for instance, when my marriage broke up and I became the sole parent of three kids under five). Sometimes, you are simply too vulnerable to let your guard down.[9]

In the late twentieth century, vocal career women, many of them journalists, came out with a firework display of outrage about the misunderstood state of motherhood. The sudden realisation that parenting is hard work, coupled with a backlash at anyone promoting infant-centred ideas, hit the news stands in a blaze. 'Motherhood: the big lie' wrote British journalist Hester Lacey.[10] We're all *Mad Cows* declared Australian novelist Kathy Lette. At last, the bad news was out of the bag . . .

> The myth that motherhood is the ultimate fulfilment for a female is the last great sacred cow, and it's time to whack it on the barbecue. There's a great conspiracy of silence between women not to tell each other how hideous motherhood is . . . I can't stress how much you love your progeny. But no one really tells you about the downside: sleep deprivation, constipation, haemorrhoids, cracked nipples, vomit, poo – and boredom.[11]

Soon the backlash had its own backlash, and letters pages offered items like this:

> I am sick and tired of whingeing careerwomen complaining about the trials of motherhood. Women only used to the relatively minor demands of office and boardroom (compared to parenting) expect children to be perfect parcels wrapped up in gold ribbon that will conveniently sleep and feed at times appropriate to the schedules of their parents . . .
> Motherhood is the most demanding, exhausting, satisfying, wonderful role I have ever undertaken but it is not a job for the self-seeking and shallow.[12]

When the backlashes have stopped and parents of all persuasions start to listen to each other, then perhaps we will gradually move towards a new consensus. As West Midlands mother Sue Cardus puts it, 'Motherhood is not a big lie but it is in this society.'[13] There is something we can do about the want of support and understanding from grandmothers; the barely-concealed mistrust between parents following different methods; the death of practical support for any parent struggling with young children.

We can go out and find the community we lack. We can admit our defeats and our difficulties, and listen to others' problems without offering judgement or advice. We can lean on neighbours and borrow our best friends for cynical washing-up or babysitting purposes. We can adopt lonely grannies from up the street on round the block and introduce them to the new generation.

We can reinvent the coffee morning to make it stimulating, forward-thinking and outward-bound. We can colonise cafés with our babes-in-arms and show them what child-friendly really means. We can team up with other parents to do one hour's evening duty a week. We can insist on Me-Time more of the time. And next dustbin day, we can put out that dusty old oil-painting of the Perfect Parent for the garbage. We just don't need it any more.

PRACTICALLY PERFECT IN EVERY WAY

Images of ideal motherhood are well-known to most of us. Portraits of a serene Madonna and child; adverts of middle-class mothers holding clean and rosy children; travellers' tales of 'primitive' mothering in glades in the rain forest; none of these have much to do with the day-to-day experience of the parents reading this book. And yet the images haunt us, for society places a moral value on positive emotion and images of perfection. Before we can start to accept ourselves, our actual situations and the fluctuating feelings of parenthood, we have to realise that the ideal does not exist: a religious portrait is fiction; an advert is propaganda; the Utopian experience is beyond our reach.

Rather than model ourselves on one or other version of perfect parenthood (and condemn ourselves to failure), we could instead start to heed the emotions that modern parenting arouses. Here one full-time mother of four speaks:

> It's the absolute, grinding relentlessness of looking after children that gets you down. You're on 24-hour call, seven days a week, fifty-two weeks a year and you can't clock off. There's always someone wanting something and you have to put them first. I can't even have a pee in peace and quiet; there's just no time left for *me* any more, no time to relax and try to recoup my energies. Sometimes I think I don't really exist except as a provider of food, comfort and clean clothes.[14]

This drained feeling is common. But instead of doing a little less, accepting support from others, trying to make her life more centred, the modern woman has discovered a novel antidote to the domestic grind. It's called going out to work. This means that, in addition to her roles as mother, cleaner, shopper, cook and home-manager, a woman can take on the responsibilities of the factory or office. The trade-off is money and status, two commodities that we have been convinced we need in ever-increasing quantities.

Following a competitive schooling, the workplace often feels more 'normal' to a woman than does the job of raising children in the home. Work offers tangible rewards, a feeling of self-worth, organised coffee-breaks, and an intelligent social life. Home, by comparison, may seem bleak.

Just think of the 'practically perfect' but highly fictional character Mary Poppins. She managed to combine all the organisational skills of a managing director with the fun-loving, charming temperament of the ideal mother. But think again. She was a nanny: childcare was her vocation, not her 24-hour destiny. Besides, she had a bottomless bag of tricks with which to wow her charges into submission. The job of the real parent has very little to do with being organised and genial from morning to night. If we model parenthood on advice from nannies, or office-style strategies, then we are likely to fail our children and ourselves.

The average working mother attempts to live up to the demands of her job *and* her baby. She splits her life sharply down the middle, all the time striving to appear as single-tracked as her male counterpart. She learns how not to appear mumsy at work, or hassled at home, but her heart may be in both places. One recent survey of 200 working mothers revealed the overwhelming strain that many feel in this fragmented life:

> 90 per cent of mothers who are in paid employment have difficulty combining the roles, according to a Gallup survey published yesterday. They faced both practical and emotional problems. The most common was lack of time for themselves and still having to do housework . . .
>
> Asked what qualities working parents most needed, they replied that they needed the 'stamina of a long-distance runner' followed by an unflappable approach to life.[15]

For unflappable, read unemotional: the working mother is expected to put her feelings on hold while she squeezes a double existence into her day. But you don't have to go out to work for a wage in order to feel stressed. Despite common misconceptions, being at home with the baby is scarcely any easier than the working option. People are apt to confront the full-time mother with questions like 'What do you *do* all day?', a challenge which shows how little understanding they have of the task. It is hard to describe to such people just how it feels to be alone all day, every day with babies and small children. Especially if you happen to live in a wet climate, with only the television for company. The typical guilty woman, should she stop for a cup of tea with a friend, spends the entire time perched on the edge of the sofa, glancing at her watch and saying 'I must get on'.

But we need not despise time spent in the company of our peers. Scientists have recently 'discovered' that the good old coffee break and its equivalents are an essential part of that delicately balanced commodity: happiness. Psychologists from

London University have created Rational Emotive Therapy, which is designed to raise our day-to-day contentedness:

'People sit in discussion groups to talk about positive experience,' says [David] Nias [psychology lecturer at London University]. 'It might be taking a walk at lunch-time or having a coffee break. The odd thing is that, although they know these things will make them happy, they often don't do them. The person who is happy is the person who acts on common sense . . .'[16]

Being a mother at home, because it involves a lot of unseen work, is often reckoned to be boring and an easy option. As a result, when mothers with no other apparent social problems try to express their deep, frightening and negative emotions, they may find themselves ridiculed or ignored. This is what happened to one middle-class mother who came close to battering her child:

The violence started simply enough. Where once I would have talked through a situation with Peter or cajoled him, a slap worked faster. Then the slaps got harder, and more often. And all the time, whether outside or in the house, we had this crying baby.

I began to dread being alone, especially at bedtimes. Every alternate week my husband was at work and it was impossible to establish a really regular routine. I would be tense, sore-shouldered from the weight of my worries, and my teeth ached from being permanently clenched.

Of course I felt for Peter. But I felt guilty, and that hurt. And sorry for myself. Tired, not recovering very well physically from the birth, never finished with chores. Never free of this bloody baby. I didn't feel I could leave him with anyone. I didn't even think it fair to leave him with my husband because he felt helpless to stop the crying.

I told the health visitors, who visited my middle-class home – with space, a garden, a helpful husband – and told me to relax. I would just smack harder. And cry when I tried to confide in a friend, who assured me everyone did it . . .

I told the doctor how hellish I was finding it. 'Yes, it is hard work, isn't it,' he pleasantly agreed.

By now, the bad times were lasting hours. I phoned the clinic and asked for a home visit. I couldn't say: 'I think I'm on the verge of battering my kid.' So I said that I couldn't stop the baby crying. A strange doctor came, and glanced at the sleeping baby. 'Wind,' he smirked.

'I can't go on. I just wish he were dead.'

'Ha, ha,' he said. 'We had one who cried for seven hours once.'

I felt like kicking him. He ignored my tears, chucked the toddler under the chin and left.[17]

Parenting brings us uncomfortably close to aspects of ourselves that we may not wish to know. We may try to deny our irritable, authoritarian, violent, fearful, angry, intolerant behaviour, which we did not realise could be a part of our personality. But everyone has a shadow side, all that varies is how well it is hidden behind the habitually sunny exterior. Just how far each of us deviates from perfection, we usually keep to ourselves.

Children, in their struggle to relate to the 'genuine' parent, are programmed to peel away our masks to reveal the worst. This is why they bear the brunt of our unpleasantness. Day after day in industrialised cultures, parents threaten, hurt and torment their children, while feeling threatened, hurt and tormented inside themselves.

LIFE OUTSIDE THE DEPARTMENT STORE

If we stopped being so busy, stopped trying to be what we thought others wanted us to be, perhaps we would be forced to attend to our inner voice. Instead, a parent may immerse herself more deeply in 'mothering', creating ever more areas of specialisation and responsibility, until her life is as segmented and over-stocked as a department store. At one moment she is the nurturing earth-mother, then judge, protector and nutritional advisor. New roles recently added to parents' lists include chauffeur, personal escort, homework monitor, safe-sex counsellor, and keeper of the infant wardrobe. It adds up to over-involvement and self-sacrifice.

'I work with parents who have never had a night out in eight to ten years,' says psychologist Solveig Sandström Taylor. 'That's what they think it means to be a good parent: but to be a good parent you have to look after the parental relationship.'

To be a good-enough parent, you need to look after all your relationships, including the way you feel about yourself. Australian mother Marion Pears, who chose to carry her babies continuum-style, breastfeed them on demand and home-school them, gives this advice:

> I would recommend to any person thinking of using 'continuum' upbringing methods, that you first take part in several kinds of therapy, and try to sort out your own problems and hang-ups as much as possible. Your children will be in your care more closely and continuously than is usual, and this provides greater opportunities for them to pick up your worst neuroses. It's quite a shock when you first see your beloved child using some of your worst adjustments! If you are going to home educate, try to do it with a group of other people who can provide the 'greater family' setting.[18]

If we are going to be good to ourselves, then we must free ourselves from the department-store mentality. 'Make sure that what you give is congruent with what you *have* to give,' said counsellor Carole Rudd. For all the grown-up 'good' boys and girls out there, it is a hard lesson to learn.

A WOMAN'S WORK

Young girls especially are trained to take care of other people's needs and to feel responsible for their feelings while ignoring their own. Often, this is their way of gaining approval. In this way, mothering becomes pathological instead of instinctive. Mother is on the nurturing war-path.

Some women find themselves mothering everyone within range: their children, their partners, their neighbours and their friends. Everyone brings their problems to these mothers, and they wonder why.

In one Posy Symmonds cartoon, Wendy, a worn-out mum, confides to her friend, 'I'm FED UP, I'm exhausted! I mean, it's TAKE, TAKE, TAKE all the time!' Wendy outlines the problems that the entire neighbourhood has laid at her door: 'There's a limit! I can't take any more! I mean . . . NO ONE *EVER* says "Are you all right, Mum?" They never ask! . . . No one ever worries about ME! Never imagine that I might have my OWN worries . . . oh no! . . .'

Her friend asks her: 'Have you got worries, Wendy?' 'Have I got worries!?' she replies, 'I'm worried about George . . . I'm worried about my mother . . . and Tamsin . . . and Sophie . . . and the cat . . . and Trina . . . and . . .'[19]

It's no wonder a woman's work is never done, if she shoulders everyone else's woes as well as her own. Mothers will become angry and frustrated if they have to keep mothering all day long. As an antidote to doing more, we might heed what continuum therapist Jean Liedloff says about early motherhood, usually considered the most intense period of a woman's life:

It would help immeasurably if we could see baby care as a non-activity. We should learn to regard it as nothing to do. Working, shopping, cooking, cleaning, walking and talking with friends are things to do, to make time for, to think of as activities. The baby (with other children) is simply brought along as a matter of course; no special time need be set aside for him, apart from the minutes devoted to changing his nappies. His bath can be part of his mother's. Breast-feeding need not stop all other activity either. It is only a matter of changing one's baby-centred thought patterns to those more suitable for a capable, intelligent being whose nature it is to enjoy work and the companionship of other adults.[20]

That mothering should be a '*non*-activity' is not entirely backed up by Liedloff's own data. The Yequana mothers she observed in the South American jungle do set aside special time for their children, absenting themselves from the hut to give attention to their babies should they become noisy at mealtimes, for instance. But it is true that in traditional societies the much-carried baby usually comes along for the ride, joining in on the mother's work and social life without expecting to be deliberately amused or stimulated.

The job of mother can only be effortless and seamless in a society that, a) takes a collective responsibility for its children, and b) welcomes those children everywhere. A Western mother has the task of conveying more acceptance to her child than society is willing to give. Perhaps we could think in terms of 'invisible mothering', rather than non-mothering.

However, it *is* possible to spend a day with a child and not adopt many of the roles that society seems to demand. Our children are happier when we do not attempt to constantly scold or regulate or praise or orchestrate or control them. Shorn of all these prickly tasks, parenting becomes a smoother affair.

WHY AM I SO ANGRY?

In the months after my father died, I found myself behaving with mounting irritation towards my family. I needed to release feelings of guilt and grief, and was not getting the opportunity. Instead I threw myself into mothering. Despite the crisis in my own life, I did not want to hand over my responsibilities. At the time, I wrote myself this note:

> Today I feel like a dreadful mother. I never wanted to shout at my children or hurt them but I find myself capable of screaming at them for tiny things. I don't hit them but I'll pick Frances up roughly by the shoulders to

304

remove her from the scene of a 'crime'. Why is it so hard to control my anger? Where does it come from? Why is it triggered off by such petty incidents? Instantly I realise my reaction is over the top and I apologise and we hug. But already Frances has had that scared look in her eyes and already she is getting to know she can 'get away' with certain things if mummy has her shout. It makes me less powerful. Why can't I remember that when I need to? And what's more important, relaying my true emotions, or controlling them?

As bio-energetic therapist Alexander Lowen said, we are not to blame for our emotions, but we are responsible for our actions. Psychotherapist Solveig Sandström Taylor expands the point: 'When your own anger and frustration come up, it isn't OK to take it out on the children. It doesn't belong there. Stay ahead and know the kinds of things that can happen – in the morning when there's a rush, for instance. Stop and think and count to ten. When the children have gone to school, you can go and bang the cushion and scream.'

Soon after I wrote the note to myself, I went for counselling, which helped me to feel and accept my grief. Once accepted, the awful feelings inside me began to subside, and the relationship between myself and my family was restored.

I still get angry, of course, but I am more aware of what is making me that way: for instance, driving along the motorway and not being able to give the girls any attention, having just had an argument with someone, or simply feeling tired. I know when my emotions need urgent attention, and I make a point of taking time to myself (or quietly with my children, if it concerns them) as soon as possible. The anger that is triggered off by my children's actions does not linger. I can generally be firm without being unkind; small incidents require small measures, and are soon forgotten.

It is not easy to alter behaviour that is learnt during childhood. If your family's pattern was to scream and shout, then that, at times of stress, is what you are liable to do with your own children. If emotions in your childhood home were suppressed, and black moods stalked the house for days, watch out for the same tendency in your adult life. If you were beaten as a child, then you may find yourself raising your hand to your children, even though you may have vowed you never would.

As the American social anthropologist Martha Wolfenstein said, 'Behaviour in adult-child relations is deeply rooted in strong and incompletely conscious feelings, not readily controllable by conscious good intentions.'[21] Solveig Sandström Taylor put it another way: 'Change is such a big word. When you accept where you are then small changes can take place.'

DEALING WITH CHANGE

Change brings with it uncomfortable feelings. As layers of negative emotions are accepted and peeled away, raw material is exposed underneath. Therapy is one route towards change, but no one claims it will be easy. People spend their lifetime keeping unwanted emotions at bay, so at first it seems they have made their lives more, not less, difficult, when they seek professional help and begin to feel worse.

In Alexander Technique lessons, for instance, pupils may initially be overwhelmed by a feeling of 'I can do nothing right'. They may be forced to confront feelings of despair. But we can survive these feelings. Alexander Technique has a lot to teach the modern parent. It always brings the student back to the important work: attending to herself. It is not selfish to look after your own emotional and physical well-being, in fact, it is essential if we are to stop taking our problems out on our children.

The first direction an Alexander student gives herself is to 'stop', which means inhibiting her usual reaction to a given order. This in itself may be very difficult at first. But if we cannot stop occasionally, we may find ourselves locked in old and possibly damaging patterns of behaviour.

We can practise stopping in our parenting. Before rushing in to complete your son's puzzle for him, before shouting 'careful' to the climbing child, before telling your daughter to stop touching herself, try telling yourself to stop. It's as simple, and yet as difficult, as that. Give yourself and your child a moment's grace, and observe what happens in the interim. Can your son do the puzzle by himself? Is your child climbing carefully according to his own instincts? Why should your daughter *not* explore her own body? And what tensions are in *your* body as you observe your child taking responsibility for himself?

'Parenting evokes your own feelings,' says Solveig Sandström Taylor. 'Children's sexuality is a big issue. How hyped up parents become when children touch themselves. Stop for a minute and think. What happened when you did it as a child? Ask yourself, "How is my sex life now?"'

Having children is an invitation to change. Many parents plan ways of continuing with their former existence before a baby arrives, only to find their plans in tatters, and the direction of their lives completely altered. As child psychologists John and Elizabeth Newson said, 'mothers find themselves adapting beyond their own expectations to meet their children's personalities.'[22] The birth of a child alters everything, and everything continues to be altered from then on. Whichever parent assumes primary responsibility for the children, priorities will never be the same again. And just when you think you are getting used to being a family, along comes the explosive change of life called adolescence which can blow everything apart.

If you cannot tolerate change in your life then you are likely to have a rough ride with your children. If we open ourselves up to experience, then change is inevitable, and the potential for inner growth enormous. Parenting affects us whether we like it or not.

We can either allow ourselves to go through the unsettling process of reassessing our beliefs and allowing our children to teach us as much as we teach them, or we can resist. Resistance is hard work, it damages the child, and it limits the potential of the parent. Irish management expert Charles Handy believes the survival of society as a whole depends on its willingness to change:

I believe that discontinuity is not a catastrophe, and that it certainly *need* not be a catastrophe. Indeed, I will argue that discontinuous change is the only way forward for a tramlined society, one that has got used to its ruts and its blinkers and prefers its own ways, however dreary, to untrodden paths and new ways of looking at things. I like the story of the Peruvian Indians who, seeing the sails of their Spanish invaders on the horizon put it down to a freak of the weather and went on about their business, having no concept of sailing ships in their limited experience. Assuming continuity, they screened out what did not fit and let disaster in. I like less the story that a frog if put in cold water will not bestir itself if that water is heated up slowly and gradually and will in the end let itself be boiled alive, too comfortable with continuity to realize that continuous change at some point becomes discontinuous and demands a change in behaviour. If we want to avoid the fate of the Peruvian Indians or the boiling frog we must learn to look for and embrace discontinuous change.[23]

Embracing change is not the same as engineering it. Sometimes parents announce that they will never do such-and-such with their children because their parents did it, and it didn't work for *them*. Issues might be as general as 'my parents were too strict', or as specific as, 'I was never allowed to go to football matches.' Whatever the gripe, parents imagine that by reversing it, they can bring happiness into their children's lives. But the attempt fails.

Reactive parenting is just another way of saying 'I know what's best for the child', which is what the parent once had said to her. What the child seeks, indeed what all children seek, is not a certain type of parent, or a specific method, but genuine, unconditional acceptance, and a readiness to listen to their side of the story. Our children have their own needs and dreams, which may have nothing to do with lenience or football matches. All they want is to be allowed to play their part in the dialogue of growing up.

LESS DOING, MORE UNDERSTANDING

Generation after generation we see reversals of parenting trends, like hem-lines going up and down. Although some methods may help parents to get in touch with their children's needs more than others, there is little we can physically *do* to make our children happier than we were. If we wish our children to move towards greater strength, we can only attend to their emotional needs and ours, and wait. Only when we acknowledge our vulnerability can feelings of strength seep in.

Moments of inspiration may come to us when we are least expecting them. You may be talking with a friend about a subject you have discussed many times: the way in which you are like your mother, for instance, or not like her, or why you find it hard to be tolerant with your children. Suddenly, you see the whole subject with new clarity and understanding. You feel invigorated by your growing awareness, and find yourself reacting slightly differently to those around you. Nothing has actually *happened*, but you move a little bit nearer to feeling OK. Alexander Lowen calls it growth:

> Change produced by the application of a force from without is the product of doing and affects being adversely. However, there is a process of change that takes place from within and requires no conscious effort. It is called growth, and it enhances being. It is not something one can do, and it is not, therefore, a function of the ego but of the body. Therapeutic change, which means a change in character, is similar to growth in that it is an inner process that cannot be accomplished by conscious effort. This is not to say that doing plays no role in the growth process. In acquiring a skill it is necessary to repeat certain actions consciously so that learning can occur, but the learning itself takes place on the unconscious level.[24]

Opportunities for growth are all around us. They are usually concealed in the circumstances that most of us try to avoid:

when someone says or does something that makes us feel uncomfortable; when we are criticised; when we notice ourselves doing something destructive or self-destructive; when we row with a friend . . . These are all moments when change is possible.

Even then, we cannot force ourselves to change, but we can get to recognise our emotions which then become clearer to us. We do not need to move straight into analysis, but can simply let our feelings be, without judgements, put-downs or negative messages that block acceptance. We might also practice not judging others, because a judgemental attitude affects us as badly as it affects the person we criticise. Healer and author Louise Hay believes

> Blame is one of the surest ways to stay *in* a problem. In blaming another, we give away our power. Understanding enables us to rise above the issue and take control of our future.
>
> The past cannot be changed. The future is shaped by our current thinking. It is imperative for our freedom to understand that our parents were doing the best they could with the understanding, awareness and knowledge they had. Whenever we blame someone else, we are not taking responsibility for ourselves.[25]

There are always better ways of doing an old thing, and we could begin by practising some of these. But we may find that altered behaviour produces new problems for us. We read a book or two, take a parent-skills course, and suddenly find ourselves in an even more impossible situation than before. At least we were comfortable in the old pattern; we may have been stuck in a destructive cycle, but that did not challenge our sense of self.

BEING OURSELVES

There are many experts who suggest that we should talk and act differently towards our children. This feels alien to us, and parents sometimes complain that they can no longer 'be themselves'. Family members may also complain when parents become more assertive and able to state their own needs.

Another common reaction is of how badly one is doing. We have to learn to forgive ourselves for whatever mistakes we think we might be making, and congratulate ourselves on the little things that go well. If we are trying out new parenting skills, we should not set our goals too high. A parent who is violent towards her children should not expect to eliminate those violent feelings overnight. On the other hand, she might ensure that the children are protected while she begins her work.

I remember feeling inspired after reading *Liberated Parents Liberated Children* by Adele Faber and Elaine Mazlish, but after a week or two of trying out their 'methods', I felt completely inept. I wrote to myself,

> All I can see is how I am going wrong. Every other phrase seems to be loaded with emotional pressure, betraying a lack of understanding and isolating Frances with her own feelings.

Much later, however, things seemed to be improving:

> As the weeks progress, my language is beginning to change. I use more 'I' sentences. Frances is getting less upset about incidents and is able to explain herself: 'Mummy, I'm upset because . . .'

Faber and Mazlish are aware that it takes a long time to incorporate new skills into the parenting repertoire. But eventually, a parent does begin to sound less like a textbook. She frees herself from all the clever, consoling, benevolent and authoritative things she used to feel she had to say. She knows she can say as much or as little as she likes, and she discovers ways of showing her children her true feelings without disturbing their emotional integrity. Perhaps for the first time, a parent finds she is able to be herself:

Mazlish: Many people will initially comment, 'Isn't it phony? Don't you have to say things in a phony way?' It is actually the opposite. Never before has a parent had such an opportunity to be so real. Parents don't have to be nice; they can be real without being hurtful. The whole approach is freeing. It's freeing to the parent and freeing to the child because you don't have to be more patient than you truly are. You know how it is when you are patient: you grit your teeth, but at some point you explode. The explosion comes from trying to hold in feelings. It's like having your foot on the brake and the gas pedal at the same time.

Faber: And you also don't have to be more articulate than you are. Different people express themselves in different ways, and each person's individual style of talking is just fine. No one has to sound like anyone but herself or himself. Whatever the language is that we exemplify in our books, it can be translated into a way of speaking that each parent is comfortable with. Our suggestions are only guidelines, not descriptions of how things must be said. Many parents find lovelier, funnier ways of putting things that we ever dreamed of.

But it takes time to change.[26]

READY TO FACE THE UNIVERSE?

So long as we feel our way through each experience, we will be on fairly safe ground. The only danger is that in applying rules mechanically, we neither listen to our own feelings, nor respond to the needs of our individual children.

There are so many things that we do automatically in life: we eat, we drive cars, we even dress mechanically. So it is not surprising that after a while we raise our children in that way, too. We shout at them out of habit, respond without thinking, react without noticing what is really going on. Discovering a good 'method' does not solve this tendency. I have heard parents saying 'I hear you' to their children, as a way of not having to listen to them. Any method requires application with feeling. This means doing a little less, and daring more. American Alexander teacher Michael Gelb describes the paradox in terms of Alexander Technique work:

> The Technique presents a formidable challenge to those of us who are used to getting results by 'trying harder.' . . . One must find the delicate balance between ends and means, control and spontaneity, doing and non-doing. This problem of balance is expressed in the paradox which is at the heart of the Technique: 'give up trying too hard, but never give up.'[27]

In planning this book, I tried to write down the principles of empowerment. These are some of the items on my list:

1. Work on feelings of guilt and blame. Let yourself off the hook.
2. A theory cannot do it all. Down with perfection.
3. There is strength in not having control. Welcome change.
4. Listen to the child. He is in touch with things you have forgotten.
5. Give yourself time, and more time. Be patient with yourself. Forgive and be forgiven.

Empowerment is a deepening of self-knowledge, which brings a sense of connection with all things. The quiet begin to use their voices, and the noisy find the power of silence. Karen Pryor, animal behaviourist and author of a book on positive reinforcement, spoke about the quality of empowerment to leaders at an annual La Leche League conference in America. She described the changes she had observed in League leaders over the years. What they had gained, she said, was more than just a growth in confidence. She called it 'an ability to deal with the universe, and to face the universe.'[28]

Through the experience of breastfeeding, of enjoying years of mutual support from other women, of meeting and accepting the feelings of other mothers, many League leaders reach the stage where nothing throws them: 'You acquire a kind of power over yourself, over your own timidities,' said Karen. 'No "little me's". You've got it in here. You know what kind of person you are, you know how you face the world . . .'

She compared the genuine face of an empowered woman with the 'many faces' of the businesswoman. She said it was known among speakers that a room-full of talking business-women produced a high-pitched noise that was almost impossible to penetrate. At League conferences, however, the hubbub was quieter and deeper, making it easier to call attention. League leaders had discovered the soft tone so admired by Shakespeare:

> Her voice was ever soft.
> Gentle and low, an excellent thing in woman.[29]

It may not be coincidental that many strong, well-centred people speak in gentle voices. Alexander Lowen explains why. He identifies the two root meanings of the word 'personality': the first is *persona*, or mask worn by an actor; the second is *per sona*, meaning 'by sound'. In his words:

> There is no question in my mind that a rich voice is a rich manner of self-expression and denotes a rich inner life . . . The essential factor is the presence of undertones and overtones that give it fullness of sound. Another factor is range. A person who speaks in a monotone has a very limited range of expression, and we tend to equate this with a limited personality.[30]

People with shrill voices may be straining to be heard. Never mind the business people – mothers and fathers in our society are often wound up so tightly, that they can no longer wind down when they need to. The over-wound parent keeps her pitch high even when it is no longer necessary. She cannot sit and do nothing. She finds it hard to relax. She does not know what it means simply to 'be'. She may not even be able to sleep. My own mother, after years of being woken up by myself and my sister in the night, carried on waking regularly at night for years after we had learnt to sleep through.

There are many ways of reaching out to ourselves, to bring back that centred feeling, to get back in touch with life without having to dominate it. We might, for instance, set aside a short time each day to be alone. I have found that after a tough day, it takes me half an hour to start relaxing, so I take an hour if I can.

When the children were small, and their father was around, I would take some solid me-time. I would close the bedroom door, but not tidy the bedroom. I might light a candle and do a five-minute meditation. I might read a magazine or do my nails. I might lie with my back on the floor and my head resting on books, Alexander Technique-style. Me-Time is up to Me. If you are planning some You-Time, only you know what you need.

We can also learn to make the most of other precious moments. Journalist Mary Morris re-evaluates time in her life:

I'm the kind of person who likes to get things done: the mail off my desk, work out into the world. I move with a frenzy that startles me at times. But then, we live in a culture that nurtures such activity – fast food and fax machines. Our purpose seems to be to do it and do it now.

But recently in my life I've begun to question all this. The rat race is fine for the rodents, but it seems to me that the important things in this world are accomplished at a different pace, a pace that our culture and ourselves hardly can abide. The evolution of a poem, the growth of love, the gestation of a baby, the cure for cancer – the things that really matter often do not come to us in a flash. By 'matter' I mean have lasting value, improving our lives and the lives of those around us.

. . . if life is a process and not a flash in the pan, then we've got to have patience. When I've got a nice seat on the slow train and I'm relaxing with the paper and suddenly the express pulls in, I have to resist the urge to make the dash. I ask myself, 'What for? I've got a seat. I'm reading the paper. What's the rush?'[31]

Alexander Lowen says 'People are so rushed that they don't have time to breathe or to be. Being takes time: time to breathe, and time to feel.'[32] He divides activities between 'being' and 'doing', which is a crucial distinction for the parent who wishes to let go.

We owe it to ourselves to increase those days of inspiration, when we wake up in harmony with the universe and ready for anything. Theatrical improviser Keith Johnstone said that when he tried to get things right, it was a disaster. Pushing, says Lowen, is a painful activity:

When an activity has the quality of *flow*, it belongs to being. When it has the quality of *push*, it belongs to doing. One pushes when the goal or end becomes more important than the means. An activity that flows is always experienced pleasurably because it stems directly from a desire and leads to the satisfaction of the need. An activity in which push is required is painful because it is against one's desires and so requires a conscious effort through the use of will . . . Unfortunately, too many of our activities are in the doing mode.[32]

We push our children, and we push ourselves. This is a plea to stop all the pushing, to be as kind to ourselves as we wish others were to us. Not to disturb the profound well of life that springs within each child. And to go with the flow.

Letting go as children grow: parents

- Being a parent involves initiating and riding change. This is extremely hard to do if we are burdened with stress and guilt
- Parents' guilt and stress increase as community breaks down. We need community support in order to do the job to the best of our ability
- If our own family are too distant or unwilling, it's up to us to create the community we seek – there is no weakness in asking for help
- Many of us live lives that are separated into many departments – the more we can streamline, the quicker we will find what works
- The only perfect parents are theorists who have yet to raise children themselves
- 'Give up trying too hard, but never give up'

NOTES

INTRODUCTION

1 Interview with Adele Faber and Elaine Mazlish, *Mothering* (US), summer 1986.
2 Antony Storr, *Human Aggression*, p. 65.
3 In a speech at Mansion House, London, 1868.
4 Alexander Lowen, *The Betrayal of the Body*, pp. 259–60.
5 Norma Jane Bumgarner, *Mothering Your Nursing Toddler*, pp. 53–4.
6 Alexander Lowen, *Fear of Life*, p. 247.
7 D.W. Winnicott, 'Breast-feeding as Communication', written for the National Childbirth Trust conference, London, November 1968. From *Babies and Their Mothers*, p. 27.

CHAPTER ONE – THE INTIMATE CONVERSATION

1 Reported by the *Evening Standard*, London and quoted in 'Talking Dirty', *Guardian*, 12 December 1996.
2 D.W. Winnicott, 'Communication between Infant and Mother, and Mother and Infant, Compared and Contrasted'; winter lectures, London, January 1968. From *Babies and Their Mothers*, pp. 100–1.
3 From *Childhood*, a television series made by Channel Four and Antelope Films, first screened in Britain in 1992.
4 Carol Tavis, 'The nature-nurture question: will it ever be answered?' *Cosmopolitan* (US), March 1990.
5 Joseph Chilton Pearce, *Magical Child*, p. 12.
6 Martin Southwold 'The Ganda of Uganda' in *Peoples of Africa*, ed. James L. Gibbs Jr., p. 107.
7 Peter Jones, An Introduction to Self-Regulation and the Continuum Concept (unpublished).
8 Frédérick Leboyer, *Birth Without Violence*, pp. 95–6.

NOTES

9 Tom Wilkie, 'Babies' relentless crying in early eveing "natural"', *Independent*, 15 September 1989; Joanna Lyall, 'Crying With Confidence', *Nursing Times*, 18 October 1989.

10 Joseph Chilton Pearce, *Magical Child*, p. 60.

11 Aletha Jauch Solter 'The Aware Baby', p. 67.

12 Sherri B. Saines, 'Do we idolize the tribe?', letter to *Mothering* (US), summer 1989.

13 Alexander Lowen, *The Betrayal of the Body*, p. 198.

14 Alexander Lowen, *Bioenergetics*, pp. 316–9.

15 John Holt, *How Children Fail*, pp. 94–5.

16 Desmond Morris, *Babywatching*, pp. 37–8.

17 Joseph Chilton Pearce, *Magical Child*, p. 61.

18 Alexander Lowen, *Bioenergetics*, pp. 282–3.

19 Deborah Jackson *Baby Wisdom*, pp. 390, 400–1.

20 Dr Daniel N. Stern, *Diary of a Baby*, pp. 19–20.

21 Alison Stallibrass, *The Self-Respecting Child*, p. 180.

22 'While the baby in the cot cries into the night and learns either the futility of expressing his needs, or how to make his parents come running, the baby in the bed is learning the value of hope. The breast is always there. He sucks on it, and at first nothing happens, but he knows that if he keeps sucking, *through his own endeavours*, the milk will come through.' Deborah Jackson, *Three in a Bed*, p. 112.

23 Bruno Bettelheim, 'The Empty Fortress: infantile autism and the birth of the self', New York, 1967. Quoted by Stallibrass, *The Self-Respecting Child*, p. 189.

24 Joseph Chilton Pearce, *Magical Child*, p. 59.

25 'Unlimited feeding is not merely a matter of "demand" (waiting for the baby to wake and cry), but of symbiosis – the "association of two different organisms living attached to each other to their mutual advantage."' Deborah Jackson, *Three in a Bed*, pp. 102–3.

26 Herbert Ratner, 'The Infant as a Human Being', La Leche League International Information Sheet no. 62, December 1984.

27 Robert Karen, 'Becoming Attached', *Atlantic Monthly* (US), February 1990.

28 Alan Sroufe, University of Minnesota, quoted in 'Becoming Attached' (see note above).

29 Maria Montessori, *The Secret of Childhood*, p. 16.

30 From a training sheet for counsellors of Families Anonymous, which supports families and friends of drug abusers.

31 Aminatta Forna 'The baby bonding myth' *Independent*, 12 July 1998

32 'Failure to bond has become one of the anxieties pre-occupying expectant mothers.' Frank Furedi in 'The burden of bonding', *Paranoid Parenting*, p. 34

33 Beverley D'Silva, 'The growing pains of separation', *Independent on Sunday*, 23 August 1992.

34 D.W. Winnicott, 'Dependence in Child Care', first published in *Your Child*, 1970. From *Babies and Their Mothers*, pp. 86–7.

CHAPTER TWO – THE SAFETY GATE

1 Headlines from *Independent* and *Today* newspapers.
2 Sources: the Home Accident Database (HADD) 1994; Home Accident Surveilence System (HASS) 1995, UK data. From the Royal Society for the Prevention of Accidents Home Safety Topic Guide: 'Child Safety in the Home'.
3 The National Safety Council (US) Home Safe Not Sorry project, 2002.
4 Maria Montessori, *The Secret of Childhood*, p. 109.
5 'Overheard', *Independent on Sunday*, 17 November 1991.
6 John Holt, *How Children Fail*, p. 82.
7 Susan Jeffers, *Feel the Fear and Do It Anyway*, p. 17.
8 *Steve Wright in the Afternoon*, Radio One, 25 June 1990.
9 Kirsty McLeod, 'Fears that can destroy freedom', 'Mother's View', *Daily Telegraph*, 3 August 1991.
10 Christina Hardyment 'The English way of death', *Independent Weekend*, 21 October 1995
11 David Brindle 'Anger at child safety drive', *Guardian*, 2 August 1999
12 Angela Phillips 'Beware the bogey mentality', *Guardian Weekend*, 15 May 1993
13 Glenda Cooper 'Tagging leaps from criminals to children' *Independent on Sunday*, 14 January 1996; Childline *Brainwaves* catalogue 1993–4 'Rest Easy with your Electronic Childminder' £29.95
14 Nancy Friday, *My Mother/My Self*, pp. 64–5.
15 Dr Brian Roet, *A Safer Place to Cry*, p. 4
16 Joseph Chilton Pearce, *Magical Child*, p. 256.
17 Alexander Lowen, *Fear of Life*, p. 63.
18 Joseph Chilton Pearce, *Magical Child*, p. 18, 24.
19 Louise J. Kaplan, *Oneness and Separateness*, p. 141.
20 Joseph Chilton Pearce, *Magical Child*, p. 113.
21 John Shedd, quoted by Susan Jeffers, *Feel the Fear and Do It Anyway*, p. 78.
22 Anthony Storr, *Human Aggression*, p. 64.
23 Alison Stallibrass, *The Self-Respecting Child*, p. 202.
24 John Holt, *How Children Fail*, p. 69.
25 Joseph Chilton Pearce, *Magical Child*, p. 181.
26 Quoted by Aline D. Wolf, *Look at the Child*, p. 36.
27 Bob Johnson 'Give a little respect' *Guardian*, 13 December 1995
28 Alison Stallibrass, *The Self-Respecting Child*, p. 195.
29 '*Only if the emotional tank is full, can a child be expected to be at his best or to do his best.*' Dr Ross Campbell, *How to Really Love Your Child*, pp. 40–1.

30 Jean Liedloff, *The Continuum Concept*, p. 87.
31 Alison Stallibrass, *The Self-Respecting Child*, pp. 199–200.
32 Maria Montessori, *The Secret of Childhood*, pp. 171–3.
33 John Adams, *Risk and Freedom*, pp. 172–3.
34 reported on Radio Four's Today programme, UK, 24 June 2002.
35 Quoted by Chris Arnot, 'The doctor prescribes white-knuckle terror', *Independent*, 4 May 1992.
36 Jean Liedloff, *The Continuum Concept*, p. 89.
37 Quoted by Aline D. Wolf, *Look at the Child*, p. 20.
38 Joseph Chilton Pearce, *Magical Child*, p. 125.

CHAPTER THREE – A CHILD REALISES HIMSELF

1 Stephen Anderton 'Little growing pains – Should children be banned from the nursery?' *The Times*, 17 June 1995
2 Hester Lacey 'Bad behaviour – Are British children a public nuisance?' ('If we are not a child-friendly nation, could it be because our kids are brats?') *Independent on Sunday*, 21 November 1993
3 Virginia M. Axline, *Play Therapy*, p. 56.
4 Alexander Lowen, *Bioenergetics*, p. 265.
5 Glen Park, *The Art of Changing*, p. 149.
6 Thérèse Bertherat, *The Body Has Its Reasons*, page ix.
7 Alexander Lowen, *The Betrayal of the Body*, p. 72.
8 Thérèse Bertherat, *The Body Has Its Reasons*, pp. 63–4.
9 Quoted by Aline D. Wolf, *Look at the Child*, p. 20.
10 Maria Montessori, *The Secret of Childhood*, pp. 81–2.
11 Dr Daniel N. Stern, *Diary of a Baby*, pp. 121–2.
12 Keith Johnstone, *Impro*, p. 77.
13 Virginia M. Axline, *Play Therapy*, p. 22.
14 Keith Johnstone, *Impro*, pp. 83–4.
15 Virginia M. Axline, *Dibs: In Search of Self*, pp. 26–7.
16 *ibid*. pp. 85–6.
17 Alison Stallibrass, *The Self-Respecting Child*, pp. 135–6.
18 Maria Montessori, *The Secret of Childhood*, p. 168.
19 David Gribble, *Considering Children*, p. 22.
20 Virginia M. Axline, *Play Therapy*, p. 111.
21 D. W. Winnicott, 'Breast-feeding as Communication' (see Introduction, note 6). From *Babies and Their Mothers*, p. 29.
22 D. W. Winnicott, 'Communication between Infant and Mother . . .' (see Chapter 1, note 1). From *Babies and Their Mothers*, p. 103.
23 Michele Hanson, 'Allowing Your Child To Profit From Play', *Observer*, 13 May 1990.
24 Maria Montessori, *The Secret of Childhood*, pp. 88–90.
25 Grethe Laub, 'Understanding Children', talk given to Alexander Technique teachers, October 1984.

26 Joseph Chilton Pearce, *Magical Child*, pp. 120–1.
27 Alison Stallibrass, *The Self-Respecting Child*, p. 151.

CHAPTER FOUR – BALANCING ACTS

1 Susan Jeffers, *Feel the Fear and Do It Anyway*, p. 17.
2 'The current expectations and pressures of our society are pushing children off balance far beyond their rhythm of readiness.' Win & Bill Sweet, *Living Joyfully With Children*, p. 69.
3 Quoted by Adele Faber and Elaine Mazlish, *Liberated Parents Liberated Children*, p. 40.
4 Alison Stallibrass, *The Self-Respecting Child*, p. 154.
5 *ibid.* p. 150.
6 Quoted in 'Through a Child's Eyes', Libby Purves, *Radio Times*, 14–20 April 1990.
7 Libby Purves, 'The First Steps', *Listener*, 21–27 April 1990.
8 David Gribble, *Considering Children*, p. 113.
9 Alison Stallibrass, *The Self-Respecting Child*, p. 29.
10 John Adams, *Risk and Freedom*, p. 163.
11 Alexander Lowen, *Bioenergetics*, p. 265.
12 A. Gardiner, 'Social isolation of talented children', letter to *Independent*, 13 March 1992.
13 'Children suffer if singled out as gifted' Sarah Cassidy, education correspondent, *Dads Against the Divorce Industry*, 7 September 2001. www.dadi.org
14 Cridge McCullogh, 'He's a very bright little fellow: a mother's tale', *Independent*, 16 June 1992.
15 Marion Pears, 'Interpreting the Continuum Concept'. *Grass Roots*, Australia (date unknown).
16 Interview by Robert Maycock, 'Rediscovering the whole musician', *Independent*, 1 October 1992.
17 Linda Hall, 'Games of Chance', *Times Educational Supplement*, 6 March 1987.
18 David Gribble, *Considering Children*, p. 116.
19 Peter Dixon, Under Fives Study Day, Manchester, July 1991.
20 Alison Stallibrass, *The Self-Respecting Child*, pp. 22–3.
21 John Holt, *How Children Fail*, pp. 83–4.
22 David Gribble, *Considering Children*, p. 73.
23 Maria Montessori, *The Secret of Childhood*, p. 196.
24 Linda Burton, 'What Do You Do All Day?' *What's a Smart Woman Like You Doing At Home?'* p. 85.
25 Jean Liedloff, *The Continuum Concept*, p. 91.
26 Juliet Solomon, *Green Parenting*, p. 64.
27 John Holt, *How Children Fail*, pp. 80–1.
28 John Holt, preface to *The Self-Respecting Child*, p. 3.
29 Alison Stallibrass, *The Self-Respecting Child*, p. 134.

NOTES

CHAPTER FIVE – HURRY UP, HARRY

1 Virginia M. Axline, *Play Therapy*, pp. 119–120.
2 Amy and Thomas Harris, *Staying OK*, pp. 247–8.
3 Maeve Haran 'Can we have our lives back, please?' *Red*, May 1999
4 Quoted by Aline D. Wolf, *Look at the Child*, p. 24.
5 Alison Stallibrass, *The Self-Respecting Child*, p. 200.
6 Juliet Solomon, *Green Parenting*, p. 67.
7 Michael Deakin, *The Children on the Hill*, p. 54.
8 *ibid*. p. 105.
9 *ibid*. p. 48.
10 Geraldine Bell, 'Whatever happened to workaholics?' *Independent on Sunday*, 19 July 1992.
11 Jean Liedloff, *The Continuum Concept* (Some Reports and Thoughts for the Second Edition), p. 14.
12 Linda Burton, Jane Dittmer, Cheri Loveless, *What's a Smart Woman Like You Doing At Home?* p. 67.
13 Deborah Jackson, 'A Contraceptive Catastrophe', *Baby Wisdom*, pp. 229–30
14 'Susanna Wesley – A Mother Who Made a Difference', In Touch Ministries, US. www.intouch.org.
15 Linda Burton, *ibid*. p. 86.
16 Dr Martha Welch, *Holding Time*, Century, London 1989
17 Linda Burton *ibid*. p. 68.
18 Maria Montessori, *The Secret of Childhood*, p. 89.
19 Juliet Solomon, *Green Parenting*, p. 68.
20 Denise Winn, *The Whole Mind Book*, p. 282.
21 Pre-Christmas divorce recovery seminars in London described by Angela Phillips in 'Is there Christmas after divorce?' *Independent*, 8 December 1993. Clare Huffington 'Making Christmas better', leaflet for Exploring Parenthood, 1994.
22 John Davy, 'Why Have Festivals?' *Lifeways*, p. 167.
23 Bons Voors, 'Birthday Parties', *Lifeways*, p. 196.
24 *ibid*. p. 197.
25 Susan Brenna, 'Family Traditions – The Power of Knowing Who You Are', *McCall's magazine* (US), April 1990.
26 Juliet Solomon, *Green Parenting*, pp. 38–9.
27 Virginia M. Axline, *Play Therapy*, p. 20.
28 Joseph Chilton Pearce, *Magical Child*, pp. 109–110.
29 Alison Stallibrass, *The Self-Respecting Child*, p. 63.
30 *ibid*. pp. 63–4.
31 Heather Welford, 'Children locked in silence', *Independent*, 21 November 1989.
32 David Gribble, *Considering Children*, p. 104.
33 Virginia M. Axline, *Play Therapy*, p. 83.

34 John Holt, *How Children Fail*, p. 187.
35 John Taylor Gatto, 'Confessions of a Teacher', *Resurgence* no. 148 (extracted from 'The Sun', an American monthly of fiction and ideas).
36 Virginia M. Axline, *Play Therapy*, p. 120.

CHAPTER SIX – THE TRAINING PROGRAMME

1 Lynette Burrows, 'The Sense in Smacking Children', *Sunday Telegraph*, 7 January 1990.
2 'On Obedience to Parents' John Wesley, Sermon 96 (text from the 1872 edition)
3 Peter Block, *The Empowered Manager*, page xiv.
4 Peter Jones, 'An Introduction to Self-Regulation and the Continuum Concept' (unpublished).
5 Alexander Lowen, *The Betrayal of the Body*, pp. 164–5.
6 Dr Ross Campbell, *How to Really Love Your Child*, p. 66.
7 La Leche League International, *The Art of Breastfeeding*, pp. 87–8.
8 Maria Montessori, *The Secret of Childhood*, pp. 166–7.
9 David Gribble, *Considering Children*, pp. 77–8.
10 Linda Gillard, 'The Age of Living Dangerously', *Ideal Home*, June 1992.
11 Herbert Ratner, 'The Infant as a Human Being', La Leche League International Information Sheet no. 62, December 1984.
12 Grethe Laub, 'Understanding Children', talk given to Alexander Technique teachers, October 1984.
13 Jerome Burne, 'Let's clear this up once and for all', *Weekend Telegraph*, 1 February 1992.
14 Leigh Minturn and John T. Hitchcock 'The Rajputs of Khalapur, India' in *Six Cultures: Studies of Childrearing*, ed. Beatrice B. Whiting p. 322.
15 Christina Hardyment, *Dream Babies*, p. 60.
16 Benjamin Spock, *Common Sense Book of Baby and Child Care*, Duell Sloan, New York, 1946
17 Christina Hardyment, *Dream Babies*, p. 269
18 Jean Liedloff, *The Continuum Concept*, pp. 67 and 104.
19 Deborah Jackson, *Baby Wisdom*, p. 271
20 '*The assumption of innate sociality* is at direct odds with the fairly universal civilised belief that a child's impulses need to be curbed in order to make him social.' Jean Leidoff, *The Continuum Concept*
21 Jane Vosper, *Good Housekeeping's Baby Book*, p. 119.
22 John Holt, *How Children Fail*, p. 79.
23 Win & Bill Sweet, *Living Joyfully With Children*, pp. 74–5.
24 John Holt, *How Children Fail*, p. 274.
25 Peter Block, *The Empowered Manager*, p. 22.
26 David Gribble, *Considering Children*, pp. 124–5.
27 Maria Montessori, *The Secret of Childhood*, pp. 117 and 123.

28 Quoted by Adele Faber and Elaine Mazlish, *Liberated Parents Liberated Children*, pp. 56–7.

29 Alison Stallibrass, *The Self-Respecting Child*, p. 203.

30 'The Blossoming Brain' 10th International SEAL conference, University of Derby, 5–7 July 2002

31 Julian Elliott quoted by Jane Mulkerrins 'Pupils held back by teachers' empty praise' *Sunday Times*, 13 January 2002

32 Virginia M. Axline, *Play Therapy*, p. 90.

33 Peter Block, *The Empowered Manager*, p. 39.

CHAPTER SEVEN – THE ROOTS OF DISCIPLINE

1 Vanessa Nicholson interviewed by Lisa O'Kelly, 'Which school for the right-on kids?' *Independent*, 14 September 1992.

2 Quoted by Christina Hardyment, *Dream Babies*, p. 19.

3 Sinichi Suzuki, *Nurtured by Love*, pp. 10–11.

4 Steve Boggan, 'Pupils used to show respect' *Independent*, 8 April 1994

5 Ralph Steadman talks to Danny Danziger, 'The sadist who destroyed me', *Independent*, 21 October 1991.

6 Maeve Binchy, 'My Old Teacher', *Independent on Sunday*, 19 May 1991.

7 John Taylor Gatto, 'Confessions of a Teacher', *Resurgence* no. 148.

8 Dr Michel Odent, 'Initiative, Submission and Health', *Montessori Today*, November 1988.

9 Maria Montessori, *The Secret of Childhood*, p. 129.

10 Howard Sharron, 'Changing Children's Minds', *Times Educational Supplement*, 22 May 1987.

11 Quoted in 'Applying the Alexander Technique to Children', excerpts from discussions held at the Society of Teachers of Alexander Technique conference, Brighton, 1984.

12 David Gribble, *Considering Children*, p. 67.

13 Virginia M. Axline, *Play Therapy*. p. 125.

14 Celia Dodd, 'At last, a school that suits Kiley', *Independent*, 13 February 1992.

15 Mem Fox and Kilmeny Niland, *Just Like That*.

16 Bronwyn Hocking, *Little Boy Lost*, pp. 51–2.

17 Michael Deakin, *The Children on the Hill*, p. 53.

18 Robin Skynner, 'Minding the Generation Gap', *Guardian*, 16–17 November 1991.

19 Robin Skynner, 'Freedom to tease and squeeze', *Guardian*, 2–3 June 1990.

20 For instance: 'After a series of studies in the Eighties showing that parents who punished their children severely were more likely to produce problem teenagers, the latest study of 1,000 three to 15-year-olds from a team of psychologists at New Zealand's Otago University suggests the opposite.

'The researchers found that children of inconsistent and lax parents are more likely to become difficult adolescents than those of strict ones. The study reinforced previous findings about the damage done to children by inconsistent parents.' Judith Judd, 'Strictly a Matter of Discipline', *Independent on Sunday*, 5 January 1992.

21 Quoted by Judith Judd, *ibid.*
22 Angela Lambert 'Slaves to tiny tyrants', *Independent*, November 1992.
23 'Fergie does it from A-D', *Daily Mail*, 24 October 1995.
24 Carol Clewlow talks to Danny Danziger, 'My mother thought I was going to the devil', *Independent*, 30 March 1992.
25 Brenda Houghton 'Stop, look, listen, think' *Independent on Sunday*, 26 September 1993.
26 *Roseanne*, Channel 4, 3 July 1992.
27 Written for the prime minister by playwright Sir Ronald Millar.
28 Dr Haim Ginott quoted by Adele Faber and Elaine Mazlish, *Liberated Parents Liberated Children*, p. 205.
29 Ushanda io Elima, 'Life with the Pygmies', *Mothering*, summer 1988.
30 Dr Ross Campbell, *How to Really Love Your Child*, p. 116.
31 David Gribble, *Considering Children*, p. 125.
32 'Temper Temper' *She*, July 1995
33 Jean Liedloff, *The Continuum Concept*, p. 103.
34 Alison Stallibrass, *The Self-Respecting Child*, p. 194.

CHAPTER EIGHT – SHOW SOME EMOTION

1 Virginia M. Axline, *Play Therapy*, p. 22.
2 Thérèse Bertherat, *The Body Has Its Reasons*, p. 64.
3 *Mothering* (US), summer 1986, pp. 19–25.
4 Linda Burton, *What's a Smart Woman Like You Doing At Home?*, pp. 65–66.
5 Virginia M. Axline, *Play Therapy*, p. 90.
6 Dorothy Wade, 'Is there love after lumpy porridge?' *Independent on Sunday*, 6 October 1991.
7 Jeremy Brett talks to Danny Danziger, 'I'd rather my nose had been smashed at school', *Independent*, 12 October 1992.
8 'Family's crash courage' *Evening Chronicle*, Bath, 4 March 1994.
9 Alexander Lowen, *The Betrayal of the Body*, p. 233.
10 David Utting, home affairs correspondent, 'Child victims are "silenced by fear"', *Sunday Correspondent*, 1 July 1990.
11 Susie Orbach, 'When fear itself is fearful', *Guardian*, 31 October 1992.
12 Angela Willans talks to Danny Danziger, 'She put us to bed and we just lay there, trembling', *Independent*, 11 June 1990.
13 Glen Park, *The Art of Changing*, p. 180.
14 Ushanda io Elima, 'Life with the Pygmies', *Mothering*, summer 1988.
15 Virginia M. Axline, *Play Therapy*, pp. 17–18.

16 Joseph Chilton Pearce, *Magical Child*, p. 138.
17 Quoted by Jane Lott, 'Talk to me like mothers do', *Observer*, 26 March 1989.
18 John and Elizabeth Newson, *Seven Years Old in the Home Environment*, pp. 44–5.
19 Sinichi Suzuki, *Nurtured by Love*, p. 45.
20 Margaret Morrison, 'Real Anguish of the Women Who Feel Smother Love', *Today*, 28 October, 1989.
21 Dr Ross Campbell, *How to Really Love Your Child*, pp. 83–93.
22 Jean Liedloff, *The Continuum Concept*, p. 125.
23 'Wake up to snap, crackle and propaganda' Beatrix Campbell, *Independent* 19 January 1994
24 Adele Faber and Elaine Mazlish, *Liberated Parents Liberated Children*, p. 154.
25 John Holt, *How Children Fail*, pp. 237–8.
26 Alexander Lowen, *Bioenergetics*, p. 339.
27 Virginia M. Axline, *Play Therapy*, p. 149.
28 'Roald Dahl's Guide to Railway Safety', pp. 1–4.
29 Quoted by Adele Faber and Elaine Mazlish, *Liberated Parents Liberated Children*, p. 10.

CHAPTER NINE – BREAKING AWAY

1 Excerpt from *Teenagers in the Family*, audio cassette available from the Trust for the Study of Adolescence, Brighton, UK.
2 Joseph Chilton Pearce, *Magical Child*, p. 25.
3 Terri Apter, *The Myth of Maturity*, p. 262.
4 Dr John Coleman, *Teenagers in the Family*, pp. 8–9.
5 Elizabeth Berg, 'Etiquette 101 for Parents – how not to embarrass your child', *Parents* (US), July 1992.
6 Win & Bill Sweet, *Living Joyfully with Children*, p. 153.
7 Peter Currie and Elin Evans, 'The Balancing Act of Parenting', *Social Work Today*, 16 November 1989.
8 Dr John Coleman, *Teenagers in the Family*, pp. 20–21.
9 David Gribble, *Considering Children*, pp. 131–2.
10 Terri Apter, *The Myth of Maturity*, p. 67.
11 Stuart Millar, 'Magic of the movies', *Guardian*, 24 June 1997.
12 Kate Figes, *The Terrible Teens*, p. 161.
13 Anne Frank, *Diary of a Young Girl – The Definitive Edition*, Viking 1997, quoted by Kate Figes (ibid) p. 69.
14 Dr John Coleman, *Teenagers in the Family*, p. 63.
15 Maria Montessori, *The Secret of Childhood*, p. 41.
16 Leon Mann, Ros Harmoni and Colin Power, 'Adolescent decision-making: the development of competence', *Journal of Adolescence*, September 1989, vol. 12 no. 3, pp. 265–278.

17 Quoted by John and Elizabeth Newson, *Seven Years Old in the Home Environment*, p. 35.

18 Kate Figes, *The Terrible Teens*, p. 39.

19 Donald MacLeod, 'Panic over exams biggest worry for teenagers, says Childline' *Guardian*, 23 April 1996.

20 Nick Fisher, 'Why some boys cry themselves to death', *The Independent*, 23 September 1995.

21 Ruth Picardie, 'An angst-free adolescence? Do us a favour, Dr Lewis', *Independent*, 26 April 1994.

22 Kim Chernin, *The Hungry Self*, pp. 101–3.

23 Carol Sarler, 'Brute force of the Law', *Sunday Times*, 5 July 1992.

24 Ivan Sokolov and Deborah Hutton, *The Parents Book*, pp. 38–9.

25 Jean Liedloff, *The Continuum Concept*, p. 90.

26 Spoken by the character Rose Nyland, *The Golden Girls*, Channel 4, 1990.

27 Spoken by the character Leland, 'father-figure' of Mackenzie Brackman, the L.A. law firm in question, *L.A. Law*, second series, ITV, 1991.

28 Alexander Lowen, *Fear of Life*, p. 121.

29 Linda Burton, *What's a Smart Woman Like You Doing At Home?* pp. 66–7.

30 Nancy Friday, *My Mother/My Self*, p. 33.

31 Anne Robinson, 'Diary', *The Times*, 18 March 1995.

32 Jean Liedloff, *The Continuum Concept*, p. 80.

33 Bernice Rubens quoted by Lynne Truss, 'All you need is love', *Independent on Sunday*, 11 February 1990.

CHAPTER TEN – A TIME AND PLACE FOR US

1 Alexander Lowen, *The Betrayal of the Body*, pp. 261–2.

2 Louise Hay, *You Can Heal Your Life*, pp. 24–5.

3 Susan Jeffers, *Feel the Fear and Do It Anyway*, pp. 57–8.

4 Dr D. W. Wall presidential address to the national conference of the Pre-School Playgroups Association, UK, 1970. (reference courtesy of Parent Link.

5 John Carvel, 'Londoners least likely to know neighbours', *Guardian*, 20 June 2002.

6 Peter Lennon, 'Friend of the dead', *Guardian*, 22 May 2002.

7 *Motherhood: From 1920 to the Present Day*, edited by Vivien Devlin, (Polygon 1996) is reviewed by Claire Harman in 'Not in front of the men', *Independent on Sunday*, 7 January 1996.

8 'Counter offensive', *Guardian Society*, 15 October 1997.

9 Susan Maushart (author of *The Mask of Motherhood*, Rivers Oram Press 1999), 'The mothers of invention', *Guardian*, 30 June 1999.

10 Hester Lacey 'Motherhood: the big lie' *Independent on Sunday*, 6 July 1997.

11 Kathy Lette (author of *Mad Cow*, Picador 1996) interviewed by Hester Lacey (*ibid.*)

12 Beverley Connolly from Woldingham, Surrey, 'Whingers and the self-seeking need not apply for motherhood', Letters pages, *Independent on Sunday*, 13 July 1997.

13 Sue Cardus from Coventry (*ibid.*)

14 Quoted by Linda Franklin, 'Why am I so tired and angry?' *She*, March 1990.

15 Barrie Clement, 'Working mothers feel the strain of dual role', *Independent*, 25 March 1992.

16 Quoted by Tim Lott, 'Bliss Artists', *Sunday Correspondent*, 25 March 1990.

17 'The demon that drives a mother to violence', *Sunday Times*, 7 July 1987.

18 Marion Pears, 'Interpreting the Continuum Concept', *Grass Roots*, Australia (date unknown)

19 Posy Simmonds, 'Who worries about the Worriers?', *She*, March 1990

20 Jean Liedloff, *The Continuum Concept*, p. 157.

21 Quoted by John and Elizabeth Newson, *Seven Years Old in the Home Environment*, p. 19.

22 *ibid.* p. 37.

23 Charles Handy, *The Age of Unreason*, pp. 7–8.

24 Alexander Lowen, *Fear of Life*, p. 35.

25 Louise Hay, *You Can Heal Your Life*, p. 35.

26 *Mothering* (US), summer 1986.

27 Michael Gelb, *Body Learning*, pp. 114–5.

28 Karen Pryor, *How LLL Empowers Women*, audio cassette available from La Leche League of Great Britain, PO Box BM 3424, London WC1N 3XX.

29 *King Lear*, Act 5, Scene 3.

30 Alexander Lowen, *Bioenergetics*, p. 270.

31 Mary Morris, 'Slow Notion', *New Woman*, October 1990.

32 Alexander Lowen, *Fear of Life*, pp. 101–2.

BIBLIOGRAPHY

John Adams, *Risk and Freedom*. Transport Publishing Projects, 1985.

Lisa Alther, *Other Women*. Penguin, 1985.

Terri Apter, The Myth of Maturity – What teenagers need from their parents to became adults, W. W. Norton, New York, 2001.

Virginia M. Axline, *Play Therapy*. (1947) Longman, 1989; *Dibs: In Search of Self*. (US 1964) Penguin, 1973.

Wilfred Barlow, *The Alexander Principle*. (1973) Victor Gollancz, 1990.

Thérèse Bertherat, *The Body Has Its Reasons – Anti-exercises and Self-awareness* (France: *Le Corps A Ses Raisons*. 1976). trans. Carol Bernstein, Cedar Books, 1988.

Peter Block, *The Empowered Manager – Positive Political Skills at Work*. (1986) Jossey-Bass Inc., 1990.

Norma Jane Bumgarner, *Mothering Your Nursing Toddler*. (1980) La Leche League International Inc., 1982.

Linda Burton, Janet Dittmer, Cheri Loveless, *What's a Smart Woman Like You Doing At Home?* Acropolis Books (US), 1986.

Dr Ross Campbell, *How to Really Love Your Child*. (1977) Scripture Press, 1991.

Kim Chernin, *The Hungry Self – Women, Eating and Identity*. (1985) Virago Press, 1986.

Joseph Chilton Pearce, *Magical Child*. (1977) Bantam, 1986.

Dr John Coleman, *Teenagers in the Family*. Tapewise booklet (and cassette), 1988.

Roald Dahl, *Roald Dahl's Guide to Railway Safety*. British Railways Board, 1991.

Gudrun Davy and Bons Voors, *Lifeways – Working with family questions*. Hawthorn Press, 1983.

Michael Deakin, *The Children on the Hill – The story of an extraordinary family*. (1972) Quartet Books, 1984.

Adele Faber and Elaine Mazlish, *Liberated Parents Liberated Children*. (1974) Avon Books (US), 1975.

BIBLIOGRAPHY

Kate Figes, *The Terrible Teens – What every parent needs to know*. Viking, London, 2002.

Mem Fox (text) and Kilmeny Niland (illustration), *Just Like That*. Hodder and Stoughton, 1986.

Nancy Friday, *My Mother/My Self*. (US 1977) Fontana, 1979.

Frank Furedi, *Paranoid Parenting – Abandon Your Anxieties and be a Good Parent*. Allen Lane, The Penguin Press, London, 2001.

Michael Gelb, *Body Learning – An Introduction to the Alexander Technique*. (1981) Aurum Press, 1983.

James L. Gibbs Jr. (ed.), *Peoples of Africa*. Holt, Rinehart and Winston, USA, 1965.

Dr Bill Gillham, *All By Myself – The Toilet Training Book*. (1986) Mandarin Paperbacks, 1989.

David Gribble, *Considering Children* – A Parents' Guide to Progressive Education. Dorling Kindersley, 1985.

Charles Handy, *The Age of Unreason*. (1989) Arrow Books, 1991.

Christina Hardyment, *Dream Babies*. (1983) Oxford University Press, 1984.

Amy and Thomas Harris, *Staying OK*. (1985) Pan, 1986.

Louise Hay, *You Can Heal Your Life*. (1984) Eden Grove Editions, 1988.

Bronwyn Hocking, *Little Boy Lost*. Bloomsbury, 1990.

John Holt, *How Children Fail*. (1964) Pelican, 1985.

Deborah Jackson, *Baby Wisdom – The world's best-kept secrets for the first year of parenting*. Hodder Mobius, London, 2002.

Deborah Jackson, *Three in a Bed*. (1989) Bloomsbury, 1990.

Susan Jeffers, *Feel the Fear and Do It Anyway*. (1987) Arrow, 1991.

Keith Johnstone, *Impro – Improvisation and the Theatre*. (1979) Methuen, 1985.

Louise J. Kaplan, *Oneness and Separateness – From Infant to Individual*. (US 1978) Jonathan Cape, 1979.

La Leche League International, *The Art of Breastfeeding: The Complete Guide for the Nursing Mother*. (1958) revised edn, Angus and Roberston, 1988.

Frédérick Leboyer, *Birth Without Violence*. (1974) Fontana Collins, 1987.

Jean Liedloff, *The Continuum Concept*. (1975) Penguin, 1986.

Alexander Lowen, *The Language of the Body*. (orig. published as *Physical Dynamics of Character Structure*. 1958) Collier Books, 1971; *The Betrayal of the Body*. (1967) Collier, 1969; *Fear of Life*. Penguin, 1980; *Bioenergetics*. (1975) Penguin, 1984.

Maria Montessori, *The Secret of Childhood*. (London 1936) Ballantine Books, 1989. (see also Aline D. Wolf)

Desmond Morris, *Babywatching*. Jonathan Cape, 1991.

John and Elizabeth Newson, *Seven Years Old in the Home Environment*. Allen and Unwin, 1976.

Glen Park, *The Art of Changing – A New Approach to the Alexander Technique*. Ashgrove Press, 1989.

Dr Brian Roet, *A Safer Place to Cry*. Macdonald Optima, London, 1989.

Ivan Sokolov and Deborah Hutton, *The Parents Book – Getting on well with our children*. Thorsons, 1988.

Juliet Solomon, *Green Parenting*. Optima, 1990.

Aletha Jauch Solter, *The Aware Baby – A new approach to parenting*. (1984) Shining Star Press, California, 1990.

Alison Stallibrass, *The Self-Respecting Child – Development through Spontaneous Play*. (1974) Addison-Wesley, 1989.

Dr Daniel N. Stern, *Diary of a Baby*. (1990) Fontana, 1991.

Anthony Storr, *Human Aggression*. (1968) Pelican, 1992.

Sinichi Suzuki, *Nurtured by Love – The Classic Approach to Talent Education*. (1969) trans. Waltraud Suzuki, Senzay Publications, 1983.

Win & Bill Sweet, *Living Joyfully With Children*. Acropolis Books, Colorado, 1997.

Jane Vosper, *Good Housekeeping's Baby Book*. (1944) Ebury Press, 1971.

Beatrice B. Whiting (ed.) *Six Cultures: Studies of Child Rearing*. John Wiley and Sons, New York, 1963.

Denise Winn, *The Whole Mind Book – An A-Z of Theories, Therapies and Facts*. Fontana, 1980.

D.W. Winnicott, *Babies and Their Mothers*. (1987) Free Association Books, 1988.

Aline D. Wolf, *Look at the Child*. Parent Child Press (US), 1978.

INDEX

LETTING GO AS CHILDREN GROW

Kagan, Jerome 13
Kaplan, Louise J. 51
Kennell, Dr John 18, 34–5
Kids' Project 203
Klaus, Dr Marshall 18, 34–5
Kolvin, Prof. Israel 153–4

labelling 85, 127, 203
Lacey, Hester 296
La Leche League 9, 165, 192, 313–14
Lambert, Angela 213
Lansdowne, Dr Richard 82
Laub, Grethe 94, 171
learning 60, 86, 99, 102, 107, 112–13, 135–6, 180
Leboyer, Frédérick 17
Lette, Kathy 296
letting go 33, 58, 168, 192, 244, 256, 267, 269, 283–4, 287, 293
Lewis, David 65
Lewis, Dr Jerry 211
Liedloff, Jean 60, 121–2, 138, 151, 171, 177, 245–6, 279–80, 282, 285, 303–4
    The Continuum Concept 57, 222
Lobi people 20
logic 15, 30, 32, 136, 242
love 11, 35, 36–7, 164–5, 190, 201, 225
    inappropriate 245–6
    unconditional 268, 269, 280, 286
Lowen, Alexander 6, 8, 21, 24, 74, 76, 107, 114, 164, 234, 249, 288–9, 305, 309, 314, 316
    Fear of Life 50, 281
Lucey, Helen 242
lying 249
lying in 35

McCullogh, Cridge 109
MacDonald, Rob 204
McLeod, Kirsty 44
Madonna 12
manipulation 160–1, 162, 181, 189
matrices 50–2, 255–6
Maushart, Susan 295
Mazlish, Elaine 227, 247, 311–12
Mellah 201
Meredith, David 73
'method' parenting 173

Montessori, Maria 30, 32–3, 41, 58, 62–3, 69, 77, 86–7, 93, 120, 132, 143, 148, 166, 183, 270
    schools 85, 106, 122, 183, 199–200
mood-sharing 247–8
moral sense 215–16, 220, 221, 224
Morris, Desmond 23
Morris, Joy 115
Morris, Mary 315
motherhood 295–8
music x, 111–12, 119

nature/nurture theories 13–14
negativity 291
neglect, benign 138
neurosis 50
neutrality 188–9
newborn baby 12–14, 17–15, 23, 27, 32–4, 35, 38
Newson, John & Elizabeth 243, 271, 307
Nias, David 300
Nicholson, Vanessa 192
non-mothering 138, 303–4
normalisation 62–3

Oberman, Wendy 244
obligatory attention 26
observation 105–6, 138, 152, 188, 190
Odent, Dr Michel 11, 145
Orbach, Susie 236
order 29–30
over-involvement 3, 38, 102, 135–7, 169, 190, 243–4, 289
over-mothering 243–6
over-parenting 263–4
over-protectiveness 43–4, 47, 54, 61, 69, 104, 170, 273, 285

pain 233, 238–9, 241
Parent Link 167, 279
Parent Network 167, 203, 278
parental roles 279–81
Park, Glen 74, 238
Partridge, Piers 232
Pearce, Joseph Chilton 23, 28, 49, 50, 56–7, 69, 116
    Magical Child 15, 95, 150, 241, 255

336

A NOTE ON THE AUTHOR

Deborah Jackson is a freelance writer who has contributed
to many newspapers, including the *Independent*, the *Daily
Mail*, and the *Guardian*. She is the author of many
childcare books including *Three In A Bed* and *Baby
Wisdom*. Deborah lives in Bath with her husband, Paul,
and their three children, Frances, Alice and Joseph.